THE CONCEPT
OF LAW

BY

H. L. A. HART

OXFORD
AT THE CLARENDON PRESS

Oxford University Press, Walton Street, Oxford OX2 6DP

OXFORD LONDON GLASGOW
NEW YORK TORONTO MELBOURNE WELLINGTON
IBADAN NAIROBI DAR ES SALAAM LUSAKA CAPE TOWN
KUALA LUMPUR SINGAPORE JAKARTA HONG KONG TOKYO
DELHI BOMBAY CALCUTTA MADRAS KARACHI

ISBN 0 19 876072 8

First published in the
Clarendon Law Series, 1961
Ninth impression 1978

Printed in Great Britain
at the University Press, Oxford
by Vivian Ridler
Printer to the University

TO J. H.

PREFACE

My aim in this book has been to further the understanding of law, coercion, and morality as different but related social phenomena. Though it is primarily designed for the student of jurisprudence, I hope it may also be of use to those whose chief interests are in moral or political philosophy, or in sociology, rather than in law. The lawyer will regard the book as an essay in analytical jurisprudence, for it is concerned with the clarification of the general framework of legal thought, rather than with the criticism of law or legal policy. Moreover, at many points, I have raised questions which may well be said to be about the meanings of words. Thus I have considered: how 'being obliged' differs from 'having an obligation'; how the statement that a rule is a valid rule of law differs from a prediction of the behaviour of officials; what is meant by the assertion that a social group observes a rule and how this differs from and resembles the assertion that its members habitually do certain things. Indeed, one of the central themes of the book is that neither law nor any other form of social structure can be understood without an appreciation of certain crucial distinctions between two different kinds of statement, which I have called 'internal' and 'external' and which can both be made whenever social rules are observed.

Notwithstanding its concern with analysis the book may also be regarded as an essay in descriptive sociology; for the suggestion that inquiries into the meanings of words merely throw light on words is false. Many important distinctions, which are not immediately obvious, between types of social situation or relationships may best be brought to light by an examination of the standard uses of the relevant expressions and of the way in which these depend on a social context, itself often left unstated. In this field of study it is particularly true that we may use, as Professor J. L. Austin said, 'a sharpened awareness of words to sharpen our perception of the phenomena'.

I am heavily and obviously indebted to other writers; indeed much of the book is concerned with the deficiencies of a simple model of a legal system, constructed along the lines of Austin's imperative theory. But in the text the reader will find very few references to other writers and very few footnotes. Instead, he will find at the end of the book extensive notes designed to be read after each chapter; here the views expressed in the text are related to those of my predecessors and contemporaries, and suggestions are made as to the way in which the argument may be further pursued in their writings. I have taken this course, partly because the argument of the book is a continuous one, which comparison with other theories would interrupt. But I have also had a pedagogic aim: I hope that this arrangement may discourage the belief that a book on legal theory is primarily a book from which one learns what other books contain. So long as this belief is held by those who write, little progress will be made in the subject; and so long as it is held by those who read, the educational value of the subject must remain very small.

I have been indebted for too long to too many friends to be capable now of identifying all my obligations. But I have a special debt to acknowledge to Mr. A. M. Honoré whose detailed criticisms exposed many confusions of thought and infelicities of style. These I have tried to eliminate, but I fear that much is left of which he would disapprove. I owe to conversations with Mr. G. A. Paul anything of value in the political philosophy of this book and in its reinterpretation of natural law, and I have to thank him for reading the proofs. I am also most grateful to Dr. Rupert Cross and Mr. P. F. Strawson, who read the text, for their beneficial advice and criticism.

H. L. A. HART

Oxford, February 1961

IN the last ten years a considerable critical literature has grown up round this book. I have taken the opportunity of a fresh reprint to add to the Notes (p. 257) a selective guide to the principal criticisms of the views expressed in the book and to the most illuminating modifications or developments of them suggested by my critics. I hope on some future occasion to add to the book a detailed discussion of these matters.

H. L. A. HART

Oxford, March 1972

CONTENTS

I. PERSISTENT QUESTIONS   1
   1. Perplexities of Legal Theory   1
   2. Three Recurrent Issues   6
   3. Definition   13

II. LAWS, COMMANDS, AND ORDERS   18
   1. Varieties of Imperatives   18
   2. Law as Coercive Orders   20

III. THE VARIETY OF LAWS   26
   1. The Content of Laws   27
   2. The Range of Application   41
   3. Modes of Origin   43

IV. SOVEREIGN AND SUBJECT   49
   1. The Habit of Obedience and the Continuity of Law   50
   2. The Persistence of Law   60
   3. Legal Limitations on Legislative Power   64
   4. The Sovereign behind the Legislature   70

V. LAW AS THE UNION OF PRIMARY AND
SECONDARY RULES   77
   1. A Fresh Start   77
   2. The Idea of Obligation   79
   3. The Elements of Law   89

VI. THE FOUNDATIONS OF A LEGAL SYSTEM   97
   1. Rule of Recognition and Legal Validity   97
   2. New Questions   107
   3. The Pathology of a Legal System   114

VII. FORMALISM AND RULE-SCEPTICISM   120
   1. The Open Texture of Law   120
   2. Varieties of Rule-Scepticism   132
   3. Finality and Infallibility in Judicial Decision   138
   4. Uncertainty in the Rule of Recognition   144

VIII. JUSTICE AND MORALITY   151
    1. Principles of Justice   153
    2. Moral and Legal Obligation   163
    3. Moral Ideals and Social Criticism   176

IX. LAWS AND MORALS   181
    1. Natural Law and Legal Positivism   181
    2. The Minimum Content of Natural Law   189
    3. Legal Validity and Moral Value   195

X. INTERNATIONAL LAW   208
    1. Sources of Doubt   208
    2. Obligations and Sanctions   211
    3. Obligation and the Sovereignty of States   215
    4. International Law and Morality   221
    5. Analogies of Form and Content   226

NOTES   232

INDEX   259

I

PERSISTENT QUESTIONS

I. PERPLEXITIES OF LEGAL THEORY

FEW questions concerning human society have been asked with
such persistence and answered by serious thinkers in so many
diverse, strange, and even paradoxical ways as the question
'What is law?' Even if we confine our attention to the legal
theory of the last 150 years and neglect classical and medieval
speculation about the 'nature' of law, we shall find a situation
not paralleled in any other subject systematically studied as a
separate academic discipline. No vast literature is dedicated to
answering the questions 'What is chemistry?' or 'What is
medicine?', as it is to the question 'What is law?' A few lines on
the opening page of an elementary textbook is all that the
student of these sciences is asked to consider; and the answers he
is given are of a very different kind from those tendered to the
student of law. No one has thought it illuminating or important
to insist that medicine is 'what doctors do about illnesses', or
'a prediction of what doctors will do', or to declare that what is
ordinarily recognized as a characteristic, central part of chemistry, say the study of acids, is not really part of chemistry at all.
Yet, in the case of law, things which at first sight look as strange
as these have often been said, and not only said but urged with
eloquence and passion, as if they were revelations of truths
about law, long obscured by gross misrepresentations of its
essential nature.

'What officials do about disputes is . . . the law itself';[1] 'The
prophecies of what the courts will do . . . are what I mean by the
law';[2] Statutes are 'sources of Law . . . not parts of the Law itself';[3]
'Constitutional law is positive morality merely';[4] 'One shall
not steal; if somebody steals he shall be punished. . . . If at all

---

[1] Llewellyn, *The Bramble Bush* (2nd edition, 1951), p. 9.
[2] O. W. Holmes, 'The Path of the Law' in *Collected Papers* (1920), p. 173.
[3] J. C. Gray, *The Nature and Sources of the Law* (1902), s. 276.
[4] Austin, *The Province of Jurisprudence Determined* (1832), Lecture VI (1954
edition, p. 259).

existent, the first norm is contained in the second norm which is the only genuine norm. . . . Law is the primary norm which stipulates the sanction'.[1]

These are only a few of many assertions and denials concerning the nature of law which at first sight, at least, seem strange and paradoxical. Some of them seem to conflict with the most firmly rooted beliefs and to be easily refutable; so that we are tempted to reply, 'Surely statutes *are* law, at least one kind of law even if there are others': 'Surely law cannot just mean what officials do or courts will do, since it takes a law to make an official or a court'.

Yet these seemingly paradoxical utterances were not made by visionaries or philosophers professionally concerned to doubt the plainest deliverances of common sense. They are the outcome of prolonged reflection on law made by men who were primarily lawyers, concerned professionally either to teach or practise law, and in some cases to administer it as judges. Moreover, what they said about law actually did in their time and place increase our understanding of it. For, understood in their context, such statements are *both* illuminating and puzzling: they are more like great exaggerations of some truths about law unduly neglected, than cool definitions. They throw a light which makes us see much in law that lay hidden; but the light is so bright that it blinds us to the remainder and so leaves us still without a clear view of the whole.

To this unending theoretical debate in books we find a strange contrast in the ability of most men to cite, with ease and confidence, examples of law if they are asked to do so. Few Englishmen are unaware that there is a law forbidding murder, or requiring the payment of income tax, or specifying what must be done to make a valid will. Virtually everyone except the child or foreigner coming across the English word 'law' for the first time could easily multiply such examples, and most people could do more. They could describe, at least in outline, how to find out whether something is the law in England; they know that there are experts to consult and courts with a final authoritative voice on all such questions. Much more than this is quite generally known. Most educated people have the idea that the laws in England form some sort of 'system,

---

[1] Kelsen, *General Theory of Law and State* (1949), p. 61.

and that in France or the United States or Soviet Russia and, indeed, in almost every part of the world which is thought of as a separate 'country' there are legal systems which are broadly similar in structure in spite of important differences. Indeed an education would have seriously failed if it left people in ignorance of these facts, and we would hardly think it a mark of great sophistication if those who knew this could also say what are the important points of similarity between different legal systems. Any educated man might be expected to be able to identify these salient features in some such skeleton way as follows. They comprise (i) rules forbidding or enjoining certain types of behaviour under penalty; (ii) rules requiring people to compensate those whom they injure in certain ways; (iii) rules specifying what must be done to make wills, contracts or other arrangements which confer rights and create obligations; (iv) courts to determine what the rules are and when they have been broken, and to fix the punishment or compensation to be paid; (v) a legislature to make new rules and abolish old ones.

If all this is common knowledge, how is it that the question 'What is law?' has persisted and so many various and extraordinary answers have been given to it? Is it because, besides the clear standard cases constituted by the legal systems of modern states, which no one in his senses doubts are legal systems, there exist also doubtful cases, and about their 'legal quality' not only ordinary educated men but even lawyers hesitate? Primitive law and international law are the foremost of such doubtful cases, and it is notorious that many find that there are reasons, though usually not conclusive ones, for denying the propriety of the now conventional use of the word 'law' in these cases. The existence of these questionable or challengeable cases has indeed given rise to a prolonged and somewhat sterile controversy, but surely they cannot account for the perplexities about the general nature of law expressed by the persistent question 'What is law?' That these cannot be the root of the difficulty seems plain for two reasons.

First, it is quite obvious why hesitation is felt in these cases. International law lacks a legislature, states cannot be brought before international courts without their prior consent, and there is no centrally organized effective system of sanctions.

Certain types of primitive law, including those out of which some contemporary legal systems may have gradually evolved, similarly lack these features, and it is perfectly clear to every-one that it is their deviation in these respects from the standard case which makes their classification appear questionable. There is no mystery about this.

Secondly, it is not a peculiarity of complex terms like 'law' and 'legal system' that we are forced to recognize both clear standard cases and challengeable borderline cases. It is now a familiar fact (though once too little stressed) that this distinction must be made in the case of almost every general term which we use in classifying features of human life and of the world in which we live. Sometimes the difference between the clear, standard case or paradigm for the use of an expression and the questionable cases is only a matter of degree. A man with a shining smooth pate is clearly bald; another with a luxuriant mop clearly is not; but the question whether a third man, with a fringe of hair here and there, is bald might be indefinitely disputed, if it were thought worth while or any practical issue turned on it.

Sometimes the deviation from the standard case is not a mere matter of degree but arises when the standard case is in fact a complex of normally concomitant but distinct elements, some one or more of which may be lacking in the cases open to challenge. Is a flying boat a 'vessel'? Is it still 'chess' if the game is played without a queen? Such questions may be instructive because they force us to reflect on, and make explicit, our con-ception of the composition of the standard case; but it is plain that what may be called the borderline aspect of things is too common to account for the long debate about law. Moreover, only a relatively small and unimportant part of the most famous and controversial theories of law are concerned with the propriety of using the expressions 'primitive law' or 'inter-national law' to describe the cases to which they are conven-tionally applied.

When we reflect on the quite general ability of people to recognize and cite examples of laws and on how much is generally known about the standard case of a legal system, it might seem that we could easily put an end to the persistent question, 'What is law?', simply by issuing a series of reminders of what is already familiar. Why should we not just repeat the skeleton account of the salient features of a municipal legal system which, perhaps optimistically, we put (on page 3) into the mouth of an educated man? We can then simply say, 'Such is the standard case of what is meant by "law" and "legal system"; remember that besides these standard cases you will also find arrangements in social life which, while sharing some of these salient features, also lack others of them. These are disputed cases where there can be no conclusive argument for or against their classification as law.'

Such a way with the question would be agreeably short. But it would have nothing else to recommend it. For, in the first place, it is clear that those who are most perplexed by the question 'What is law?' have not forgotten and need no reminder of the familiar facts which this skeleton answer offers them. The deep perplexity which has kept alive the question, is not ignorance or forgetfulness or inability to recognize the phenomena to which the word 'law' commonly refers. Moreover, if we consider the terms of our skeleton account of a legal system, it is plain that it does little more than assert that in the standard, normal case laws of various sorts go together. This is so because both a court and a legislature, which appear in this short account as typical elements of a standard legal system, are themselves creatures of law. Only when there are certain types of laws giving men jurisdiction to try cases and authority to make laws do they constitute a court or a legislature.

This short way with the question, which does little more than remind the questioner of the existing conventions governing the use of the words 'law' and 'legal system', is therefore useless. Plainly the best course is to defer giving any answer to the query 'What is law?' until we have found out what it is about law that has in fact puzzled those who have asked or attempted to answer it, even though their familiarity with the law and their ability to recognize examples are beyond question. What more do they want to know and why do they want to know it? To *this* question something like a general answer can be given. For there are certain recurrent main themes which have formed a constant focus of argument and counter-argument about the nature of law, and provoked exaggerated and paradoxical assertions about law such as those we have already cited.

Speculation about the nature of law has a long and complicated history; yet in retrospect it is apparent that it has centred almost continuously upon a few principal issues. These were not gratuitously chosen or invented for the pleasure of academic discussion; they concern aspects of law which seem naturally, at all times, to give rise to misunderstanding, so that confusion and a consequent need for greater clarity about them may coexist even in the minds of thoughtful men with a firm mastery and knowledge of the law.

2. THREE RECURRENT ISSUES

We shall distinguish here three such principal recurrent issues, and show later why they come together in the form of a request for a *definition* of law or an answer to the question 'What is law?', or in more obscurely framed questions such as 'What is the nature (or the essence) of law?'

Two of these issues arise in the following way. The most prominent general feature of law at all times and places is that its existence means that certain kinds of human conduct are no longer optional, but in *some* sense obligatory. Yet this apparently simple characteristic of law is not in fact a simple one; for within the sphere of non-optional obligatory conduct we can distinguish different forms. The first, simplest sense in which conduct is no longer optional, is when one man is forced to do what another tells him, not because he is physically compelled in the sense that his body is pushed or pulled about, but because the other threatens him with unpleasant consequences if he refuses. The gunman orders his victim to hand over his purse and threatens to shoot if he refuses; if the victim complies we refer to the way in which he was forced to do so by saying that he was *obliged* to do so. To some it has seemed clear that in this situation where one person gives another an order backed by threats, and, in this sense of 'oblige', obliges him to comply, we have the essence of law, or at least 'the key to the science of jurisprudence'.[1] This is the starting-point of Austin's analysis by which so much English jurisprudence has been influenced.

There is of course no doubt that a legal system often presents this aspect among others. A penal statute declaring certain conduct to be an offence and specifying the punishment to

---

[1] Austin, op. cit., Lecture I, p. 13. He adds 'and morals'.

which the offender is liable, may appear to be the gunman situation writ large; and the only difference to be the relatively minor one, that in the case of statutes, the orders are addressed generally to a group which customarily obeys such orders. But attractive as this reduction of the complex phenomena of law to this simple element may seem, it has been found, when examined closely, to be a distortion and a source of confusion even in the case of a penal statute where an analysis in these simple terms seems most plausible. How then do law and legal obligation differ from, and how are they related to, orders backed by threats? This at all times has been one cardinal issue latent in the question 'What is law?'.

A second such issue arises from a second way in which conduct may be not optional but obligatory. Moral rules impose obligations and withdraw certain areas of conduct from the free option of the individual to do as he likes. Just as a legal system obviously contains elements closely connected with the simple cases of orders backed by threats, so equally obviously it contains elements closely connected with certain aspects of morality. In both cases alike there is a difficulty in identifying precisely the relationship and a temptation to see in the obviously close connexion an identity. Not only do law and morals share a vocabulary so that there are both legal and moral obligations, duties, and rights; but all municipal legal systems reproduce the substance of certain fundamental moral requirements. Killing and the wanton use of violence are only the most obvious examples of the coincidence between the prohibitions of law and morals. Further, there is one idea, that of justice which seems to unite both fields: it is both a virtue specially appropriate to law and the most legal of the virtues. We think and talk of 'justice *according to* law' and yet also of the justice or injustice *of* the laws.

These facts suggest the view that law is best understood as a 'branch' of morality or justice and that its congruence with the principles of morality or justice rather than its incorporation of orders and threats is of its 'essence'. This is the doctrine characteristic not only of scholastic theories of natural law but of some contemporary legal theory which is critical of the legal 'positivism' inherited from Austin. Yet here again theories that make this close assimilation of law to morality

seem, in the end, often to confuse one kind of obligatory conduct with another, and to leave insufficient room for differences in kind between legal and moral rules and for divergences
in their requirements. These are at least as important as
the similarity and convergence which we may also find. So
the assertion that 'an unjust law is not a law'[1] has the same
ring of exaggeration and paradox, if not falsity, as 'statutes are
not laws' or 'constitutional law is not law'. It is characteristic
of the oscillation between extremes, which make up the history
of legal theory, that those who have seen in the close assimilation of law and morals nothing more than a mistaken inference
from the fact that law and morals share a common vocabulary
of rights and duties, should have protested against it in terms
equally exaggerated and paradoxical. 'The prophecies of what
the courts will do in fact, and nothing more pretentious, are
what I mean by the law.'[2]

The third main issue perennially prompting the question
'What is law?' is a more general one. At first sight it might seem
that the statement that a legal system consists, in general at any
rate, of *rules* could hardly be doubted or found difficult to understand. Both those who have found the key to the understanding
of law in the notion of orders backed by threats, and those who
have found it in its relation to morality or justice, alike speak of
law as containing, if not consisting largely of, rules. Yet dis-
satisfaction, confusion, and uncertainty concerning this seemingly unproblematic notion underlies much of the perplexity
about the nature of law. What *are* rules? What does it mean to
say that a rule *exists*? Do courts really apply rules or merely
pretend to do so? Once the notion is queried, as it has been
especially in the jurisprudence of this century, major diver-
gencies in opinion appear. These we shall merely outline here.

It is of course true that there are rules of many different
types, not only in the obvious sense that besides legal rules there
are rules of etiquette and of language, rules of games and clubs,
but in the less obvious sense that even within any one of these
spheres, what are called rules may originate in different ways
and may have very different relationships to the conduct with
which they are concerned. Thus even within the law some rules

---

[1] 'Non videtur esse lex quae justa non fuerit': St. Augustine I, *De Libero Arbitrio*,
5; Aquinas, *Summa Theologica*, Qu. xcv, Arts. 2, 4.   [2] Holmes, loc. cit.

are made by legislation; others are not made by any such deliberate act. More important, some rules are mandatory in the sense that they require people to behave in certain ways, e.g. abstain from violence or pay taxes, whether they wish to or not; other rules such as those prescribing the procedures, formalities, and conditions for the making of marriages, wills, or contracts indicate what people should do to give effect to the wishes they have. The same contrast between these two types of rule is also to be seen between those rules of a game which veto certain types of conduct under penalty (foul play or abuse of the referee) and those which specify what must be done to score or to win. But even if we neglect for the moment this complexity and consider only the first sort of rule (which is typical of the criminal law) we shall find, even among contemporary writers, the widest divergence of view as to the meaning of the assertion that a rule of this simple mandatory type exists. Some indeed find the notion utterly mysterious.

The account which we are at first perhaps naturally tempted to give of the apparently simple idea of a mandatory rule has soon to be abandoned. It is that to say that a rule exists means only that a group of people, or most of them, behave 'as a rule' i.e. *generally*, in a specified similar way in certain kinds of circumstances. So to say that in England there is a rule that a man must not wear a hat in church or that one must stand up when 'God Save the Queen' is played means, on this account of the matter, only that most people generally do these things. Plainly this is not enough, even though it conveys part of what is meant. Mere convergence in behaviour between members of a social group may exist (all may regularly drink tea at breakfast or go weekly to the cinema) and yet there may be no rule *requiring* it. The difference between the two social situations of mere convergent behaviour and the existence of a social rule shows itself often linguistically. In describing the latter we may, though we need not, make use of certain words which would be misleading if we meant only to assert the former. These are the words 'must', 'should', and 'ought to', which in spite of differences share certain common functions in indicating the presence of a rule requiring certain conduct. There is in England no rule, nor is it true, that everyone must or ought to or should go to the cinema each week: it is only true that there is regular resort to the cinema each week. But there *is* a rule that a man must bare his head in church.

What then is the crucial difference between merely convergent habitual behaviour in a social group and the existence of a rule of which the words 'must', 'should', and 'ought to' are often a sign? Here indeed legal theorists have been divided, especially in our own day when several things have forced this issue to the front. In the case of legal rules it is very often held that the crucial difference (the element of 'must' or 'ought') consists in the fact that deviations from certain types of behaviour will probably meet with hostile reaction, and in the case of legal rules be punished by officials. In the case of what may be called mere group habits, like that of going weekly to the cinema, deviations are not met with punishment or even reproof; but wherever there are rules requiring certain conduct, even non-legal rules like that requiring men to bare their heads in church, something of this sort is likely to result from deviation. In the case of legal rules this predictable consequence is definite and officially organized, whereas in the non-legal case, though a similar hostile reaction to deviation is probable, this is not organized or definite in character.

It is obvious that predictability of punishment is one important aspect of legal rules; but it is not possible to accept this as an exhaustive account of what is meant by the statement that a social rule exists or of the element of 'must' or 'ought' involved in rules. To such a predictive account there are many objections, but one in particular, which characterizes a whole school of legal theory in Scandinavia, deserves careful consideration. It is that if we look closely at the activity of the judge or official who punishes deviations from legal rules (or those private persons who reprove or criticize deviations from non-legal rules), we see that rules are involved in this activity in a way which this predictive account leaves quite unexplained. For the judge, in punishing, takes the rule as his *guide* and the breach of the rule as his *reason* and *justification* for punishing the offender. He does not look upon the rule as a statement that he and others are likely to punish deviations, though a spectator might look upon the rule in just this way. The predictive aspect of the rule (though real enough) is irrelevant to his purposes, whereas its status as a guide and justification is essential. The same is true of informal reproofs administered for the breach of non-legal rules. These too are not merely predictable reactions to deviations, but something which existence of the rule guides and is held to justify. So we say that we reprove or punish a man *because* he has broken the rule: and not merely that it was probable that we would reprove or punish him.

Yet among critics who have pressed these objections to the predictive account some confess that there is something obscure here; something which resists analysis in clear, hard, factual terms. What *can* there be in a rule apart from regular and hence predictable punishment or reproof of those who deviate from the usual patterns of conduct, which distinguishes it from a mere group habit? Can there really be something over and above these clear ascertainable facts, some extra element, which guides the judge and justifies or gives him a reason for punishing? The difficulty of saying what exactly this extra element is has led these critics of the predictive theory to insist at this point that all talk of rules, and the corresponding use of words like 'must', 'ought', and 'should', is fraught with a confusion which perhaps enhances their importance in men's eyes but has no rational basis. We merely *think*, so such critics claim, that there is something in the rule which binds us to do certain things and guides or justifies us in doing them, but this is an illusion even if it is a useful one. All that there is, over and above the clear ascertainable facts of group behaviour and predictable reaction to deviation, are our own powerful 'feelings' of compulsion to behave in accordance with the rule and to act against those who do not. We do not recognize these feelings for what they are but imagine that there is something external, some invisible part of the fabric of the universe guiding and controlling us in these activities. We are here in the realm of fiction, with which it is said the law has always been connected. It is only because we adopt this fiction that we can talk solemnly of the government 'of laws not men'. This type of criticism, whatever the merits of its positive contentions, at least calls for further elucidation of the distinction between social rules and mere convergent habits of behaviour. This distinction is crucial for the understanding of law, and much of the early chapters of this book is concerned with it.

Scepticism about the character of legal rules has not, how-

ever, always taken the extreme form of condemning the very
notion of a binding rule as confused or fictitious. Instead, the
most prevalent form of scepticism in England and the United
States invites us to reconsider the view that a legal system
wholly, or even *primarily*, consists of rules. No doubt the courts so
frame their judgments as to give the impression that their decisions are the necessary consequence of predetermined rules
whose meaning is fixed and clear. In very simple cases this may
be so; but in the vast majority of cases that trouble the courts,
neither statutes nor precedents in which the rules are allegedly
contained allow of only one result. In most important cases
there is always a choice. The judge has to choose between
alternative meanings to be given to the words of a statute or
between rival interpretations of what a precedent 'amounts
to'. It is only the tradition that judges 'find' and do not 'make'
law that conceals this, and presents their decisions as if they
were deductions smoothly made from clear pre-existing rules
without intrusion of the judge's choice. Legal rules may have a
central core of undisputed meaning, and in some cases it may
be difficult to imagine a dispute as to the meaning of a rule
breaking out. The provision of s. 9 of the Wills Act 1837 that
there must be two witnesses to a will may not seem likely to
raise problems of interpretation. Yet all rules have a penumbra
of uncertainty where the judge must choose between alternatives. Even the meaning of the innocent-seeming provision of
the Wills Act that the testator must *sign* the will may prove
doubtful in certain circumstances. What if the testator used a
pseudonym? Or if his hand was guided by another? Or if he
wrote his initials only? Or if he put his full, correct, name unaided,
but at the top of the first page instead of at the bottom of the
last? Would all these cases be 'signing' within the meaning of
the legal rule?

If so much uncertainty may break out in humble spheres of
private law, how much more shall we find in the magniloquent
phrases of a constitution such as the Fifth and Fourteenth
Amendments to the Constitution of the United States, providing that no person shall be 'deprived of life liberty or property without due process of law'? Of this one writer[1] has said

[1] J. D. March,'Sociological Jurisprudence Revisited', 8 *Stanford Law Review* (1956),
p. 518.

that the true meaning of this phrase is really quite clear. It means 'no *w* shall be *x* or *y* without *z* where *w*, *x*, *y*, and *z* can assume any values within a wide range'. To cap the tale sceptics remind us that not only are the rules uncertain, but the court's interpretation of them may be not only authoritative but final. In view of all this, is not the conception of law as essentially a matter of rules a gross exaggeration if not a mistake? Such thoughts lead to the paradoxical denial which we have already cited: 'Statutes are sources of law, not part of the law itself.'[1]

3. DEFINITION

Here then are the three recurrent issues: How does law differ from and how is it related to orders backed by threats? How does legal obligation differ from, and how is it related to, moral obligation? What are rules and to what extent is law an affair of rules? To dispel doubt and perplexity on these three issues has been the chief aim of most speculation about the 'nature' of law. It is possible now to see why this speculation has usually been conceived as a search for the definition of law, and also why at least the familiar forms of definition have done so little to resolve the persistent difficulties and doubts. Definition, as the word suggests, is primarily a matter of drawing lines or distinguishing between one kind of thing and another, which language marks off by a separate word. The need for such a drawing of lines is often felt by those who are perfectly at home with the day-to-day use of the word in question, but cannot state or explain the distinctions which, they sense, divide one kind of thing from another. All of us are sometimes in this predicament: it is fundamentally that of the man who says, 'I can recognize an elephant when I see one but I cannot define it.' The same predicament was expressed by some famous words of St. Augustine[2] about the notion of time. 'What then is time? If no one asks me I know: if I wish to explain it to one that asks I know not.' It is in this way that even skilled lawyers have felt that, though they know the law, there is much about law and its relations to other things that they cannot explain and do not fully understand. Like a man who can get from one point to another in a familiar town but cannot

---

[1] Gray, loc. cit.   [2] *Confessiones*, xiv. 17.

explain or show others how to do it, those who press for a definition need a map exhibiting clearly the relationships dimly felt to exist between the law they know and other things.

Sometimes in such cases a definition of a word can supply such a map: at one and the same time it may make explicit the latent principle which guides our use of a word, and may exhibit relationships between the type of phenomena to which we apply the word and other phenomena. It is sometimes said that definition is 'merely verbal' or 'just about words'; but this may be most misleading where the expression defined is one in current use. Even the definition of a triangle as a 'three-sided rectilinear figure', or the definition of an elephant as a 'quadruped distinguished from others by its possession of a thick skin, tusks, and trunk', instructs us in a humble way both as to the standard use of these words and about the things to which the words apply. A definition of this familiar type does two things at once. It simultaneously provides a code or formula translating the word into other well-understood terms and locates for us the kind of thing to which the word is used to refer, by indicating the features which it shares in common with a wider family of things and those which mark it off from others of that same family. In searching for and finding such definitions we 'are looking not merely at words . . . but also at the realities we use words to talk about. We are using a sharpened awareness of words to sharpen our perception of the phenomena.'[1]

This form of definition (*per genus et differentiam*) which we see in the simple case of the triangle or elephant is the simplest and to some the most satisfying, because it gives us a form of words which can always be substituted for the word defined. But it is not always available nor, when it is available, always illuminating. Its success depends on conditions which are often not satisfied. Chief among these is that there should be a wider family of things or *genus*, about the character of which we are clear, and within which the definition locates what it defines; for plainly a definition which tells us that something is a member of a family cannot help us if we have only vague or confused ideas as to the character of the family. It is this requirement that in the case of law renders this form of definition useless, for

[1] J. L. Austin, 'A Plea for Excuses', *Proceedings of the Aristotelian Society*, vol. 57 (1956–7), 8.

here there is no familiar well-understood general category of which law is a member. The most obvious candidate for use in this way in a definition of law is the general family of *rules of behaviour*; yet the concept of a rule as we have seen is as perplexing as that of law itself, so that definitions of law that start by identifying laws as a species of rule usually advance our understanding of law no further. For this, something more fundamental is required than a form of definition which is successfully used to locate some special, subordinate, kind within some familiar, well-understood, general kind of thing.

There are, however, further formidable obstacles to the profitable use of this simple form of definition in the case of law. The supposition that a general expression can be defined in this way rests on the tacit assumption that all the instances of what is to be defined as triangles and elephants have common characteristics which are signified by the expression defined. Of course, even at a relatively elementary stage, the existence of borderline cases is forced upon our attention, and this shows that the assumption that the several instances of a general term must have the same characteristics may be dogmatic. Very often the ordinary, or even the technical, usage of a term is quite 'open' in that it does not *forbid* the extension of the term to cases where only some of the normally concomitant characteristics are present. This, as we have already observed, is true of international law and of certain forms of primitive law, so that it is always possible to argue with plausibility for and against such an extension. What is more important is that, apart from such borderline cases, the several instances of a general term are often linked together in quite different ways from that postulated by the simple form of definition. They may be linked by analogy as when we speak of the 'foot' of a man and also of the 'foot' of a mountain. They may be linked by *different* relationships to a central element. Such a unifying principle is seen in the application of the word 'healthy' not only to a man but to his complexion and to his morning exercise; the second being a *sign* and the third a *cause* of the first central characteristic. Or again—and here perhaps we have a principle similar to that which unifies the different types of rules which make up a legal system—the several instances may be different constituents of some complex activity. The use of the adjectival expression 'railway' not only of a train but also of the lines, of a station, of a porter, and of a limited company, is governed by this type of unifying principle.

There are of course many other kinds of definition besides the very simple traditional form which we have discussed, but it seems clear, when we recall the character of the three main issues which we have identified as underlying the recurrent question 'What is law?', that nothing concise enough to be recognized as a definition could provide a satisfactory answer to it. The underlying issues are too different from each other and too fundamental to be capable of this sort of resolution. This the history of attempts to provide concise definitions has shown. Yet the instinct which has often brought these three questions together under a single question or request for definition has not been misguided; for, as we shall show in the course of this book, it is possible to isolate and characterize a central set of elements which form a common part of the answer to all three. What these elements are and why they deserve the important place assigned to them in this book will best emerge, if we first consider, in detail, the deficiencies of the theory which has dominated so much English jurisprudence since Austin expounded it. This is the claim that the key to the understanding of law is to be found in the simple notion of an order backed by threats, which Austin himself termed a 'command'. The investigation of the deficiencies of this theory occupies the next three chapters. In criticizing it first and deferring to the later chapters of this book consideration of its main rival, we have consciously disregarded the historical order in which modern legal theory has developed; for the rival claim that law is best understood through its 'necessary' connexion with morality is an older doctrine which Austin, like Bentham before him, took as a principal object of attack. Our excuse, if one is needed, for this unhistorical treatment, is that the errors of the simple imperative theory are a better pointer to the truth than those of its more complex rivals.

At various points in this book the reader will find discussions of the borderline cases where legal theorists have felt doubts about the application of the expression 'law' or 'legal system', but the suggested resolution of these doubts, which he will also find here, is only a secondary concern of the book. For its purpose

is not to provide a definition of law, in the sense of a rule by
reference to which the correctness of the use of the word can
be tested; it is to advance legal theory by providing an im-
proved analysis of the distinctive structure of a municipal legal
system and a better understanding of the resemblances and
differences between law, coercion, and morality, as types of
social phenomena. The set of elements identified in the course
of the critical discussion of the next three chapters and described in detail in Chapters V and VI serve this purpose in
ways which are demonstrated in the rest of the book. It is for
this reason that they are treated as the central elements in the
concept of law and of prime importance in its elucidation.

II

LAWS, COMMANDS, AND ORDERS

1. VARIETIES OF IMPERATIVES

THE clearest and the most thorough attempt to analyse the concept of law in terms of the apparently simple elements of commands and habits, was that made by Austin in the *Province of Jurisprudence Determined*. In this and the next two chapters we shall state and criticize a position which is, in substance, the same as Austin's doctrine but probably diverges from it at certain points. For our principal concern is not with Austin but with the credentials of a certain type of theory which has perennial attractions whatever its defects may be. So we have not hesitated where Austin's meaning is doubtful or where his views seem inconsistent to ignore this and to state a clear and consistent position. Moreover, where Austin merely gives hints as to ways in which criticisms might be met, we have developed these (in part along the lines followed by later theorists such as Kelsen) in order to secure that the doctrine we shall consider and criticize is stated in its strongest form.

In many different situations in social life one person may express a wish that another person should do or abstain from doing something. When this wish is expressed not merely as a piece of interesting information or deliberate self-revelation but with the intention that the person addressed should conform to the wish expressed, it is customary in English and many other languages, though not necessary, to use a special linguistic form called the *imperative mood*, 'Go home!' 'Come here!' 'Stop!' 'Do not kill him!' The social situations in which we thus address others in imperative form are extremely diverse; yet they include some recurrent main types, the importance of which is marked by certain familiar classifications. 'Pass the salt, please', is usually a mere *request*, since normally it is addressed by the speaker to one who is able to render him a service, and there is no suggestion either of any great urgency or any hint of what may follow on failure to comply. 'Do not

kill me', would normally be uttered as a *plea* where the speaker
is at the mercy of the person addressed or in a predicament from
which the latter has the power to release him. 'Don't move', on
the other hand, may be a *warning* if the speaker knows of some
impending danger to the person addressed (a snake in the
grass) which his keeping still may avert.

The varieties of social situation in which use is characteristically, though not invariably, made of imperative forms of
language are not only numerous but shade into each other; and
terms like 'plea', 'request', or 'warning', serve only to make a
few rough discriminations. The most important of these situations is one to which the word 'imperative' seems specially
appropriate. It is that illustrated by the case of the gunman
who says to the bank clerk, 'Hand over the money or I will
shoot.' Its distinctive feature which leads us to speak of the
gunman *ordering* not merely *asking*, still less *pleading with* the
clerk to hand over the money, is that, to secure compliance
with his expressed wishes, the speaker threatens to do something
which a normal man would regard as harmful or unpleasant,
and renders keeping the money a substantially less eligible
course of conduct for the clerk. If the gunman succeeds, we
would describe him as having *coerced* the clerk, and the clerk as
in that sense being in the gunman's power. Many nice linguistic questions may arise over such cases: we might properly
say that the gunman *ordered* the clerk to hand over the money
and the clerk obeyed, but it would be somewhat misleading to
say that the gunman *gave an order* to the clerk to hand it over,
since this rather military-sounding phrase suggests some right
or authority to give orders not present in our case. It would,
however, be quite natural to say that the gunman gave an
order to his henchman to guard the door.

We need not here concern ourselves with these subtleties.
Although a suggestion of authority and deference to authority
may often attach to the words 'order' and 'obedience', we shall
use the expressions 'orders backed by threats' and 'coercive
orders' to refer to orders which, like the gunman's, are supported only by threats, and we shall use the words 'obedience'
and 'obey' to include compliance with such orders. It is, however, important to notice, if only because of the great influence
on jurists of Austin's definition of the notion of a command, that

the simple situation, where threats of harm and nothing else is used to force obedience, is *not* the situation where we naturally speak of 'commands'. This word, which is not very common outside military contexts, carries with it very strong implications that there is a relatively stable hierarchical organization of men, such as an army or a body of disciples in which the commander occupies a position of pre-eminence. Typically it is the general (not the sergeant) who is the commander and gives commands, though other forms of special pre-eminence are spoken of in these terms, as when Christ in the New Testament is said to command his disciples. More important—for this is a crucial distinction between different forms of 'imperative'—is the point that it need not be the case, where a command is given, that there should be a latent threat of harm in the event of disobedience. To command is characteristically to exercise authority over men, not power to inflict harm, and though it may be combined with threats of harm a command is primarily an appeal not to fear but to respect for authority.

It is obvious that the idea of a command with its very strong connexion with authority is much closer to that of law than our gunman's order backed by threats, though the latter is an instance of what Austin, ignoring the distinctions noticed in the last paragraph, misleadingly calls a command. A command is, however, too close to law for our purpose; for the element of authority involved in law has always been one of the obstacles in the path of any easy explanation of what law is. We cannot therefore profitably use, in the elucidation of law, the notion of a command which also involves it. Indeed it is a virtue of Austin's analysis, whatever its defects, that the elements of the gunman situation are, unlike the element of authority, not themselves obscure or in need of much explanation; and hence we shall follow Austin in an attempt to build up from it the idea of law. We shall not, however, hope, as Austin did, for success, but rather to learn from our failure.

2. LAW AS COERCIVE ORDERS

Even in a complex large society, like that of a modern state, there are occasions when an official, face to face with an individual, orders him to do something. A policeman orders a particular motorist to stop or a particular beggar to move on.

But these simple situations are not, and could not be, the standard way in which law functions, if only because no society could support the number of officials necessary to secure that every member of the society was officially and separately informed of every act which he was required to do. Instead such particularized forms of control are either exceptional or are ancillary accompaniments or reinforcements of general forms of directions which do not name, and are not addressed to, particular individuals, and do not indicate a particular act to be done. Hence the *standard* form even of a criminal statute (which of all the varieties of law has the closest resemblance to an order backed by threats) is general in two ways; it indicates a general type of conduct and applies to a general class of persons who are expected to see that it applies to them and to comply with it. Official individuated face-to-face directions here have a secondary place: if the primary general directions are not obeyed by a particular individual, officials may draw his attention to them and demand compliance, as a tax inspector does, or the disobedience may be officially identified and recorded and the threatened punishment imposed by a court.

Legal control is therefore primarily, though not exclusively, control by directions which are in this double sense *general*. This is the first feature which we must add to the simple model of the gunman if it is to reproduce for us the characteristics of law. The range of persons affected and the manner in which the range is indicated may vary with different legal systems and even different laws. In a modern state it is normally understood that, in the absence of special indications widening or narrowing the class, its general laws extend to all persons within its territorial boundaries. In canon law there is a similar understanding that normally all the members of the church are within the range of its law except when a narrower class is indicated. In all cases the range of application of a law is a question of interpretation of the particular law aided by such general understandings. It is here worth noticing that though jurists, Austin among them, sometimes speak of laws being *addressed*[1] to classes of persons this is misleading in suggesting a parallel to the face-to-face situation which really does not exist and is not intended by those who use this expression. Ordering people to do

---

[1] 'Addressed to the community at large', Austin, op. cit., p. 22.

things is a form of communication and does entail actually 'addressing' them, i.e. attracting their attention or taking steps to attract it, but making laws for people does not. Thus the gunman by one and the same utterance, 'Hand over those notes', expresses his wish that the clerk should do something and actually *addresses* the clerk, i.e. he does what is normally sufficient to bring this expression to the clerk's attention. If he did not do the latter but merely said the same words in an empty room, he would not have addressed the clerk at all and would not have *ordered* him to do anything: we might describe the situation as one where the gunman merely said the words, 'Hand over those notes'. In this respect making laws differs from ordering people to do things, and we must allow for this difference in using this simple idea as a model for law. It may indeed be desirable that laws should as soon as may be after they are made, be brought to the attention of those to whom they apply. The legislator's purpose in making laws would be defeated unless this were generally done, and legal systems often provide, by special rules concerning promulgation, that this shall be done. But laws may be complete as laws before this is done, and even if it is not done at all. In the absence of special rules to the contrary, laws are validly made even if those affected are left to find out for themselves what laws have been made and who are affected thereby. What is usually intended by those who speak of laws being 'addressed' to certain persons, is that these are the persons to whom the particular law applies, i.e. whom it requires to behave in certain ways. If we use the word 'addressed' here we may both fail to notice an important difference between the making of a law and giving a face-to-face order, and we may confuse the two distinct questions: 'To whom does the law apply?' and 'To whom has it been published?'

Besides the introduction of the feature of generality a more fundamental change must be made in the gunman situation if we are to have a plausible model of the situation where there is law. It is true there is a sense in which the gunman has an ascendancy or superiority over the bank clerk; it lies in his temporary ability to make a threat, which might well be sufficient to make the bank clerk do the particular thing he is told to do. There is no other form of relationship of superiority and inferiority between the two men except this short-lived coercive one. But for the gunman's purposes this may be enough; for the simple face-to-face order 'Hand over those notes or I'll shoot' dies with the occasion. The gunman does not issue to the bank clerk (though he may to his gang of followers) *standing orders* to be followed time after time by classes of persons. Yet laws pre-eminently have this 'standing' or persistent characteristic. Hence if we are to use the notion of orders backed by threats as explaining what laws are, we must endeavour to reproduce this enduring character which laws have.

We must therefore suppose that there is a general belief on the part of those to whom the general orders apply that disobedience is likely to be followed by the execution of the threat not only on the first promulgation of the order, but continuously until the order is withdrawn or cancelled. This continuing belief in the consequences of disobedience may be said to keep the original orders alive or 'standing', though as we shall see later there is difficulty in analysing the persistent quality of laws in these simple terms. Of course the concurrence of many factors which could not be reproduced in the gunman situation may, in fact, be required if such a general belief in the continuing likelihood of the execution of the threat is to exist: it may be that the power to carry out threats attached to such standing orders affecting large numbers of persons could only in fact exist, and would only be thought to exist, if it was known that some considerable number of the population were prepared both themselves to obey voluntarily, i.e. independently of fear of the threat, and to co-operate in the execution of the threats on those who disobeyed.

Whatever the basis of this general belief in the likelihood of the execution of the threats, we must distinguish from it a further necessary feature which we must add to the gunman situation if it is to approximate to the settled situation in which there is law. We must suppose that, whatever the motive, most of the orders are more often obeyed than disobeyed by most of those affected. We shall call this here, following Austin, 'a general habit of obedience' and note, with him, that like many other aspects of law it is an essentially vague or imprecise notion. The question how many people must obey how many such general orders, and for how long, if there is to be law, no more admits of definite answers than the question how few hairs must a man have to be bald. Yet in this fact of general obedience lies a crucial distinction between laws and the original simple case of the gunman's order. Mere temporary ascendancy of one person over another is naturally thought of as the polar opposite of law, with its relatively enduring and settled character, and, indeed, in most legal systems to exercise such short-term coercive power as the gunman has would constitute a criminal offence. It remains indeed to be seen whether this simple, though admittedly vague, notion of general habitual obedience to general orders backed by threats is really enough to reproduce the settled character and continuity which legal systems possess.

The concept of general orders backed by threats given by one generally obeyed, which we have constructed by successive additions to the simple situation of the gunman case, plainly approximates closer to a penal statute enacted by the legislature of a modern state than to any other variety of law. For there are types of law which seem prima facie very unlike such penal statutes, and we shall have later to consider the claim that these other varieties of law also, in spite of appearances to the contrary, are really just complicated or disguised versions of this same form. But if we are to reproduce the features of even a penal statute in our constructed model of general orders generally obeyed, something more must be said about the person who gives the orders. The legal system of a modern state is characterized by a certain kind of *supremacy* within its territory and *independence* of other systems which we have not yet reproduced in our simple model. These two notions are not as simple as they may appear, but what, on a common-sense view (which may not prove adequate) is essential to them, may be expressed as follows. English law, French law, and the law of any modern country regulates the conduct of populations inhabiting territories with fairly well-defined geographical limits. Within the territory of each country there may be many different persons or bodies of persons giving general orders backed by threats and receiving habitual obedience. But we should distinguish some of these persons or bodies (e.g. the L.C.C. or a minister exercising what we term powers of delegated legislation) as *subordinate* lawmakers in contrast to the Queen in Parliament who is supreme. We can express this relationship in the simple terminology of habits by saying that whereas the Queen in Parliament in making laws obeys no one habitually, the subordinate lawmakers keep within limits statutorily prescribed and so may be said in making law to be agents of the Queen in Parliament. If they did not do so we should not have one system of law in England but a plurality of systems; whereas in fact just because the Queen in Parliament is supreme in relation to all within the territory in this sense and the other bodies are not, we have in England a single system in which we can distinguish a hierarchy of supreme and subordinate elements.

The same negative characterization of the Queen in Parliament, as *not* habitually obeying the orders of others, roughly defines the notion of *independence* which we use in speaking of the separate legal systems of different countries. The supreme legislature of the Soviet Union is not in the habit of obeying the Queen in Parliament, and whatever the latter enacted about Soviet affairs (though it would constitute part of the law of England) would not form part of the law of the U.S.S.R. It would do so only if the Queen in Parliament were habitually obeyed by the legislature of the U.S.S.R.

On this simple account of the matter, which we shall later have to examine critically, there must, wherever there is a legal system, be some persons or body of persons issuing general orders backed by threats which are generally obeyed, and it must be generally believed that these threats are likely to be implemented in the event of disobedience. This person or body must be internally supreme and externally independent. If, following Austin, we call such a supreme and independent person or body of persons the sovereign, the laws of any country will be the general orders backed by threats which are issued either by the sovereign or subordinates in obedience to the sovereign.

III

THE VARIETY OF LAWS

I F we compare the varieties of different kinds of law to be found in a modern system such as English Law with the simple model of coercive orders constructed in the last chapter, a crowd of objections leap to mind. Surely not all laws order people to do or not to do things. Is it not misleading so to classify laws which confer powers on private individuals to make wills, contracts, or marriages, and laws which give powers to officials, e.g. to a judge to try cases, to a minister to make rules, or a county council to make by-laws? Surely not all laws are enacted nor are they all the expression of someone's desire like the general orders of our model. This seems untrue of custom which has a genuine though modest place in most legal systems. Surely laws, even when they are statutes deliberately made, need not be orders given only to *others*. Do not statutes often bind the legislators themselves? Finally, must enacted laws to be laws really express any legislator's actual desires, intentions, or wishes? Would an enactment duly passed not be law if (as must be the case with many a section of an English Finance Act) those who voted for it did not know what it meant?

These are some of the most important of many possible objections. Plainly some modification of the original simple model will be necessary to deal with them and, when they have all been accommodated, we may find that the notion of general orders backed by threats has been transformed out of recognition.

The objections we have mentioned fall into three main groups. Some of them concern the *content* of laws, others their *mode of origin*, and others again their *range of application*. All legal systems, at any rate, *seem* to contain laws which in respect of one or more of these three matters diverge from the model of general orders which we have set up. In the rest of this chapter we shall consider separately these three types of objection. We shall leave to the next chapter a more fundamental criticism that apart from these objections on the score of content, mode of origin, and range of application, the whole conception of a supreme and independent sovereign habitually obeyed, on which the model rests, is misleading, since there is little in any actual legal system which corresponds to it.

1. THE CONTENT OF LAWS

The criminal law is something which we either obey or disobey and what its rules require is spoken of as a 'duty'. If we disobey we are said to 'break' the law and what we have done is legally 'wrong', a 'breach of duty', or an 'offence'. The social function which a criminal statute performs is that of setting up and defining certain kinds of conduct as something to be avoided or done by those to whom it applies, irrespective of their wishes. The punishment or 'sanction' which is attached by the law to breaches or violations of the criminal law is (whatever other purpose punishment may serve) intended to provide one motive for abstaining from these activities. In all these respects there is at least a strong analogy between the criminal law and its sanctions and the general orders backed by threats of our model. There is some analogy (notwithstanding many important differences) between such general orders and the law of torts, the primary aim of which is to provide individuals with compensation for harm suffered as the result of the conduct of others. Here too the rules which determine what types of conduct constitute actionable wrongs are spoken of as imposing on persons, irrespective of their wishes, 'duties' (or more rarely 'obligations') to abstain from such conduct. This conduct is itself termed a 'breach of duty' and the compensation or other legal remedies a 'sanction'. But there are important classes of law where this analogy with orders backed by threats altogether fails, since they perform a quite different social function. Legal rules defining the ways in which valid contracts or wills or marriages are made do not require persons to act in certain ways whether they wish to or not. Such laws do not impose duties or obligations. Instead, they provide individuals with *facilities* for realizing their wishes, by conferring legal powers upon them to create, by certain specified procedures and subject to certain conditions, structures of rights and duties within the coercive framework of the law.

The power thus conferred on individuals to mould their legal relations with others by contracts, wills, marriages, &c., is one of the great contributions of law to social life; and it is a feature of law obscured by representing all law as a matter of orders backed by threats. The radical difference in function between laws that confer such powers and the criminal statute is reflected in much of our normal ways of speaking about this class of laws. We may or may not 'comply' in making our will with the provision of s. 9 of the Wills Act, 1837, as to the number of witnesses. If we do not comply the document we have made will not be a 'valid' will creating rights and duties; it will be a 'nullity' without legal 'force' or 'effect'. But, though it is a nullity our failure to comply with the statutory provision is not a 'breach' or a 'violation' of any obligation or duty nor an 'offence' and it would be confusing to think of it in such terms.

If we look into the various legal rules that confer legal powers on private individuals we find that these themselves fall into distinguishable kinds. Thus behind the power to make wills or contracts are rules relating to *capacity* or minimum personal qualification (such as being adult or sane) which those exercising the power must possess. Other rules detail the manner and form in which the power is to be exercised, and settle whether wills or contracts may be made orally or in writing, and if in writing the form of execution and attestation. Other rules delimit the variety, or maximum or minimum duration, of the structure of rights and duties which individuals may create by such acts-in-the-law. Examples of such rules are those of public policy in relation to contract, or the rules against accumulations in wills or settlements.

We shall consider later the attempts made by jurists to assimilate those laws which provide facilities or powers and say, 'If you wish to do this, this is the way to do it' to the criminal laws which, like orders backed by threats, say, 'Do this whether you wish to or not.' Here, however, we shall consider a further class of laws which also confer legal powers but, in contrast to those just discussed, the powers are of a public or official rather than a private nature. Examples of these are to be found in all the three departments, judicial, legislative, and administrative, into which government is customarily though vaguely divided.

Consider first those laws which lie behind the operation of a law court. In the case of a court some rules specify the subject-matter and content of the judge's jurisdiction or, as we say, give him 'power to try' certain types of case. Other rules specify the manner of appointment, the qualifications for, and tenure of judicial office. Others again will lay down canons of correct judicial behaviour and determine the procedure to be followed in the court. Examples of such rules, forming something like a judicial code, are to be found in the County Courts Act, 1959, the Court of Criminal Appeal Act, 1907, or Title 28 of the United States Code. It is salutary to observe the variety of provisions made in these statutes for the constitution and normal operation of a law court. Few of these seem at first sight to be orders given to the judge to do or abstain from doing anything; for though of course there is no reason why the law should not also by special rules prohibit a judge under penalty from exceeding his jurisdiction or trying a case in which he has a financial interest, these rules imposing such legal duties would be additional to those conferring judicial powers on him and defining his jurisdiction. For the concern of rules conferring such powers is not to deter judges from improprieties but to define the conditions and limits under which the court's decisions shall be valid.

It is instructive to examine in a little detail a typical provision specifying the extent of a court's jurisdiction. We may take as a very simple example the section of the County Courts Act, 1959 as amended, which confers jurisdiction on the county courts to try actions for the recovery of land. Its language which is very remote from that of 'orders', is as follows:

A county court shall have jurisdiction to hear and determine any action for the recovery of land where the net annual value for rating of the land in question does not exceed one hundred pounds.[1]

If a county court judge exceeds his jurisdiction by trying a case for the recovery of land with an annual value greater than £100 and makes an order concerning such land, neither he nor the parties to the action commit an *offence*. Yet the position is not quite like that which arises when a private person does something which is a 'nullity' for lack of compliance with

[1] Section 48 (1).

some condition essential for the valid exercise of some legal power. If a would-be testator omits to sign or obtain two witnesses to his will, what he writes has no legal status or effect. A court's order is not, however, treated in this way even if it is plainly one outside the jurisdiction of the court to make. It is obviously in the interests of public order that a court's decision should have legal authority until a superior court certifies its invalidity, even if it is one which the court should not legally have given. Hence, until it is set aside on appeal as an order given in excess of jurisdiction, it stands as a legally effective order between the parties which will be enforced. But it has a legal defect: it *is liable* to be set aside or 'quashed' on appeal because of the lack of jurisdiction. It is to be noted that there is an important difference between what is ordinarily spoken of in England as a 'reversal' by a superior court of an inferior court's order and the 'quashing' of an order for lack of jurisdiction. If an order is reversed, it is because what the lower court has said either about the law applicable to the case or the facts, is considered wrong. But an order of the lower court which is quashed for lack of jurisdiction may be impeccable in both these respects. It is not *what* the judge in the lower court has said or ordered that is wrong, but *his* saying or ordering of it. He has purported to do something which he is not legally empowered to do though other courts may be so empowered. But for the complication that, in the interests of public order a decision given in excess of jurisdiction stands till quashed by a superior court, conformity or failure to conform to rules of jurisdiction is like conformity and failure to conform to rules defining the conditions for the valid exercise of legal powers by private individuals. The relationship between the conforming action and the rule is ill-conveyed by the words 'obey' and 'disobey', which are more apposite in the case of the criminal law where the rules are analogous to orders.

A statute conferring legislative powers on a subordinate legislative authority similarly exemplifies a type of legal rule that cannot, except at the cost of distortion, be assimilated to a general order. Here too, as in the exercise of private powers, conformity with the conditions specified by the rules conferring the legislative powers is a step which is like a 'move' in a game such as chess; it has consequences definable in terms of the rules, which the system enables persons to achieve. Legislation is an exercise of legal powers 'operative' or effective in creating legal rights and duties. Failure to conform to the conditions of the enabling rule makes what is done ineffective and so a nullity for this purpose.

The rules which lie behind the exercise of legislative powers are themselves even more various than those which lie behind the jurisdiction of a court, for provision must be made by them for many different aspects of legislation. Thus some rules specify the subject-matter over which the legislative power may be exercised; others the qualifications or identity of the members of the legislative body; others the manner and form of legislation and the procedure to be followed by the legislature. These are only a few of the relevant matters; a glance at any enactment such as the Municipal Corporations Act, 1882, conferring and defining the powers of an inferior legislature or rule-making body will reveal many more. The consequence of failure to conform to such rules may not always be the same, but there will always be some rules, failure to conform to which renders a purported exercise of legislative power a nullity or, like the decision of an inferior court, liable to be declared invalid. Sometimes a certificate that the required procedures have been followed may by law be made conclusive as to matters of internal procedure, and sometimes persons not qualified under the rules, who participate in legislative proceedings, may be liable to a penalty under special criminal rules making this an offence. But, though partly hidden by these complications, there is a radical difference between rules conferring and defining the manner of exercise of legislative powers and the rules of criminal law, which at least resemble orders backed by threats.

In some cases it would be grotesque to assimilate these two broad types of rule. If a measure before a legislative body obtains the required majority of votes and is thus duly passed, the voters in favour of the measure have not 'obeyed' the law requiring a majority decision nor have those who voted against it either obeyed or disobeyed it: the same is of course true if the measure fails to obtain the required majority and so no law is passed. The radical difference in function between such rules as these prevents the use here of the terminology appropriate to conduct in its relation to rules of the criminal law.

A full detailed taxonomy of the varieties of law comprised in a modern legal system, free from the prejudice that all *must* be reducible to a single simple type, still remains to be accomplished. In distinguishing certain laws under the very rough head of laws that confer powers from those that impose duties and are analogous to orders backed by threats, we have made only a beginning. But perhaps enough has been done to show that some of the distinctive features of a legal system lie in the provision it makes, by rules of this type, for the exercise of private and public legal powers. If such rules of this distinctive kind did not exist we should lack some of the most familiar concepts of social life, since these logically presuppose the existence of such rules. Just as there could be no crimes or offences and so no murders or thefts if there were no criminal laws of the mandatory kind which do resemble orders backed by threats, so there could be no buying, selling, gifts, wills, or marriages if there were no power-conferring rules; for these latter things, like the orders of courts and the enactments of law-making bodies, just consist in the valid exercise of legal powers.

Nevertheless the itch for uniformity in jurisprudence is strong: and since it is by no means disreputable, we must consider two alternative arguments in favour of it which have been sponsored by great jurists. These arguments are designed to show that the distinction between varieties of law which we have stressed is superficial, if not unreal, and that 'ultimately' the notion of orders backed by threats is adequate for the analysis of rules conferring powers as well as for the rules of criminal law. As with most theories which have persisted long in jurisprudence there is an element of truth in these arguments. There certainly are points of resemblance between the legal rules of the two sorts which we have distinguished. In both cases actions may be criticized or assessed by reference to the rules as legally the 'right' or 'wrong' thing to do. Both the power-conferring rules concerning the making of a will and the rule of criminal law prohibiting assault under penalty constitute *standards* by which particular actions may be thus critically appraised. So much is perhaps implied in speaking of them both as rules. Further it is important to realize that rules of the power-conferring sort, though different from rules which impose duties and so have some analogy to orders backed by threats, are always related to such rules; for the powers which they confer are powers to make general rules of the latter sort or to impose duties on particular persons who would otherwise not be subject to them. This is most obviously the case when the power conferred is what would ordinarily be termed a power to legislate. But, as we shall see, it is also true in the case of other legal powers. It might be said, at the cost of some inaccuracy, that whereas rules like those of the criminal law impose duties, power-conferring rules are recipes for creating duties.

Nullity as a sanction

The first argument, designed to show the fundamental identity of the two sorts of rule and to exhibit both as coercive orders, fastens on the 'nullity' which ensues when some essential condition for the exercise of the power is not fulfilled. This, it is urged, is like the punishment attached to the criminal law, a threatened evil or sanction exacted by law for breach of the rule; though it is conceded that in certain cases this sanction may only amount to a slight inconvenience. It is in this light that we are invited to view the case of one who seeks to enforce by law, as contractually binding, a promise made to him, and finds, to his chagrin, that, since it is not under seal and he gave no consideration for the promise, the written promise is legally a nullity. Similarly we are to think of the rule providing that a will without two witnesses will be inoperative, as moving testators to compliance with s. 9 of the Wills Act, just as we are moved to obedience to the criminal law by the thought of imprisonment.

No one could deny that there are, in some cases, these associations between nullity and such psychological factors as disappointment of the hope that a transaction will be valid. Nonetheless the extension of the idea of a sanction to include nullity is a source (and a sign) of confusion. Some minor objections to it are well known. Thus, in many cases, nullity may not be an 'evil' to the person who has failed to satisfy some condition required for legal validity. A judge may have no material interest in and may be indifferent to the validity of his order; a party who finds that the contract on which he is sued is not binding on him, because he was under age or did not sign the memorandum in writing required for certain contracts, might not recognize here a 'threatened evil' or 'sanction'. But apart from these trivialities, which might be accommodated with some ingenuity, nullity cannot, for more important reasons, be assimilated to a punishment attached to a rule as an inducement to abstain from the activities which the rule forbids. In the case of a rule of criminal law we can identify and distinguish two things: a certain type of conduct which the rule prohibits, and a sanction intended to discourage it. But how could we consider in this light such desirable social activities as men making each other promises which do not satisfy legal requirements as to form? This is not like the conduct discouraged by the criminal law, something which the legal rules stipulating legal forms for contracts are designed to suppress. The rules merely withhold legal recognition from them. Even more absurd is it to regard as a sanction the fact that a legislative measure, if it does not obtain the required majority, fails to attain the status of a law. To assimilate this fact to the sanctions of the criminal law would be like thinking of the scoring rules of a game as designed to eliminate all moves except the kicking of goals or the making of runs. This, if successful, would be the end of all games; yet only if we think of power-conferring rules as designed to make people behave in certain ways and as adding 'nullity' as a motive for obedience, can we assimilate such rules to orders backed by threats.

The confusion inherent in thinking of nullity as similar to the threatened evil or sanctions of the criminal law may be brought out in another form. In the case of the rules of the criminal law, it is logically possible and might be desirable that there should be such rules even though no punishment or other evil were threatened. It may of course be argued that in that case they would not be *legal* rules; nonetheless, we can distinguish clearly the rule prohibiting certain behaviour from the provision for penalties to be exacted if the rule is broken, and suppose the first to exist without the latter. We can, in a sense, subtract the sanction and still leave an intelligible standard of behaviour which it was designed to maintain. But we cannot logically make such a distinction between the rule requiring compliance with certain conditions, e.g. attestation for a valid will, and the so-called sanction of 'nullity'. In this case, if failure to comply with this essential condition did not entail nullity, the rule itself could not be intelligibly said to exist without sanctions even as a non-legal rule. The provision for nullity is *part* of this type of rule itself in a way which punish-ment attached to a rule imposing duties is not. If failure to get the ball between the posts did not mean the 'nullity' of not scoring, the scoring rules could not be said to exist.

The argument which we have here criticized is an attempt to show the fundamental identity of power-conferring rules with coercive orders by *widening* the meaning of a sanction or threatened evil, so as to include the nullity of a legal transac-tion when it is vitiated by non-compliance with such rules. The second argument which we shall consider takes a different, indeed an opposite, line. Instead of attempting to show that these rules are a species of coercive orders, it denies them the status of 'law'. To exclude them it *narrows* the meaning of the word 'law'. The general form of this argument, which appears in a more or less extreme form in different jurists, is to assert that what are loosely or in popular modes of expression referred to as complete rules of law, are really incomplete fragments of coercive rules which are the only 'genuine' rules of law.

Power-conferring rules as fragments of laws

In its extreme form this argument would deny that even the rules of the criminal law, in the words in which they are often stated, are genuine laws. It is in this form that the argument is adopted by Kelsen: 'Law is the primary norm which stipulates the sanction'.[1] There is no law prohibiting murder: there is only a law directing officials to apply certain sanctions in certain circumstances to those who do murder. On this view, what is ordinarily thought of as the content of law, designed to guide the conduct of ordinary citizens, is merely the antecedent or 'if-clause' in a rule which is directed not to them but to officials, and orders them to apply certain sanctions if certain conditions are satisfied. All genuine laws, on this view, are con-ditional orders to officials to apply sanctions. They are all of the form, 'If anything of a kind X is done or omitted or happens, then apply sanction of a kind Y.'

By greater and greater elaboration of the antecedent or if-clauses, legal rules of every type, including the rules conferring and defining the manner of exercise of private or public powers, can be restated in this conditional form. Thus, the provisions

---

[1] *General Theory of Law and State*, p. 63. See above, p. 2.

of the Wills Act requiring two witnesses would appear as a common part of many different directions to courts to apply sanctions to an executor who, in breach of the provisions of the will, refuses to pay the legacies: 'if and only if there is a will duly witnessed containing these provisions and if . . . then sanctions must be applied to him.' Similarly, a rule specifying the extent of a court's jurisdiction would appear as a common part of the conditions to be satisfied before it applies any sanctions. So too, the rules conferring legislative powers and defining the manner and form of legislation (including the provisions of a constitution concerning the supreme legislature) can also be restated and exhibited as specifying certain common conditions on the fulfilment of which (among others) the courts are to apply the sanctions mentioned in the statutes. Thus, the theory bids us disentangle the substance from the obscuring forms; then we shall see that constitutional forms such as 'what the Queen in Parliament enacts is law', or the provisions of the American constitution as to the law-making power of Congress, merely specify the general conditions under which courts are to apply sanctions. These forms are essentially 'if-clauses', not complete rules: '*If* the Queen in Parliament has so enacted . . .' or '*if* Congress within the limits specified in the Constitution has so enacted . . .' are forms of conditions common to a vast number of directions to courts to apply sanctions or punish certain types of conduct.

This is a formidable and interesting theory, purporting to disclose the true, uniform nature of law latent beneath a variety of common forms and expressions which obscure it. Before we consider its defects it is to be observed that, in this extreme form, the theory involves a shift from the original conception of law as consisting of orders backed by threats of sanctions which are to be exacted when the orders are disobeyed. Instead, the central conception now is that of orders to officials to apply sanctions. On this view it is not necessary that a sanction be prescribed for the *breach* of every law; it is only necessary that every 'genuine' law shall direct the application of some sanction. So it may well be the case that an official who disregards such directions will not be punishable; and of course this is in fact often the case in many legal systems.

This general theory may, as we have said, take one of two

forms, one less extreme than the other. In the less extreme form the original conception of law (which many find intuitively more acceptable) as orders backed by threats directed to ordinary citizens, among others, is preserved at least for those rules that, on a common-sense view, refer primarily to the conduct of ordinary citizens, and not merely to officials. The rules of the criminal law, on this more moderate view, are laws as they stand, and need no recasting as fragments of other complete rules; for they are already orders backed by threats. Recasting is, however, needed in other cases. Rules which confer legal powers on private individuals are, for this as for the more extreme theory, mere fragments of the real complete laws—the orders backed by threats. These last are to be discovered by asking: what persons does the law order to do things, subject to a penalty if they do not comply? When this is known the provisions of such rules as those of the Wills Act, 1837, in relation to witnesses, and other rules conferring on individuals powers and defining the conditions for valid exercise of them, may be recast as specifying some of the conditions under which ultimately such a legal duty arises. They will then appear as part of the antecedent or 'if-clause' of conditional orders backed by threats or rules imposing duties. 'If and only if a will has been signed by the testator and witnessed by two witnesses in the specified manner and if . . . then the executor (or other legal representative) shall give effect to the provisions of the will.' Rules relating to the formation of contract will similarly appear as mere fragments of rules ordering persons, if certain things are the case or have been said or done (if the party is of full age, has covenanted under seal or been promised consideration) to do the things which by the contract are to be done.

A recasting of rules conferring legislative powers (including the provisions of a constitution as to the supreme legislature), so as to represent them as fragments of the 'real' rules, may be carried through along the lines similar to those explained on page 36 in the case of the more extreme version of this theory. The only difference is that on the more moderate view the power-conferring rules are represented by the antecedents or if-clauses of rules ordering ordinary citizens, under threat of sanctions, to do things and not merely (as in the more extreme theory) as the if-clauses of directions to officials to apply sanctions.

Both versions of this theory attempt to reduce apparently distinct varieties of legal rule to a single form alleged to convey the quintessence of law. Both, in different ways, make the sanction a centrally important element, and both will fail if it is shown that law without sanctions is perfectly conceivable. This general objection must be, however, left till later. The specific criticism of both forms of the theory which we shall develop here is that they purchase the pleasing uniformity of pattern to which they reduce all laws at too high a price: that of distorting the different social functions which different types of legal rule perform. This is true of both forms of the theory, but is most evident in the recasting of the criminal law demanded by the theory in its more extreme form.

Distortion as the price of uniformity

The distortion effected by this recasting is worth considering for it illuminates many different aspects of law. There are many techniques by which society may be controlled, but the characteristic technique of the criminal law is to designate by rules certain types of behaviour as standards for the guidance either of the members of society as a whole or of special classes within it: they are expected without the aid or intervention of officials to understand the rules and to see that the rules apply to them and to conform to them. Only when the law is broken, and this primary function of the law fails, are officials concerned to identify the fact of breach and impose the threatened sanctions. What is distinctive of this technique, as compared with individuated face-to-face orders which an official, like a policeman on traffic duty, might give to a motorist, is that the members of society are left to discover the rules and conform their behaviour to them; in this sense they 'apply' the rules themselves to themselves, though they are provided with a motive for conformity in the sanction added to the rule. Plainly we shall conceal the characteristic way in which such rules function if we concentrate on, or make primary, the rules requiring the courts to impose the sanctions in the event of disobedience; for these latter rules make provision for the breakdown or failure of the primary purpose of the system. They may indeed be indispensable but they are ancillary.

The idea that the substantive rules of the criminal law have

as their function (and, in a broad sense, their meaning) the
guidance not merely of officials operating a system of penalties,
but of ordinary citizens in the activities of non-official life,
cannot be eliminated without jettisoning cardinal distinctions
and obscuring the specific character of law as a means of social
control. A punishment for a crime, such as a fine, is not the
same as a tax on a course of conduct, though both involve
directions to officials to inflict the same money loss. What
differentiates these ideas is that the first involves, as the second
does not, an offence or breach of duty in the form of a violation
of a rule set up to guide the conduct of ordinary citizens. It is
true that this generally clear distinction may in certain circumstances be blurred. Taxes may be imposed not for revenue
purposes but to discourage the activities taxed, though the law
gives no express indications that these are to be abandoned as
it does when it 'makes them criminal'. Conversely the fines
payable for some criminal offence may, because of the deprecia-
tion of money, become so small that they are cheerfully paid.
They are then perhaps felt to be 'mere taxes', and 'offences' are
frequent, precisely because in these circumstances the sense is
lost that the rule is, like the bulk of the criminal law, meant to
be taken seriously as a standard of behaviour.

It is sometimes urged in favour of theories like the one under
consideration that, by recasting the law in a form of a direction
to apply sanctions, an advance in clarity is made, since this form
makes plain all that the 'bad man' wants to know about the law.
This may be true but it seems an inadequate defence for the
theory. Why should not law be equally if not more concerned
with the 'puzzled man' or 'ignorant man' who is willing to do
what is required, if only he can be told what it is? Or with the
'man who wishes to arrange his affairs' if only he can be told
how to do it? It is of course very important, if we are to understand the law, to see how the courts administer it when they
come to apply its sanctions. But this should not lead us to think
that all there is to understand is what happens in courts. The
principal functions of the law as a means of social control are
not to be seen in private litigation or prosecutions, which
represent vital but still ancillary provisions for the failures of
the system. It is to be seen in the diverse ways in which the law
is used to control, to guide, and to plan life out of court.

We may compare the inversion of ancillary and principal, which this extreme form of the theory makes, to the following suggestion for recasting the rules of a game. A theorist, considering the rules of cricket or baseball, might claim that he had discovered a uniformity hidden by the terminology of the rules and by the conventional claim that some were primarily addressed to players, some primarily to officials (umpire and scorer), some to both. 'All rules', the theorist might claim, 'are *really* rules directing officials to do certain things under certain conditions.' The rules that certain motions after hitting the ball constitute a 'run', or that being caught makes a man 'out', are really just complex directions to officials; in the one case to the scorer to write down 'a run' in the scoring-book and in the other to the umpire to order the man 'off the field'. The natural protest is that the uniformity imposed on the rules by this transformation of them conceals the ways in which the rules operate, and the manner in which the players use them in guiding purposive activities, and so obscures their function in the co-operative, though competitive, social enterprise which is the game.

The less extreme form of the theory would leave the criminal law and all other laws which impose duties untouched, since these already conform to the simple model of coercive orders. But it would reduce all rules conferring and defining the manner of exercise of legal powers to this single form. It is open here to the same criticism as the extreme form of the theory. If we look at all law simply from the point of view of the persons on whom its duties are imposed, and reduce all other aspects of it to the status of more or less elaborate conditions in which duties fall on them, we treat as something merely subordinate, elements which are at least as characteristic of law and as valuable to society as duty. Rules conferring private powers must, if they are to be understood, be looked at from the point of view of those who exercise them. They appear then as an additional element introduced by the law into social life over and above that of coercive control. This is so because possession of these legal powers makes of the private citizen, who, if there were no such rules, would be a mere duty-bearer, a private legislator. He is made competent to determine the course of the law within the sphere of his contracts, trusts, wills, and other structures of rights and duties which he is enabled to build. Why should rules which are used in this special way, and confer this huge and distinctive amenity, not be recognized as distinct from rules which impose duties, the incidence of which is indeed in part determined by the exercise of such powers? Such power-conferring rules are thought of, spoken of, and used in social life differently from rules which impose duties, and they are valued for different reasons. What other tests for difference in character could there be?

The reduction of rules conferring and defining legislative and judicial powers to statements of the conditions under which duties arise has, in the public sphere, a similar obscuring vice. Those who exercise these powers to make authoritative enactments and orders use these rules in a form of purposive activity utterly different from performance of duty or submission to coercive control. To represent such rules as mere aspects or fragments of the rules of duty is, even more than in the private sphere, to obscure the distinctive characteristics of law and of the activities possible within its framework. For the introduction into society of rules enabling legislators to change and add to the rules of duty, and judges to determine when the rules of duty have been broken, is a step forward as important to society as the invention of the wheel. Not only was it an important step; but it is one which, as we shall argue in Chapter IV, may fairly be considered as the step from the pre-legal into the legal world.

2. THE RANGE OF APPLICATION

Plainly a penal statute, of all the varieties of law, approximates most closely to the simple model of coercive orders. Yet even these laws have certain characteristics, examined in this section, to which the model is apt to blind us, and we shall not understand them till we shake off its influence. The order backed by threats is essentially the expression of a wish that *others* should do or abstain from doing certain things. It is, of course, possible that legislation might take this exclusively other-regarding form. An absolute monarch wielding legislative power may, in certain systems, always be considered exempt from the scope of the laws he makes; and even in a democratic system laws may be made which do not apply to those who made them, but only to special classes indicated in the law. But the range of application of a law is always a question of its interpretation. It may or may not be found on interpretation to exclude those who made it, and, of course, many a law is now made which imposes legal obligations on the makers of the law. Legislation, as distinct from just ordering *others* to do things under threats, may perfectly well have such a self-binding force. There is nothing *essentially* other-regarding about it. This is a legal phenomenon which is puzzling only so long as we think, under the influence of the model, of the laws as always laid down by a man or men above the law for others subjected to it.

This vertical or 'top-to-bottom' image of law making, so attractive in its simplicity, is something which can only be reconciled with the realities by the device of distinguishing between the legislator in his official capacity as one person and in his private capacity as another. Acting in the first capacity he then makes law which imposes obligations on other persons, including himself in his 'private capacity'. There is nothing objectionable in these forms of expression, but the notion of different capacities, as we shall see in Chapter IV, is intelligible only in terms of power-conferring rules of law which cannot be reduced to coercive orders. Meanwhile it is to be observed that this complicated device is really quite unnecessary; we can explain the self-binding quality of legislative enactment without it. For we have to hand, both in daily life and in the law, something which will enable us to understand it far better. This is the operation of a *promise* which in many ways is a far better model than that of coercive orders for understanding many, though not all, features of law.

To promise is to say something which creates an obligation for the promisor: in order that words should have this kind of effect, rules must exist providing that if words are used by appropriate persons on appropriate occasions (i.e. by sane persons understanding their position and free from various sorts of pressure) those who use these words shall be bound to do the things designated by them. So, when we promise, we make use of specified procedures to change our own moral situation by imposing obligations on ourselves and conferring rights on others; in lawyers' parlance we exercise 'a power' conferred by rules to do this. It would be indeed possible, but not helpful, to distinguish two persons 'within' the promisor: one acting in the capacity of creator of obligations and the other in the capacity of person bound: and to think of one as ordering the other to do something.

Equally we can dispense with this device for understanding the self-binding force of legislation. For the making of a law, like the making of a promise, presupposes the existence of certain rules which govern the process: words said or written by the persons qualified by these rules, and following the procedure specified by them, create obligations for all within the ambit designated explicitly or implicitly by the words. These may include those who take part in the legislative process.

Of course, though there is this analogy which explains the self-binding character of legislation, there are many differences between the making of promises and the making of laws. The rules governing the latter are very much more complex and the bilateral character of a promise is not present. There is usually no person in the special position of the promisee *to whom* the promise is made and who has a special, if not the only, claim to its performance. In these respects certain other forms of self-imposition of obligation known to English law, such as that whereby a person declares himself trustee of property for other persons, offer a closer analogy to the self-binding aspect of legislation. Yet, in general, making of law by enactment is something we shall understand best by considering such private ways of creating particular legal obligations.

What is most needed as a corrective to the model of coercive orders or rules, is a fresh conception of legislation as the introduction or modification of general standards of behaviour to be followed by the society generally. The legislator is not necessarily like the giver of orders to another: someone by definition outside the reach of what he does. Like the giver of a promise he exercises powers conferred by rules: very often he may, as the promisor *must*, fall within their ambit.

3. MODES OF ORIGIN

So far we have confined our discussion of the varieties of law to statutes which, in spite of the differences we have emphasized, have one salient point of analogy with coercive orders. The enactment of a law, like the giving of an order, *is* a deliberate datable act. Those who take part in legislation consciously operate a procedure for making law, just as the man who gives an order consciously uses a form of words to secure recognition of, and compliance with, his intentions. Accordingly, theories which use the model of coercive orders in the analysis of law make the claim that all law can be seen, if we strip away the disguises, to have this point of resemblance to legislation and to owe its status as law to a deliberate law-creating act. The type of law which most obviously conflicts with this claim is custom; but the discussion whether custom is 'really' law has often been confused by the failure to disentangle two distinct issues. The first is whether 'custom as such' is law or not. The meaning and good sense of the denial that custom, as such, is law lie in the simple truth that, in any society, there are many customs which form no part of its law. Failure to take off a hat to a lady is not a breach of any rule of law; it has no legal status save that of being permitted by law. This shows that custom is law only if it is one of a class of customs which is 'recognized' as law by a particular legal system. The second issue concerns the meaning of 'legal recognition'. What is it for a custom to be legally recognized? Does it, as the model of coercive orders requires, consist in the fact that someone, perhaps 'the sovereign' or his agent, has ordered the custom to be obeyed, so that its status as law is due to something which, in this respect, resembles the act of legislation?

Custom is not in the modern world a very important 'source' of law. It is usually a subordinate one, in the sense that the legislature may by statute deprive a customary rule of legal status; and in many systems the tests which courts apply, in determining whether a custom is fit for legal recognition, incorporate such fluid notions as that of 'reasonableness' which provide at least some foundation for the view that in accepting or rejecting a custom courts are exercising a virtually uncontrolled discretion. Even so, to attribute the legal status of a custom to the fact that a court or the legislature or the sovereign has so 'ordered' is to adopt a theory which can only be carried through if a meaning is given to 'order' so extended as to rob the theory of its point.

In order to present this doctrine of legal recognition we must recall the part played by the sovereign in the conception of law as coercive orders. According to this theory, law is the order of either the sovereign or of his subordinate whom he may choose to give orders on his behalf. In the first case law is made by the order of the sovereign in the most literal sense of 'order'. In the second case the order given by the subordinate will only rank as law if it is, in its own turn, given in pursuance of some order issued by the sovereign. The subordinate must have some authority delegated by the sovereign to issue orders on his behalf. Sometimes this may be conferred by an express direction to a minister to 'make orders' on a certain subject-matter. If the theory stopped here, plainly it could not account for the facts; so it is extended and claims that sometimes the sovereign may express his will in less direct fashion. His orders may be 'tacit'; he may, without giving an express order, signify his intentions that his subjects should do certain things, by not interfering when his subordinates both give orders to his subjects and punish them for disobedience.

A military example may make the idea of a 'tacit order' as clear as it is possible to make it. A sergeant who himself regularly obeys his superiors, orders his men to do certain fatigues and punishes them when they disobey. The general, learning of this, allows things to go on, though if he had ordered the sergeant to stop the fatigues he would have been obeyed. In these circumstances the general may be considered tacitly to have expressed his will that the men should do the fatigues. His non-interference, when he could have interfered, is a silent substitute for the words he might have used in ordering the fatigues.

It is in this light that we are asked to view customary rules which have the status of law in a legal system. Till the courts apply them in particular cases such rules are *mere* customs, in no sense law. When the courts use them, and make orders in accordance with them which are enforced, then for the first time these rules receive legal recognition. The sovereign who might have interfered has tacitly ordered his subjects to obey the judges' orders 'fashioned' on pre-existing custom.

This account of the legal status of custom is open to two different criticisms. The first is that it is not *necessarily* the case that until they are used in litigation customary rules have no status as law. The assertion that this is necessarily the case is either merely dogmatic or fails to distinguish what is necessary from what may be the case in certain systems. Why, if statutes made in certain defined ways are law before they are applied by the courts in particular cases, should not customs of certain defined kinds also be so? Why should it not be true that, just as the courts recognize as binding the general principle that what the legislature enacts is law, they also recognize as binding another general principle: that customs of certain defined sorts are law? What absurdity is there in the contention that, when particular cases arise, courts apply custom, as they apply statute, as something which is already law and because it is law? It is, of course, *possible* that a legal system should provide that no customary rule should have the status of law until the courts, in their uncontrolled discretion, declared that it should. But this would be just *one* possibility, which cannot exclude the possibility of systems in which the courts have no such discretion. How can it establish the general contention that a customary rule *cannot* have the status of law till applied in court?

The answers made to these objections sometimes reduce to no more than the reassertion of the dogma that nothing can be law unless and until it has been *ordered* by someone to be so. The suggested parallel between the relationships of courts to statute and to custom is then rejected on the ground that, before it is applied by a court, a statute has already been 'ordered' but a custom has not. Less dogmatic arguments are inadequate because they make too much of the particular arrangements of particular systems. The fact that in English law a custom may be rejected by the courts if it fails to pass the test of 'reasonableness' is sometimes said to show that it is not law till applied by the courts. This again could at the most only prove something about custom in English law. Even this cannot be established, unless it is true, as some claim, that it is meaningless to distinguish a system in which courts are only bound to apply certain customary rules if they are reasonable from a system in which they have an uncontrolled discretion.

The second criticism of the theory that custom, when it is law, owes its legal status to the sovereign's tacit order is more fundamental. Even if it is conceded that it is not law till enforced by the court in the particular case, is it possible to treat the failure of the sovereign to interfere as a tacit expression of the wish that the rules should be obeyed? Even in the very simple military example on page 45 it is not a necessary inference from the fact that the general did not interfere with the sergeant's orders that he wished them to be obeyed. He may merely have wished to placate a valued subordinate and hoped that the men would find some way of evading the fatigues. No doubt we might in some cases draw the inference that he wished the fatigues to be done, but if we did this, a material part of our evidence would be the fact that the general knew that the orders had been given, had time to consider them, and decided to do nothing. The main objection to the use of the idea of tacit expressions of the sovereign's will to explain the legal status of custom is that, in any modern state, it is rarely possible to ascribe such knowledge, consideration and decision not to interfere to the 'sovereign', whether we identify the sovereign with the supreme legislature or the electorate. It is, of course, true that in most legal systems custom is a source of law subordinate to statute. This means that the legislature *could* take away their legal status; but failure to do this may not be a sign of the legislator's wishes. Only very rarely is the attention of a legislature, and still more rarely that of the electorate, turned to the customary rules applied by courts. Their non-interference can therefore not be compared to the general's non-interference with his sergeant; even if, in his case, we are prepared to infer from it a wish that his subordinate's orders be obeyed.

In what then does the legal recognition of custom consist? To what does a customary rule owe its legal status, if it is not to the order of the court which applied it to a particular case or to the tacit order of the supreme law-making power? How can it, like statute, be law before the court applies it? These questions can only be fully answered when we have scrutinized in detail, as we shall in the next chapter, the doctrine that, where there is law, there must be some sovereign person or persons whose general orders, explicit or tacit, alone are law. Meanwhile we may summarize the conclusions of this chapter as follows:

The theory of law as coercive orders meets at the outset with the objection that there are varieties of law found in all systems which, in three principal respects, do not fit this description. First, even a penal statute, which comes nearest to it, has often a range of application different from that of orders given to others; for such a law may impose duties on those who make it as well as on others. Secondly, other statutes are unlike orders in that they do not require persons to do things, but may confer powers on them; they do not impose duties but offer facilities for the free creation of legal rights and duties within the coercive framework of the law. Thirdly, though the enactment of a statute is in some ways analogous to the giving of an order, some rules of law originate in custom and do not owe their legal status to any such conscious law-creating act.

To defend the theory against these objections a variety of expedients have been adopted. The originally simple idea of a threat of evil or 'sanction' has been stretched to include the nullity of a legal transaction; the notion of a legal rule has been narrowed so as to exclude rules which confer powers, as being mere fragments of law; within the single natural person of the legislator whose enactments are self-binding two persons have been discovered; the notion of an order has been extended from a verbal to a 'tacit' expression of will, consisting in non-interference with orders given by subordinates. Notwithstanding the ingenuity of these devices, the model of orders backed by threats obscures more of law than it reveals; the effort to reduce to this single simple form the variety of laws ends by imposing upon them a spurious uniformity. Indeed, to look for uniformity here may be a mistake, for, as we shall argue in Chapter V, a distinguishing, if not the distinguishing, characteristic of law lies in its fusion of different types of rule.

IV

SOVEREIGN AND SUBJECT

IN criticizing the simple model of law as coercive orders we have so far raised no questions concerning the 'sovereign' person or persons whose general orders constitute, according to this conception, the law of any society. Indeed in discussing the adequacy of the idea of an order backed by threats as an account of the different varieties of law, we provisionally assumed that in any society where there is law, there actually is a sovereign, characterized affirmatively and negatively by reference to the habit of obedience: a person or body of persons whose orders the great majority of the society habitually obey and who does not habitually obey any other person or persons.

We must now consider in some detail this general theory concerning the foundations of all legal systems; for in spite of its extreme simplicity the doctrine of sovereignty is nothing less than this. The doctrine asserts that in every human society, where there is law, there is ultimately to be found latent beneath the variety of political forms, in a democracy as much as in an absolute monarchy, this simple relationship between subjects rendering habitual obedience and a sovereign who renders habitual obedience to no one. This vertical structure composed of sovereign and subjects is, according to the theory, as essential a part of a society which possesses law, as a backbone is of a man. Where it is present, we may speak of the society, together with its sovereign, as a single independent state, and we may speak of *its* law: where it is not present, we can apply none of these expressions, for the relation of sovereign and subject forms, according to this theory, part of their very meaning.

Two points in this doctrine are of special importance and we shall emphasize them here in general terms in order to indicate the lines of criticism pursued in detail in the rest of the chapter. The first concerns the idea of a *habit* of obedience, which is all that is required on the part of those to whom the sovereign's laws apply. Here we shall inquire whether such a habit is sufficient to account for two salient features of most legal systems: the *continuity* of the authority to make law possessed by a succession of different legislators, and the *persistence* of laws long after their maker and those who rendered him habitual obedience have perished. Our second point concerns the position occupied by the sovereign above the law: he creates law for others and so imposes legal duties or 'limitations' upon them whereas he is said himself to be legally unlimited and illimitable. Here we shall inquire whether this legally illimitable status of the supreme law-giver is necessary for the existence of law, and whether either the presence or the absence of legal limits on legislative power can be understood in the simple terms of habit and obedience into which this theory analyses these notions.

I. THE HABIT OF OBEDIENCE AND THE CONTINUITY OF LAW

The idea of obedience, like many other apparently simple ideas used without scrutiny, is not free from complexities. We shall disregard the complexity already noticed[1] that the word 'obedience' often suggests deference to authority and not merely compliance with orders backed by threats. Even so, it is not easy to state, even in the case of a single order given face to face by one man to another, precisely what connexion there must be between the giving of the order and the performance of the specified act in order that the latter should constitute obedience. What, for example, is the relevance of the fact, when it is a fact, that the person ordered would certainly have done the very same thing without any order? These difficulties are particularly acute in the case of laws, some of which prohibit people from doing things which many of them would never think of doing. Till these difficulties are settled the whole idea of a 'general habit of obedience' to the laws of a country must remain somewhat obscure. We may, however, for our present purposes imagine a very simple case to which the words 'habit' and 'obedience' would perhaps be conceded to have a fairly obvious application.

[1] See p. 19 above.

We shall suppose that there is a population living in a territory in which an absolute monarch (Rex) reigns for a very long time: he controls his people by general orders backed by threats requiring them to do various things which they would not otherwise do, and to abstain from doing things which they would otherwise do; though there was trouble in the early years of the reign, things have long since settled down and, in general, the people can be relied on to obey him. Since what Rex requires is often onerous, and the temptation to disobey and risk the punishment is considerable, it is hardly to be supposed that the obedience, though generally rendered, is a 'habit' or 'habitual' in the full sense or most usual sense of that word. Men can indeed quite literally acquire the habit of complying with certain laws: driving on the left-hand side of the road is perhaps a paradigm, for Englishmen, of such an acquired habit. But where the law runs counter to strong inclinations as, for example, do laws requiring the payment of taxes, our eventual compliance with them, even though regular, has not the unreflective, effortless, engrained character of a habit. Nonetheless, though the obedience accorded to Rex will often lack this element of habit, it will have other important ones. To say of a person that he has a habit, e.g. of reading a newspaper at breakfast, entails that he has for some considerable time past done this and that he is likely to repeat this behaviour. If so, it will be true of most people in our imagined community, at any time after the initial period of trouble, that they have generally obeyed the orders of Rex and are likely to continue to do so.

It is to be noted that, on this account of the social situation under Rex, the habit of obedience is a personal relationship between each subject and Rex: each regularly does what Rex orders him, among others, to do. If we speak of the *population* as 'having such a habit', this, like the assertion that people habitually frequent the tavern on Saturday nights, will mean only that the habits of most of the people are convergent: they each habitually obey Rex, just as they might each habitually go to the tavern on Saturday night.

It is to be observed that in this very simple situation all that is required from the community to constitute Rex the sovereign are the personal acts of obedience on the part of the population. Each of them need, for his part, only obey; and, so long as obedience is regularly forthcoming, no one in the community need have or express any views as to whether his own or others' obedience to Rex is in any sense right, proper, or legitimately demanded. Plainly, the society we have described, in order to give as literal application as possible to the notion of a habit of obedience, is a very simple one. It is probably far too simple ever to have existed anywhere, and it is certainly not a primitive one; for primitive society knows little of absolute rulers like Rex, and its members are not usually concerned merely to obey but have pronounced views as to the rightness of obedience on the part of all concerned. Nonetheless the community under Rex has certainly some of the important marks of a society governed by law, at least during the lifetime of Rex. It has even a certain unity, so that it may be called 'a state'. This unity is constituted by the fact that its members obey the same person, even though they may have no views as to the rightness of doing so.

Let us now suppose that, after a successful reign, Rex dies leaving a son Rex II who then starts to issue general orders. The mere fact that there was a general habit of obedience to Rex I in his lifetime does not by itself even render probable that Rex II will be habitually obeyed. Hence if we have nothing more to go on than the fact of obedience to Rex I and the likelihood that *he* would continue to be obeyed, we shall not be able to say of Rex II's first order, as we could have said of Rex I's last order, that it was given by one who was sovereign and was therefore law. There is as yet no established habit of obedience to Rex II. We shall have to wait and see whether such obedience will be accorded to Rex II, as it was to his father, before we can say, in accordance with the theory, that he is now sovereign and his orders are law. There is nothing to make him sovereign from the start. Only after we know that his orders have been obeyed for some time shall we be able to say that a habit of obedience has been established. Then, but not till then, we shall be able to say of any further order that it is already law as soon as it is issued and before it is obeyed. Till this stage is reached there will be an interregnum in which no law can be made.

Such a state of affairs is of course possible and has occasionally been realized in troubled times: but the dangers of discontinuity are obvious and not usually courted. Instead, it is characteristic of a legal system, even in an absolute monarchy, to secure the uninterrupted continuity of law-making power by rules which bridge the transition from one law-giver to another: these regulate the succession *in advance*, naming or specifying in general terms the qualifications of and mode of determining the law-giver. In a modern democracy the qualifications are highly complex and relate to the composition of a legislature with a frequently changing membership, but the essence of the rules required for continuity can be seen in the simpler forms appropriate to our imaginary monarchy. If the rule provides for the succession of the eldest son, then Rex II has a *title* to succeed his father. He will have the *right* to make law on his father's death, and when his first orders are issued we may have good reason for saying that they are already law, before any relationship of habitual obedience between him personally and his subjects has had time to establish itself. Indeed such a relationship may never be established. Yet his word may be law; for Rex II may himself die immediately after issuing his first orders; he will not have lived to receive obedience, yet he may have had the *right* to make law and his orders may be law.

In explaining the continuity of law-making power through a changing succession of individual legislators, it is natural to use the expressions 'rule of succession', 'title', 'right to succeed', and 'right to make law'. It is plain, however, that with these expressions we have introduced a new set of elements, of which no account can be given in terms of habits of obedience to general orders, out of which, following the prescription of the theory of sovereignty, we constructed the simple legal world of Rex I. For in that world there were no rules, and so no rights or titles, and hence *a fortiori* no right or title to succeed: there were just the facts that orders were given by Rex I, and his orders were habitually obeyed. To constitute Rex sovereign during his lifetime and to make his orders law, no more was needed; but this is not enough to account for his successor's *rights*. In fact, the idea of habitual obedience fails, in two different though related ways, to account for the continuity to be observed in every normal legal system, when one legislator succeeds another. First, mere habits of obedience to orders given by one legislator cannot confer on the new legislator any *right* to succeed the old and give orders in his place. Secondly, habitual obedience to the old law-giver cannot by itself render probable, or found any presumption, that the new legislator's orders will be obeyed. If there is to be this right and this presumption at the moment of succession there must, during the reign of the earlier legislator, have been somewhere in the society a general social practice more complex than any that can be described in terms of habit of obedience: there must have been the acceptance of the rule under which the new legislator is entitled to succeed.

What is this more complex practice? What is the acceptance of a rule? Here we must resume the inquiry already outlined in Chapter I. To answer it we must, for the moment, turn aside from the special case of legal rules. How does a habit differ from a rule? What is the difference between saying of a group that they have the habit, e.g. of going to the cinema on Saturday nights, and saying that it is the rule with them that the male head is to be bared on entering a church? We have already mentioned in Chapter I some of the elements which must be brought into the analysis of this type of rule, and here we must pursue the analysis further.

There is certainly one point of similarity between social rules and habits: in both cases the behaviour in question (e.g. baring the head in church) must be general though not necessarily invariable; this means that it is repeated when occasion arises by most of the group: so much is, as we have said, implied in the phrase, 'They do it *as a rule*.' But though there is this similarity there are three salient differences.

First, for the group to have a *habit* it is enough that their behaviour in fact converges. Deviation from the regular course need not be a matter for any form of criticism. But such general convergence or even identity of behaviour is not enough to constitute the existence of a rule requiring that behaviour: where there is such a rule deviations are generally regarded as lapses or faults open to criticism, and threatened deviations meet with pressure for conformity, though the forms of criticism and pressure differ with different types of rule.

Secondly, where there are such rules, not only is such criticism in fact made but deviation from the standard is generally accepted as a *good reason* for making it. Criticism for deviation is regarded as legitimate or justified in this sense, as are demands for compliance with the standard when deviation is threatened. Moreover, except by a minority of hardened offenders, such criticism and demands are generally regarded as legitimate, or made with good reason, both by those who make them and those to whom they are made. How many of the group must in these various ways treat the regular mode of behaviour as a standard of criticism, and how often and for how long they must do so to warrant the statement that the group has a rule, are not definite matters; they need not worry us more than the question as to the number of hairs a man may have and still be bald. We need only remember that the statement that a group has a certain rule is compatible with the existence of a minority who not only break the rule but refuse to look upon it as a standard either for themselves or others.

The third feature distinguishing social rules from habits is implicit in what has already been said, but it is one so important and so frequently disregarded or misrepresented in jurisprudence that we shall elaborate it here. It is a feature which throughout this book we shall call the *internal aspect* of rules. When a habit is general in a social group, this generality is merely a fact about the observable behaviour of most of the group. In order that there should be such a habit no members of the group need in any way think of the general behaviour, or even know that the behaviour in question is general; still less need they strive to teach or intend to maintain it. It is enough that each for his part behaves in the way that others also in fact do. By contrast, if a social rule is to exist some at least must look upon the behaviour in question as a general standard to be followed by the group as a whole. A social rule has an 'internal' aspect, in addition to the external aspect which it shares with a social habit and which consists in the regular uniform behaviour which an observer could record.

This internal aspect of rules may be simply illustrated from the rules of any game. Chess players do not merely have similar habits of moving the Queen in the same way which an external observer, who knew nothing about their attitude to the moves which they make, could record. In addition, they have a reflective critical attitude to this pattern of behaviour: they regard it as a standard for all who play the game. Each not only moves the Queen in a certain way himself but 'has views' about the propriety of all moving the Queen in that way. These views are manifested in the criticism of others and demands for conformity made upon others when deviation is actual or threatened, and in the acknowledgement of the legitimacy of such criticism and demands when received from others. For the expression of such criticisms, demands, and acknowledgements a wide range of 'normative' language is used. 'I (You) ought not to have moved the Queen like that', 'I (You) must do that', 'That is right', 'That is wrong'.

The internal aspect of rules is often misrepresented as a mere matter of 'feelings' in contrast to externally observable physical behaviour. No doubt, where rules are generally accepted by a social group and generally supported by social criticism and pressure for conformity, individuals may often have psychological experiences analogous to those of restriction or compulsion. When they say they 'feel bound' to behave in certain ways they may indeed refer to these experiences. But such feelings are neither necessary nor sufficient for the existence of 'binding' rules. There is no contradiction in saying that people accept certain rules but experience no such feelings of compulsion. What is necessary is that there should be a critical reflective attitude to certain patterns of behaviour as a common standard, and that this should display itself in criticism (including self-criticism), demands for conformity, and in acknowledgements that such criticism and demands are justified, all of which find their characteristic expression in the normative terminology of 'ought', 'must', and 'should', 'right' and 'wrong'.

These are the crucial features which distinguish social rules from mere group habits, and with them in mind we may return to the law. We may suppose that our social group has not only rules which, like that concerning baring the head in church, makes a specific kind of behaviour standard, but a rule which provides for the identification of standards of behaviour in a less direct fashion, by reference to the words, spoken or written, of a given person. In its simplest form this rule will be to the effect that whatever actions Rex specifies (perhaps in certain formal ways) are to be done. This transforms the situation which we first depicted in terms of mere habits of obedience to Rex; for where such a rule is accepted Rex will not only in fact specify what is to be done but will have the *right* to do this; and not only will there be general obedience to his orders, but it will be generally accepted that it is *right* to obey him. Rex will in fact be a legislator with the *authority* to legislate, i.e. to introduce new standards of behaviour into the life of the group, and there is no reason, since we are now concerned with standards, not 'orders', why he should not be bound by his own legislation.

The social practices which underlie such legislative authority will be, in all essentials, the same as those which underlie the simple direct rules of conduct, like that concerning baring the head in church, which we may now distinguish as mere customary rules, and they will differ in the same way from general habits. Rex's *word* will now be a standard of behaviour so that deviations from the behaviour he designates will be open to criticism; his word will now generally be referred to and accepted as justifying criticism and demands for compliance.

In order to see how such rules explain the continuity of legislative authority, we need only notice that in some cases, even before a new legislator has begun to legislate, it may be clear that there is a firmly established rule giving him, as one of a *class* or line of persons, the right to do this in his turn. Thus we may find it generally accepted by the group, during the lifetime of Rex I, that the person whose word is to be obeyed is not limited to the individual Rex I but is that person who, for the time being, is qualified in a certain way, e.g. as the eldest living descendant in the direct line of a certain ancestor: Rex I is merely the particular person so qualified at a particular time. Such a rule, unlike the habit of obeying Rex I, looks forward, since it refers to future possible lawgivers as well as the present actual lawgiver.

The acceptance, and so the existence, of such a rule will be manifested during Rex I's lifetime in part by obedience to him, but also by acknowledgements that obedience is something to which he has a right by virtue of his qualification under the general rule. Just because the scope of a rule accepted at a given time by a group may look forward in general terms to successors in the office of legislator in this way, its acceptance affords us grounds *both* for the statement of law that the successor has a right to legislate, even before he starts to do so, and for the statement of fact that he is likely to receive the same obedience as his predecessor does.

Of course, acceptance of a rule by a society at one moment does not *guarantee* its continued existence. There may be a revolution: the society may cease to accept the rule. This may happen either during the lifetime of one legislator, Rex I, or at the point of transition to a new one, Rex II, and, if it does happen, Rex I will lose or Rex II will not acquire, the right to legislate. It is true that the position may be obscure: there may be intermediate confused stages, when it is not clear whether we are faced with a mere insurrection or temporary interruption of the old rule, or a full-scale effective abandonment of it. But in principle the matter is clear. The statement that a new legislator has a right to legislate presupposes the existence, in the social group, of the rule under which he has this right. If it is clear that the rule which now qualifies him was accepted during the lifetime of his predecessor, whom it also qualified, it is to be assumed, in the absence of evidence to the contrary, that it has not been abandoned and still exists. A similar continuity is to be observed in a game when the scorer, in the absence of evidence that the rules of the game have been changed since the last innings, credits the new batsman with the runs which he makes, assessed in the usual way.

Consideration of the simple legal worlds of Rex I and Rex II is perhaps enough to show that the continuity of legislative authority which characterizes most legal systems depends on that form of social practice which constitutes the acceptance of a rule, and differs, in the ways we have indicated, from the simpler facts of mere habitual obedience. We may summarize the argument as follows. Even if we concede that a person, such as Rex, whose general orders are habitually obeyed, may be called a legislator and his orders laws, habits of obedience to each of a succession of such legislators are not enough to account for the *right* of a successor to succeed and for the consequent continuity in legislative power. First, because habits are not 'normative'; they cannot confer rights or authority on anyone. Secondly, because habits of obedience to one individual cannot, though accepted rules can, refer to a class or line of future successive legislators as well as to the current legislator, or render obedience to them likely. So the fact that there is habitual obedience to one legislator neither affords grounds for the statement that his successor has the right to make law, nor for the factual statement that he is likely to be obeyed. At this point, however, an important point must be noticed which we shall develop fully in a later chapter. It constitutes one of the strong points of Austin's theory. In order to reveal the essential differences between accepted rules and habits we have taken a very simple form of society. Before we leave this aspect of sovereignty we must inquire how far our account of the acceptance of a rule conferring authority to legislate could be transferred to a modern state. In referring to our simple society we spoke as if most ordinary people not only obeyed the law but understood and accepted the rule qualifying a succession of lawgivers to legislate. In a simple society this might be the case; but in a modern state it would be absurd to think of the mass of the population, however law abiding, as having any clear realization of the rules specifying the qualifications of a continually changing body of persons entitled to legislate. To speak of the populace 'accepting' these rules, in the same way as the members of some small tribe might accept the rule giving authority to its successive chiefs, would involve putting into the heads of ordinary citizens an understanding of constitutional matters which they might not have. We would only require such an understanding of the officials or experts of the system; the courts, which are charged with the responsibility of determining what the law is, and the lawyers whom the ordinary citizen consults when he wants to know what it is.

These differences between a simple tribal society and a modern state deserve attention. In what sense, then, are we to think of the continuity of the legislative authority of the Queen in Parliament, preserved throughout the changes of successive legislators, as resting on some fundamental rule or rules generally accepted? Plainly, general acceptance is here a complex phenomenon, in a sense divided between official and ordinary citizens, who contribute to it and so to the *existence* of a legal system in different ways. The officials of the system may be said to acknowledge explicitly such fundamental rules conferring legislative authority: the legislators do this when they make laws in accordance with the rules which empower them to do so: the courts when they identify, as laws to be applied by them, the laws made by those thus qualified, and the experts when they guide the ordinary citizens by reference to the laws so made. The ordinary citizen manifests his acceptance largely by acquiescence in the results of these official operations. He keeps the law which is made and identified in this way, and also makes claims and exercises powers conferred by it. But he may know little of its origin or its makers: some may know nothing more about the laws than that they are 'the law'. It forbids things ordinary citizens want to do, and they know that they may be arrested by a policeman and sentenced to prison by a judge if they disobey. It is the strength of the doctrine which insists that habitual obedience to orders backed by threats is the foundation of a legal system that it forces us to think in realistic terms of this relatively passive aspect of the complex phenomenon which we call the existence of a legal system. The weakness of the doctrine is that it obscures or distorts the other relatively active aspect, which is seen primarily, though not exclusively, in the law-making, law-identifying, and law-applying operations of the officials or experts of the system. Both aspects must be kept in view if we are to see this complex social phenomenon for what it actually is.

2. THE PERSISTENCE OF LAW

In 1944 a woman was prosecuted in England and convicted for telling fortunes in violation of the Witchcraft Act, 1735.[1] This is only a picturesque example of a very familiar legal phenomenon: a statute enacted centuries ago may still be law today. Yet familiar though it is, the persistence of laws in this way is something which cannot be made intelligible in terms of the simple scheme which conceives of laws as orders given by a person habitually obeyed. We have in fact here the converse of the problem of the continuity of law-making authority which we have just considered. There the question was how, on the basis of the simple scheme of habits of obedience, it could be said that the first law made by a successor to the office of legislator is *already* law before he personally had received habitual obedience. Here the question is: how can law made

---

[1] *R.* v. *Duncan*, [1944] 1 K.B. 713.

by an earlier legislator, long dead, *still* be law for a society that cannot be said habitually to obey him? As in the first case, no difficulty arises for the simple scheme if we confine our view to the lifetime of the legislator. Indeed, it seems to explain admirably why the Witchcraft Act was law in England but would not have been law in France, even if its terms extended to French citizens telling fortunes in France, though of course it could have been applied to those Frenchmen who had the misfortune to be brought before English courts. The simple explanation would be that in England there was a habit of obedience to those who enacted this law whereas in France there was not. Hence it was law for England but not for France.

We cannot, however, narrow our view of laws to the lifetime of their makers, for the feature which we have to explain is just their obdurate capacity to survive their makers and those who habitually obeyed them. Why is the Witchcraft Act law still for us, if it was not law for the contemporary French? Surely, by no stretch of language can we, the English of the twentieth century, now be said habitually to obey George II and his Parliament. In this respect, the English now and the French then are alike: neither habitually obey or obeyed the maker of this law. The Witchcraft Act might be the sole Act surviving from this reign and yet it would still be law in England now. The answer to this problem of 'Why law still?' is in principle the same as the answer to our first problem of 'Why law already?' and it involves the substitution, for the too simple notion of habits of obedience to a sovereign person, of the notion of currently accepted fundamental rules specifying a class or line of persons whose word is to constitute a standard of behaviour for the society, i.e. who have the *right* to legislate. Such a rule, though it must exist now, may in a sense be timeless in its reference: it may not only look forward and refer to the legislative operation of a future legislator but it may also look back and refer to the operations of a past one.

Presented in the simple terms of the Rex dynasty the position is this. Each of a line of legislators, Rex I, II, and III, may be qualified under the same general rule that confers the right to legislate on the eldest living descendant in the direct line. When the individual ruler dies his legislative work lives on; for it rests upon the foundation of a general rule which successive generations of the society continue to respect regarding each legislator whenever he lived. In the simple case Rex I, II, and III, are each entitled, under the same general rule, to introduce standards of behaviour by legislation. In most legal systems matters are not quite so simple, for the presently accepted rule under which past legislation is recognized as law may differ from the rule relating to contemporary legislation. But, given the present acceptance of the underlying rule, the persistence of laws is no more mysterious than the fact that the decision of the umpire, in the first round of a tournament between teams whose membership has changed, should have the same relevance to the final result as those of the umpire who took his place in the third round. Nonetheless, if not mysterious, the notion of an accepted rule conferring authority on the orders of past and future, as well as present, legislators, is certainly more complex and sophisticated than the idea of habits of obedience to a present legislator. Is it possible to dispense with this complexity, and by some ingenious extension of the simple conception of orders backed by threats show that the persistence of laws rests, after all, on the simpler facts of habitual obedience to the present sovereign?

One ingenious attempt to do this has been made: Hobbes, echoed here by Bentham and Austin, said that 'the legislator is he, not by whose authority the laws were first made, but by whose authority they now continue to be laws'.[1] It is not immediately clear, if we dispense with the notion of a rule in favour of the simpler idea of habit, what the 'authority' as distinct from the 'power' of a legislator can be. But the general argument expressed by this quotation is clear. It is that, though as a matter of history the source or origin of a law such as the Witchcraft Act was the legislative operation of a past sovereign, its present status as law in twentieth-century England is due to its recognition as law by the present sovereign. This recognition does not take the form of an *explicit* order, as in the case of statutes made by the now living legislators, but of a *tacit* expression of the sovereign's will. This consists in the fact that, though he could, he does not interfere with the enforcement by his agents (the courts and possibly the executive) of the statute made long ago.

---

[1] *Leviathan*, chap. xxvi.

This is, of course, the same theory of tacit orders already considered, which was invoked to explain the legal status of certain customary rules, which appeared not to have been ordered by any one at any time. The criticisms which we made of this theory in Chapter III apply even more obviously when it is used to explain the continued recognition of past legislation as law. For though, owing to the wide discretion accorded to the courts to reject unreasonable customary rules, there may be some plausibility in the view that until the courts actually apply a customary rule in a given case, it has no status as law, there is very little plausibility in the view that a statute made by a past 'sovereign' is not law until it is actually applied by the courts in the particular case, and enforced with the acquiescence of the present sovereign. If this theory is right it follows that the courts do not enforce it because it is already law: yet this would be an absurd inference to draw from the fact that the present legislator could repeal the past enactments but has not exercised this power. For Victorian statutes and those passed by the Queen in Parliament today surely have precisely the same legal status in present-day England. Both are law even before cases to which they are applied arise in the courts and, when such cases do arise, the courts apply both Victorian and modern statutes because they are already law. In neither case are these law only after they are applied by the courts; and in both cases alike their status as law is due to the fact that they were enacted by persons whose enactments are now authoritative under presently accepted rules, irrespective of the fact that these persons are alive or dead.

The incoherence of the theory that past statutes owe their present status as law to the acquiescence of the present legislature in their application by the courts, may be seen most clearly in its incapacity to explain why the courts of the present day should distinguish between a Victorian statute which has not been repealed as still law, and one which was repealed under Edward VII as no longer law. Plainly, in drawing such distinctions the courts (and with them any lawyer or ordinary citizen who understands the system) use as a criterion a fundamental rule or rules of what is to count as law which embraces past as well as present legislative operations: they do not rest their discrimination between the two statutes on knowledge that the present sovereign has tacitly commanded (i.e. allowed to be enforced) one but not the other.

Again, it seems that the only virtue in the theory we have rejected is that of a blurred version of a realistic reminder. In this case it is the reminder that unless the officials of the system and above all the courts accept the rule that certain legislative operations, *past or present*, are authoritative, something essential to their status as law will be lacking. But realism of this humdrum sort must not be inflated into the theory sometimes known as Legal Realism, the main features of which are discussed in detail later,[1] and which, in some versions, holds *no* statute to be law until it is actually applied by a court. There is a difference, crucial for the understanding of law, between the truth that if a statute is to be law, the courts must accept the rule that certain legislative operations make law, and the misleading theory that nothing is law till it is applied in a particular case by a court. Some versions of the theory of Legal Realism of course go far beyond the false explanation of the persistence of laws which we have criticized; for they go the full length of denying that the status of law can belong to any statute whether made by a past or *present* sovereign, before the courts have actually applied it. Yet an explanation of the persistence of laws which stops short of the full Realist theory and acknowledges that statutes of the present sovereign, as distinguished from past sovereigns, are law before they are applied by the courts has the worst of both worlds and is surely quite absurd. This half-way position is untenable because there is nothing to distinguish the legal status of a statute of the present sovereign and an unrepealed statute of an earlier one. Either both (as ordinary lawyers would acknowledge) or neither, as the full Realist theory claims, are law before they are applied by the courts of the present day to a particular case.

3. LEGAL LIMITATIONS ON LEGISLATIVE POWER

In the doctrine of sovereignty the general habit of obedience of the subject has, as its complement, the absence of any such habit in the sovereign. He makes law for his subjects and makes it from a position outside any law. There are, and can be, no

[1] See pp. 132–44 below.

legal limits on his law-creating power. It is important to understand that the legally unlimited power of the sovereign is his by definition: the theory simply asserts that there could only be legal limits on legislative power if the legislator were under the orders of another legislator whom he habitually obeyed; and in that case he would no longer be sovereign. If he is sovereign he does not obey any other legislator and hence there can be no legal limits on his legislative power. The importance of the theory does not of course lie in these definitions and their simple necessary consequences which tell us nothing about the facts. It lies in the claim that in every society where there is law there is a sovereign with these attributes. We may have to look behind legal or political forms, which suggest that all legal powers are limited and that no person or persons occupy the position outside the law ascribed to the sovereign. But if we are resolute in our search we shall find the reality which, as the theory claims, exists behind the forms.

We must not misinterpret the theory as making either a weaker or a stronger claim than it in fact makes. The theory does not merely state that there are *some* societies where a sovereign subject to no legal limits is to be found, but that everywhere the existence of law implies the existence of such a sovereign. On the other hand the theory does not insist that there are no limits on the sovereign's power but only that there are no *legal* limits on it. So the sovereign may in fact defer, in exercising legislative power, to popular opinion either from fear of the consequences of flouting it, or because he thinks himself morally bound to respect it. Very many different factors may influence him in this, and, if a fear of popular revolt or moral conviction leads him not to legislate in ways which he otherwise would, he may indeed think and speak of these factors as 'limits' on his power. But they are not legal limits. He is under no legal duty to abstain from such legislation, and the law courts, in considering whether they have before them a law of the sovereign, would not listen to the argument that its divergence from the requirements of popular opinion or morality prevented it from ranking as law, unless there was an order of the sovereign that they should.

The attractions of this theory as a general account of law are manifest. It seems to give us in satisfying simple form an answer to two major questions. When we have found the sovereign who receives habitual obedience but yields it to no one, we can do two things. First, we can identify in his general orders the law of a given society and distinguish it from many other rules, principles, or standards, moral or merely customary, by which the lives of its members are also governed. Secondly, within the area of law we can determine whether we are confronted with an independent legal system or merely a subordinate part of some wider system.

It is usually claimed that the Queen in Parliament, considered as a single continuing legislative entity, fills the requirements of this theory and the sovereignty of Parliament consists in the fact that it does so. Whatever the accuracy of this belief (some aspects of which we later consider in Chapter VI), we can certainly reproduce quite coherently in the imaginary simple world of Rex I what the theory demands. It is instructive to do this before considering the more complex case of a modern state, since the full implications of the theory are best brought out in this way. To accommodate the criticisms made in Section 1 of the notion of habits of obedience we can conceive of the situation in terms of rules rather than habits. On this footing we shall imagine a society in which there is a rule generally accepted by courts, officials, and citizens that, whenever Rex orders anything to be done, his word constitutes a standard of behaviour for the group. It may well be that, in order to distinguish among these orders those expressions of 'private' wishes, which Rex does not wish to have 'official' status, from those which he does, ancillary rules will also be adopted specifying a special style which the monarch is to use when he legislates 'in the character of a monarch' but not when he gives private orders to his wife or mistress. Such rules concerning the manner and form of legislation must be taken seriously if they are to serve their purpose, and they may at times inconvenience Rex. Nonetheless, though we may well rank them as legal rules, we need not count them as 'limits' on his legislative power, since if he does follow the required form there is no subject on which he cannot legislate so as to give effect to his wishes. The 'area' if not the 'form' of his legislative power is unlimited by law.

The objection to the theory as a general theory of law is that the existence of a sovereign such as Rex in this imagined society, who is subject to no legal limitations, is not a necessary condition or presupposition of the existence of law. To establish this we need not invoke disputable or challengeable types of law. Our argument therefore is not drawn from systems of customary law or international law, to which some wish to deny the title of law just because they lack a legislature. Appeal to these cases is quite unnecessary; for the conception of the legally unlimited sovereign misrepresents the character of law in many modern states where no one would question that there is law. Here there are legislatures but sometimes the supreme legislative power within the system is far from unlimited. A written constitution may restrict the competence of the legislature not merely by specifying the form and manner of legislation (which we may allow not to be limitations) but by excluding altogether certain matters from the scope of its legislative competence, thus imposing limitations of substance.

Again, before examining the complex case of a modern state, it is useful to see what, in the simple world where Rex is the supreme legislator, 'legal limitations on his legislative power' would actually mean, and why it is a perfectly coherent notion.

In the simple society of Rex it may be the accepted rule (whether embodied in a written constitution or not) that no law of Rex shall be valid if it excludes native inhabitants from the territory or provides for their imprisonment without trial, and that any enactment contrary to these provisions shall be void and so treated by all. In such a case Rex's powers to legislate would be subject to limitations which surely would be legal, even if we are disinclined to call such a fundamental constitutional rule 'a law'. Unlike disregard of popular opinion or popular moral convictions to which he might often defer even against his inclinations, disregard of these specific restrictions would render his legislation void. The courts would therefore be concerned with these in a way in which they would not be concerned with the other merely moral or *de facto* limits on the legislator's exercise of his power. Yet, in spite of these legal limitations, surely Rex's enactments within their scope are laws, and there is an independent legal system in his society.

It is important to dwell a little longer on this imaginary

simple case in order to see precisely what legal limits of this type are. We might often express the position of Rex by saying that he 'cannot' pass laws providing for imprisonment without trial; it is illuminating to contrast this sense of 'cannot' with that which signifies that a person is under some legal duty or obligation not to do something. 'Cannot' is used in this latter sense when we say, 'You cannot ride a bicycle on the pavement.' A constitution which effectively restricts the legislative powers of the supreme legislature in the system does not do so by imposing (or at any rate need not impose) duties on the legislature not to attempt to legislate in certain ways; instead it provides that any such purported legislation shall be void. It imposes not legal duties but legal disabilities. 'Limits' here implies not the presence of *duty* but the absence of legal power.

Such restrictions on the legislative power of Rex may well be called constitutional: but they are not mere conventions or moral matters with which courts are unconcerned. They are parts of the rule conferring authority to legislate and they vitally concern the courts, since they use such a rule as a criterion of the validity of purported legislative enactments coming before them. Yet though such restrictions are legal and not merely moral or conventional, their presence or absence cannot be expressed in terms of the presence or absence of a habit of obedience on the part of Rex to other persons. Rex may well be subject to such restrictions and never seek to evade them; yet there may be no one whom he habitually obeys. He merely fulfils the conditions for making valid law. Or he may try to evade the restrictions by issuing orders inconsistent with them; yet if he does this he will not have disobeyed any one; he will not have broken any superior legislators' law or violated a legal duty. He will surely have failed to make (though he does not break) a valid law. Conversely, if in the constitutional rule qualifying Rex to legislate there are no legal restrictions on Rex's authority to legislate, the fact that he habitually obeys the orders of Tyrannus, the king of the neighbouring territory, will neither deprive Rex's enactments of their status as law nor show that they are subordinate parts of a single system in which Tyrannus has supreme authority.

The foregoing very obvious considerations establish a number of points much obscured by the simple doctrine of sovereignty yet vital for the understanding of the foundation of a legal system. These we may summarize as follows: First, legal limitations on legislative authority consist not of duties imposed on the legislator to obey some superior legislator but of disabilities contained in rules which qualify him to legislate.

Secondly, in order to establish that a purported enactment is law we do not have to trace it back to the enactment, express or tacit, of a legislator who is 'sovereign' or 'unlimited' either in the sense that his authority to legislate is legally unrestricted or in the sense that he is a person who obeys no one else habitually. Instead we have to show that it was made by a legislator who was qualified to legislate under an existing rule and that either no restrictions are contained in the rule or there are none affecting this particular enactment.

Thirdly, in order to show that we have before us an independent legal system we do not have to show that its supreme legislator is legally unrestricted or obeys no other person habitually. We have to show merely that the rules which qualify the legislator do not confer superior authority on those who have also authority over other territory. Conversely, the fact that he is not subject to such foreign authority does not mean that he has unrestricted authority within his own territory.

Fourthly, we must distinguish between a legally unlimited legislative authority and one which, though limited, is supreme in the system. Rex may well have been the highest legislating authority known to the law of the land, in the sense that all other legislation may be repealed by his, even though his own is restricted by a constitution.

Fifthly, and last, whereas the presence or absence of rules limiting the legislator's competence to legislate is crucial, the legislator's habits of obedience are at the most of some indirect evidential importance. The only relevance of the fact, if it be the fact, that the legislator is not in a habit of obedience to other persons is that sometimes it may afford some, though far from conclusive, evidence that his authority to legislate is not subordinate, by constitutional or legal rule, to that of others. Similarly, the only relevance of the fact that the legislator does habitually obey someone else is that this is some evidence that under the rules his authority to legislate is subordinate to that of others.

4. THE SOVEREIGN BEHIND THE LEGISLATURE

There are in the modern world many legal systems in which the body, normally considered to be the supreme legislature within the system, is subject to legal limitations on the exercise of its legislative powers; yet, as both lawyer and legal theorist would agree, the enactments of such a legislature within the scope of its limited powers are plainly law. In these cases, if we are to maintain the theory that wherever there is law there is a sovereign incapable of legal limitation, we must search for such a sovereign behind the legally limited legislature. Whether he is there to be found is the question which we must now consider.

We may neglect for the moment the provisions, which every legal system must make in one form or another, though not necessarily by a written constitution, as to the qualification of the legislators and 'the manner and form' of legislation. These may be considered as specifications of the identity of the legislative body and of what it must do to legislate rather than legal limitations on the scope of its legislative power; though, in fact, as the experience of South Africa has shown,[1] it is difficult to give general criteria which satisfactorily distinguish mere provisions as to 'manner and form' of legislation or definitions of the legislative body from 'substantial' limitations.

Plain examples of substantive limitations are, however, to be found in federal constitutions such as those of the United States or Australia, where the division of powers between the central government and the member states, and also certain individual rights, cannot be changed by the ordinary processes of legislation. In these cases an enactment, either of the state or federal legislature, purporting to alter or inconsistent with the federal division of powers or with the individual rights protected in this way, is liable to be treated as *ultra vires*, and declared legally invalid by the courts to the extent that it conflicts with the constitutional provisions. The most famous of such legal limitations on legislative powers is the Fifth Amendment to the constitution of the United States. This provides, among other things, that no person shall be deprived 'of life liberty or property without due process of law'; and statutes of Congress have been declared invalid by the courts when found to conflict

[1] See *Harris v. Dönges*, [1952] 1 T.L.R. 1245.

with these or with other restrictions placed by the constitution on their legislative powers.

There are, of course, many different devices for protecting the provisions of a constitution from the operations of the legislature. In some cases, such as that of Switzerland, some provisions as to the rights of the member states of a federation and the rights of individuals, though mandatory in form, are treated as 'merely political' or hortatory. In such cases the courts are not accorded jurisdiction to 'review' the enactment of the federal legislature and to declare it invalid even though it may be in plain conflict with the provisions of the constitution as to the proper scope of the legislature's operations.[1] Certain provisions of the United States constitution have been held to raise 'political questions', and where a case falls within this category the courts will not consider whether a statute violates the constitution.

Where legal limitations on the normal operations of the supreme legislature are imposed by a constitution, these themselves may or may not be immune from certain forms of legal change. This depends on the nature of the provision made by the constitution for its amendment. Most constitutions contain a wide amending power to be exercised either by a body distinct from the ordinary legislature, or by the members of the ordinary legislature using a special procedure. The provision of Article V of the constitution of the United States for amendments ratified by the legislatures of three-fourths of the States or by conventions in three-fourths thereof is an example of the first type of amending power; and the provision for amendment in the South Africa Act of 1909 s. 152 is an example of the second. But not all constitutions contain an amending power, and sometimes even where there is such an amending power certain provisions of the constitution which impose limits on the legislature are kept outside its scope; here the amending power is itself limited. This may be observed (though some limitations are no longer of practical importance) even in the constitution of the United States. For Article V provides that 'no amendment made prior to the Year 1808 shall in any Manner affect the first and fourth Clauses in the Ninth Section of the first Article and that no State without its consent shall be deprived of its equal suffrage in the Senate'.

[1] See Art. 113 of the Constitution of Switzerland.

Where the legislature is subject to limitations which can, as in South Africa, be removed by the members of the legislature operating a special procedure, it is arguable that it may be identified with the sovereign incapable of legal limitation which the theory requires. The difficult cases for the theory are those where the restrictions on the legislature can, as in the United States, only be removed by the exercise of an amending power entrusted to a special body, or where the restrictions are altogether outside the scope of any amending power.

In considering the claim of the theory to account consistently for these cases we must recall, since it is often overlooked, that Austin himself in elaborating the theory did *not* identify the sovereign with the legislature even in England. This was his view although the Queen in Parliament is, according to the normally accepted doctrine, free from legal limitations on its legislative power, and so is often cited as a paradigm of what is meant by 'a sovereign legislature' in contrast with Congress or other legislatures limited by a 'rigid' constitution. Nonetheless, Austin's view was that in any democracy it is not the elected representatives who constitute or form part of the sovereign body but the electors. Hence in England 'speaking accurately the members of the commons house are merely trustees for the body by which they are elected and appointed: and consequently the sovereignty always resides in the Kings Peers and the electoral body of the commons'.[1] Similarly, he held that in the United States sovereignty of each of the states and 'also of the larger state arising from the Federal Union resided in the states' governments as forming one aggregate body, meaning by a state's government not its ordinary legislature but the body of citizens which appoints its ordinary legislature'.[2]

Viewed in this perspective, the difference between a legal system in which the ordinary legislature is free from legal limitations, and one where the legislature is subject to them, appears merely as a difference between the manner in which the sovereign electorate chooses to exercise its sovereign powers. In England, on this theory, the only direct exercise made by the electorate of their share in the sovereignty consists in their

[1] Austin, *Province of Jurisprudence Determined*, Lecture VI, pp. 230–1.
[2] Ibid., p. 251.

election of representatives to sit in Parliament and the delegation to them of their sovereign power. This delegation is, in a
sense, absolute since, though a trust is reposed in them not to
abuse the powers thus delegated to them, this trust in such cases
is a matter only for moral sanctions and the courts are not
concerned with it, as they are with legal limitations on legislative power. By contrast, in the United States, as in every democracy where the ordinary legislature is legally limited, the
electoral body has not confined its exercise of sovereign power
to the election of delegates, but has subjected them to legal
restrictions. Here the electorate may be considered an 'extraordinary and ulterior legislature' superior to the ordinary
legislature which is legally 'bound' to observe the constitutional
restrictions and, in cases of conflict, the courts will declare the
Acts of the ordinary legislature invalid. Here then, in the
electorate, is the sovereign free from all legal limitations which
the theory requires.

It is plain that in these further reaches of the theory the
initial, simple conception of the sovereign has undergone a
certain sophistication, if not a radical transformation. The
description of the sovereign as 'the person or persons to whom
the bulk of the society are in the habit of obedience' had, as we
showed in Section 1 of this chapter, an almost literal application
to the simplest form of society, in which Rex was an absolute
monarch and no provision was made for the succession to him
as legislator. Where such a provision was made, the consequent
continuity of legislative authority, which is such a salient
feature of a modern legal system, could not be expressed in the
simple terms of habits of obedience, but required for its expression the notion of an accepted rule under which the
successor had the right to legislate before actually doing so and
receiving obedience. But the present identification of the
sovereign with the electorate of a democratic state has no
plausibility whatsoever, unless we give to the key words 'habit
of obedience' and 'person or persons' a meaning which is quite
different from that which they had when applied to the simple
case; and it is a meaning which can only be made clear if the
notion of an accepted rule is surreptitiously introduced. The
simple scheme of habits of obedience and orders cannot suffice
for this.

That this is so may be shown in many different ways. It emerges most clearly if we consider a democracy in which the electorate excludes only infants and mental defectives and so itself constitutes 'the bulk' of the population, or if we imagine a simple social group of sane adults where all have the right to vote. If we attempt to treat the electorate in such cases as the sovereign and apply to it the simple definitions of the original theory, we shall find ourselves saying that here the 'bulk' of the society habitually obey themselves. Thus the original clear image of a society divided into two segments: the sovereign free from legal limitation who gives orders, and the subjects who habitually obey, has given place to the blurred image of a society in which the majority obey orders given by the majority or by all. Surely we have here neither 'orders' in the original sense (expression of intention that *others* shall behave in certain ways) or 'obedience'.

To meet this criticism, a distinction may be made between the members of the society in their private capacity as individuals and the same persons in their official capacity as electors or legislators. Such a distinction is perfectly intelligible; indeed many legal and political phenomena are most naturally presented in such terms; but it cannot rescue the theory of sovereignty even if we are prepared to take the further step of saying that the individuals in their official capacity constitute *another person* who is habitually obeyed. For if we ask what is meant by saying of a group of persons that in electing a representative or in issuing an order, they have acted not 'as individuals' but 'in their official capacity', the answer can only be given in terms of their qualifications under certain rules and their compliance with other rules, which define what is to be done by them to make a valid election or a law. It is only by reference to such rules that we can identify something as an election or a law made by this body of persons. Such things are to be attributed to the body 'making' them not by the same simple natural test which we use in attributing an individual's spoken or written orders to him.

What then is it for such rules to exist? Since they are rules defining what the members of the society must do to function as an electorate (and so for the purposes of the theory as a sovereign) they cannot themselves have the status of orders issued by the sovereign, for nothing can count as orders issued by the sovereign unless the rules already exist and have been followed.

Can we then say that these rules are just parts of the description of the population's *habits* of obedience? In a simple case where the sovereign is a single person whom the bulk of the society obey if, and only if, he gives his orders in a certain form, e.g. in writing signed and witnessed, we might say (subject to the objections made in Section 1 to the use here of the notion of habit) that the rule that he must legislate in this fashion is just part of the description of the society's habit of obedience: they habitually obey him *when* he gives orders in this way. But, where the sovereign person is not identifiable independently of the rules, we cannot represent the rules in this way as merely the terms or conditions under which the society habitually obeys the sovereign. The rules are *constitutive* of the sovereign, not merely things which we should have to mention in a description of the habits of obedience to the sovereign. So we cannot say that in the present case the rules specifying the procedure of the electorate represent the conditions under which the society, as so many individuals, obeys itself as an electorate; for 'itself as an electorate' is not a reference to a person identifiable apart from the rules. It is a condensed reference to the fact that the electors have complied with rules in electing their representatives. At the most we might say (subject to the objections in Section 1) that the rules set forth the conditions under which the *elected persons* are habitually obeyed: but this would take us back to a form of the theory in which the legislature, not the electorate, is sovereign, and all the difficulties, arising from the fact that such a legislature might be subject to legal limitations on its legislative powers, would remain unsolved.

These arguments against the theory, like those of the earlier section of this chapter, are fundamental in the sense that they amount to the contention that the theory is not merely mistaken in detail, but that the simple idea of orders, habits, and obedience, cannot be adequate for the analysis of law. What is required instead is the notion of a rule conferring powers, which may be limited or unlimited, on persons qualified in certain ways to legislate by complying with a certain procedure.

Apart from what may be termed the general conceptual

inadequacy of the theory, there are many ancillary objections to this attempt to accommodate within it the fact that what would ordinarily be regarded as the supreme legislature may be legally limited. If in such cases the sovereign is to be identified with the electorate, we may well ask, even where the electorate has an unlimited amending power by which the restrictions on the ordinary legislature could all be removed, if it is true that these restrictions are legal because the electorate has given orders which the ordinary legislature habitually obeys. We might waive our objection that legal limitations on legislative power are misrepresented as orders and so as *duties* imposed on it. Can we, even so, suppose that these restrictions are duties which the electorate has even *tacitly* ordered the legislature to fulfil? All the objections taken in earlier chapters to the idea of tacit orders apply with even greater force to its use here. Failure to exercise an amending power as complex in its manner of exercise as that in the United States constitution, may be a poor sign of the wishes of the electorate, though often a reliable sign of its ignorance and indifference. We are a long way indeed from the general who may, perhaps plausibly, be considered tacitly to have ordered his men to do what he knows the sergeant tells them to do.

Again, what are we to say, in the terms of the theory, if there are some restrictions on the legislature which are altogether outside the scope of the amending power entrusted to the electorate? This is not merely conceivable but actually is the position in some cases. Here the electorate is subject to legal limitations, and though it may be called an extraordinary legislature it is not free from legal limitation and so is not sovereign. Are we to say here that the society as a whole is sovereign and these legal limitations have been tacitly ordered by *it*, since it has failed to revolt against them? That this would make the distinction between revolution and legislation untenable is perhaps a sufficient reason for rejecting it.

Finally, the theory treating the electorate as sovereign only provides at the best for a limited legislature in a democracy where an electorate exists. Yet there is no absurdity in the notion of an hereditary monarch like Rex enjoying limited legislative powers which are both limited and supreme within the system.

V

LAW AS THE UNION OF PRIMARY AND SECONDARY RULES

1. A FRESH START

In the last three chapters we have seen that, at various crucial ʿ points, the simple model of law as the sovereign's coercive orders failed to reproduce some of the salient features of a legal system. To demonstrate this, we did not find it necessary to invoke (as earlier critics have done) international law or primitive law which some may regard as disputable or borderline examples of law; instead we pointed to certain familiar features of municipal law in a modern state, and showed that these were either distorted or altogether unrepresented in this over-simple theory.

The main ways in which the theory failed are instructive enough to merit a second summary. First, it became clear that though of all the varieties of law, a criminal statute, forbidding or enjoining certain actions under penalty, most resembles orders backed by threats given by one person to others, such a statute nonetheless differs from such orders in the important respect that it commonly applies to those who enact it and not merely to others. Secondly, there are other varieties of law, notably those conferring legal powers to adjudicate or legislate (public powers) or to create or vary legal relations (private powers) which cannot, without absurdity, be construed as orders backed by threats. Thirdly, there are legal rules which differ from orders in their mode of origin, because they are not brought into being by anything analogous to explicit prescription. Finally, the analysis of law in terms of the sovereign, habitually obeyed and necessarily exempt from all legal limitation, failed to account for the continuity of legislative authority characteristic of a modern legal system, and the sovereign person or persons could not be identified with either the electorate or the legislature of a modern state.

It will be recalled that in thus criticizing the conception of law as the sovereign's coercive orders we considered also a number of ancillary devices which were brought in at the cost of corrupting the primitive simplicity of the theory to rescue it from its difficulties. But these too failed. One device, the notion of a *tacit* order, seemed to have no application to the complex actualities of a modern legal system, but only to very much simpler situations like that of a general who deliberately refrains from interfering with orders given by his subordinates. Other devices, such as that of treating power-conferring rules as mere fragments of rules imposing duties, or treating all rules as directed only to officials, distort the ways in which these are spoken of, thought of, and actually used in social life. This had no better claim to our assent than the theory that all the rules of a game are 'really' directions to the umpire and the scorer. The device, designed to reconcile the self-binding character of legislation with the theory that a statute is an order given to *others*, was to distinguish the legislators acting in their official capacity, as *one* person ordering *others* who include themselves in their private capacities. This device, impeccable in itself, involved supplementing the theory with something it does not contain: this is the notion of a rule defining what must be done to legislate; for it is only in conforming with such a rule that legislators have an official capacity and a separate personality to be contrasted with themselves as private individuals.

The last three chapters are therefore the record of a failure and there is plainly need for a fresh start. Yet the failure is an instructive one, worth the detailed consideration we have given it, because at each point where the theory failed to fit the facts it was possible to see at least in outline why it was bound to fail and what is required for a better account. The root cause of failure is that the elements out of which the theory was constructed, viz. the ideas of orders, obedience, habits, and threats, do not include, and cannot by their combination yield, the idea of a rule, without which we cannot hope to elucidate even the most elementary forms of law. It is true that the idea of a rule is by no means a simple one: we have already seen in Chapter III the need, if we are to do justice to the complexity of a legal system, to discriminate between two different though related types. Under rules of the one type, which may well be considered the basic or primary type, human beings are required to do or abstain from certain actions, whether they wish to or not. Rules of the other type are in a sense parasitic upon or secondary to the first; for they provide that human beings may by doing or saying certain things introduce new rules of the primary type, extinguish or modify old ones, or in various ways determine their incidence or control their operations. Rules of the first type impose duties; rules of the second type confer powers, public or private. Rules of the first type concern actions involving physical movement or changes; rules of the second type provide for operations which lead not merely to physical movement or change, but to the creation or variation of duties or obligations.

We have already given some preliminary analysis of what is involved in the assertion that rules of these two types exist among a given social group, and in this chapter we shall not only carry this analysis a little farther but we shall make the general claim that in the combination of these two types of rule there lies what Austin wrongly claimed to have found in the notion of coercive orders, namely, 'the key to the science of jurisprudence'. We shall not indeed claim that wherever the word 'law' is 'properly' used this combination of primary and secondary rules is to be found; for it is clear that the diverse range of cases of which the word 'law' is used are not linked by any such simple uniformity, but by less direct relations—often of analogy of either form or content—to a central case. What we shall attempt to show, in this and the succeeding chapters, is that most of the features of law which have proved most perplexing and have both provoked and eluded the search for definition can best be rendered clear, if these two types of rule and the interplay between them are understood. We accord this union of elements a central place because of their explanatory power in elucidating the concepts that constitute the framework of legal thought. The justification for the use of the word 'law' for a range of apparently heterogeneous cases is a secondary matter which can be undertaken when the central elements have been grasped.

2. THE IDEA OF OBLIGATION

It will be recalled that the theory of law as coercive orders, notwithstanding its errors, started from the perfectly correct

appreciation of the fact that where there is law, there human
conduct is made in some sense non-optional or obligatory. In
choosing this starting-point the theory was well inspired, and in
building up a new account of law in terms of the interplay of
primary and secondary rules we too shall start from the same
idea. It is, however, here, at this crucial first step, that we have
perhaps most to learn from the theory's errors.

Let us recall the gunman situation. A orders B to hand over
his money and threatens to shoot him if he does not comply.
According to the theory of coercive orders this situation illustrates the notion of obligation or duty in general. Legal obligation is to be found in this situation writ large; A must be the
sovereign habitually obeyed and the orders must be general,
prescribing courses of conduct not single actions. The plausibility of the claim that the gunman situation displays the meaning of obligation lies in the fact that it is certainly one in which
we would say that B, if he obeyed, was 'obliged' to hand over
his money. It is, however, equally certain that we should misdescribe the situation if we said, on these facts, that B 'had an
obligation' or a 'duty' to hand over the money. So from the
start it is clear that we need something else for an understanding of the idea of obligation. There is a difference, yet to be
explained, between the assertion that someone *was obliged* to do
something and the assertion that he *had an obligation* to do it.
The first is often a statement about the beliefs and motives with
which an action is done: B was obliged to hand over his money
may simply mean, as it does in the gunman case, that he
believed that some harm or other unpleasant consequences
would befall him if he did not hand it over and he handed it
over to avoid those consequences. In such cases the prospect of
what would happen to the agent if he disobeyed has rendered
something he would otherwise have preferred to have done (keep
the money) less eligible.

Two further elements slightly complicate the elucidation of
the notion of being obliged to do something. It seems clear that
we should not think of B as obliged to hand over the money if
the threatened harm was, according to common judgments,
trivial in comparison with the disadvantage or serious consequences, either for B or for others, of complying with the
orders, as it would be, for example, if A merely threatened to

pinch B. Nor perhaps should we say that B was obliged, if there were no reasonable grounds for thinking that A could or would probably implement his threat of relatively serious harm. Yet, though such references to common judgments of comparative harm and reasonable estimates of likelihood, are implicit in this notion, the statement that a person was obliged to obey someone is, in the main, a psychological one referring to the beliefs and motives with which an action was done. But the statement that someone *had an obligation* to do something is of a very different type and there are many signs of this difference. Thus not only is it the case that the facts about B's action and his beliefs and motives in the gunman case, though sufficient to warrant the statement that B was obliged to hand over his purse, are *not sufficient* to warrant the statement that he had an obligation to do this; it is also the case that facts of this sort, i.e. facts about beliefs and motives, are *not necessary* for the truth of a statement that a person had an obligation to do something. Thus the statement that a person had an obligation, e.g. to tell the truth or report for military service, remains true even if he believed (reasonably or unreasonably) that he would never be found out and had nothing to fear from disobedience. Moreover, whereas the statement that he had this obligation is quite independent of the question whether or not he in fact reported for service, the statement that someone was obliged to do something, normally carries the implication that he actually did it.

Some theorists, Austin among them, seeing perhaps the general irrelevance of the person's beliefs, fears, and motives to the question whether he had an obligation to do something, have defined this notion not in terms of these subjective facts, but in terms of the *chance* or *likelihood* that the person having the obligation will suffer a punishment or 'evil' at the hands of others in the event of disobedience. This, in effect, treats statements of obligation not as psychological statements but as predictions or assessments of chances of incurring punishment or 'evil'. To many later theorists this has appeared as a revelation, bringing down to earth an elusive notion and restating it in the same clear, hard, empirical terms as are used in science. It has, indeed, been accepted sometimes as the only alternative to metaphysical conceptions of obligation or duty as invisible objects mysteriously existing 'above' or 'behind' the world of ordinary, observable facts. But there are many reasons for rejecting this interpretation of statements of obligation as predictions, and it is not, in fact, the only alternative to obscure metaphysics.

The fundamental objection is that the predictive interpretation obscures the fact that, where rules exist, deviations from them are not merely grounds for a prediction that hostile reactions will follow or that a court will apply sanctions to those who break them, but are also a reason or justification for such reaction and for applying the sanctions. We have already drawn attention in Chapter IV to this neglect of the internal aspect of rules and we shall elaborate it later in this chapter.

There is, however, a second, simpler, objection to the predictive interpretation of obligation. If it were true that the statement that a person had an obligation meant that *he* was likely to suffer in the event of disobedience, it would be a contradiction to say that he had an obligation, e.g. to report for military service but that, owing to the fact that he had escaped from the jurisdiction, or had successfully bribed the police or the court, there was not the slightest chance of his being caught or made to suffer. In fact, there is no contradiction in saying this, and such statements are often made and understood.

It is, of course, true that in a normal legal system, where sanctions are exacted for a high proportion of offences, an offender usually runs a risk of punishment; so, usually the statement that a person has an obligation and the statement that he is likely to suffer for disobedience will both be true together. Indeed, the connexion between these two statements is somewhat stronger than this: at least in a municipal system it may well be true that, unless *in general* sanctions were likely to be exacted from offenders, there would be little or no point in making particular statements about a person's obligations. In this sense, such statements may be said to presuppose belief in the continued normal operation of the system of sanctions much as the statement 'he is out' in cricket presupposes, though it does not assert, that players, umpire, and scorer will probably take the usual steps. Nonetheless, it is crucial for the understanding of the idea of obligation to see that in individual cases the statement that a person has an obligation under some rule and the prediction that he is likely to suffer for disobedience may diverge.

It is clear that obligation is not to be found in the gunman situation, though the simpler notion of being obliged to do something may well be defined in the elements present there. To understand the general idea of obligation as a necessary preliminary to understanding it in its legal form, we must turn to a different social situation which, unlike the gunman situation, includes the existence of social rules; for this situation contributes to the meaning of the statement that a person has an obligation in two ways. First, the existence of such rules, making certain types of behaviour a standard, is the normal, though unstated, background or proper context for such a statement; and, secondly, the distinctive function of such statement is to apply such a general rule to a particular person by calling attention to the fact that his case falls under it. We have already seen in Chapter IV that there is involved in the existence of any social rules a combination of regular conduct with a distinctive attitude to that conduct as a standard. We have also seen the main ways in which these differ from mere social habits, and how the varied normative vocabulary ('ought', 'must', 'should') is used to draw attention to the standard and to deviations from it, and to formulate the demands, criticisms, or acknowledgements which may be based on it. Of this class of normative words the words 'obligation' and 'duty' form an important sub-class, carrying with them certain implications not usually present in the others. Hence, though a grasp of the elements generally differentiating social rules from mere habits is certainly indispensable for understanding the notion of obligation or duty, it is not sufficient by itself.

The statement that someone has or is under an obligation does indeed imply the existence of a rule; yet it is not always the case that where rules exist the standard of behaviour required by them is conceived of in terms of obligation. 'He ought to have' and 'He had an obligation to' are not always interchangeable expressions, even though they are alike in carrying an implicit reference to existing standards of conduct or are used in drawing conclusions in particular cases from a general rule. Rules of etiquette or correct speech are certainly rules: they are more than convergent habits or regularities of behaviour; they are taught and efforts are made to maintain them; they are used in criticizing our own and other people's behaviour in the characteristic normative vocabulary. 'You ought to take your hat off', 'It is wrong to say "you was"'. But to use in connexion with rules of this kind the words 'obligation' or 'duty' would be misleading and not merely stylistically odd. It would misdescribe a social situation; for though the line separating rules of obligation from others is at points a vague one, yet the main rationale of the distinction is fairly clear.

Rules are conceived and spoken of as imposing obligations when the general demand for conformity is insistent and the social pressure brought to bear upon those who deviate or threaten to deviate is great. Such rules may be wholly customary in origin: there may be no centrally organized system of punishments for breach of the rules; the social pressure may take only the form of a general diffused hostile or critical reaction which may stop short of physical sanctions. It may be limited to verbal manifestations of disapproval or of appeals to the individuals' respect for the rule violated; it may depend heavily on the operation of feelings of shame, remorse, and guilt. When the pressure is of this last-mentioned kind we may be inclined to classify the rules as part of the morality of the social group and the obligation under the rules as moral obligation. Conversely, when physical sanctions are prominent or usual among the forms of pressure, even though these are neither closely defined nor administered by officials but are left to the community at large, we shall be inclined to classify the rules as a primitive or rudimentary form of law. We may, of course, find both these types of serious social pressure behind what is, in an obvious sense, the same rule of conduct; sometimes this may occur with no indication that one of them is peculiarly appropriate as primary and the other secondary, and then the question whether we are confronted with a rule of morality or rudimentary law may not be susceptible of an answer. But for the moment the possibility of drawing the line between law and morals need not detain us. What is important is that the insistence on importance or *seriousness* of social pressure behind the rules is the primary factor determining whether they are thought of as giving rise to obligations.

Two other characteristics of obligation go naturally together with this primary one. The rules supported by this serious pressure are thought important because they are believed to be necessary to the maintenance of social life or some highly prized feature of it. Characteristically, rules so obviously essential as those which restrict the free use of violence are thought of in terms of obligation. So too rules which require honesty or truth or require the keeping of promises, or specify what is to be done by one who performs a distinctive role or function in the social group are thought of in terms of either 'obligation' or perhaps more often 'duty'. Secondly, it is generally recognized that the conduct required by these rules may, while benefiting others, conflict with what the person who owes the duty may wish to do. Hence obligations and duties are thought of as characteristically involving sacrifice or renunciation, and the standing possibility of conflict between obligation or duty and interest is, in all societies, among the truisms of both the lawyer and the moralist.

The figure of a *bond* binding the person obligated, which is buried in the word 'obligation', and the similar notion of a debt latent in the word 'duty' are explicable in terms of these three factors, which distinguish rules of obligation or duty from other rules. In this figure, which haunts much legal thought, the social pressure appears as a chain binding those who have obligations so that they are not free to do what they want. The other end of the chain is sometimes held by the group or their official representatives, who insist on performance or exact the penalty: sometimes it is entrusted by the group to a private individual who may choose whether or not to insist on performance or its equivalent in value to him. The first situation typifies the duties or obligations of criminal law and the second those of civil law where we think of private individuals having rights correlative to the obligations.

Natural and perhaps illuminating though these figures or metaphors are, we must not allow them to trap us into a misleading conception of obligation as essentially consisting in some feeling of pressure or compulsion experienced by those who have obligations. The fact that rules of obligation are generally supported by serious social pressure does not entail that to have an obligation under the rules is to experience feelings of compulsion or pressure. Hence there is no contradiction in saying of some hardened swindler, and it may often be true, that he had an obligation to pay the rent but felt no pressure to pay when he made off without doing so. To *feel* obliged and to have an obligation are different though frequently concomitant things. To identify them would be one way of misinterpreting, in terms of psychological feelings, the important internal aspect of rules to which we drew attention in Chapter III.

Indeed, the internal aspect of rules is something to which we must again refer before we can dispose finally of the claims of the predictive theory. For an advocate of that theory may well ask why, if social pressure is so important a feature of rules of obligation, we are yet so concerned to stress the inadequacies of the predictive theory; for it gives this very feature a central place by defining obligation in terms of the likelihood that threatened punishment or hostile reaction will follow deviation from certain lines of conduct. The difference may seem slight between the analysis of a statement of obligation as a prediction, or assessment of the chances, of hostile reaction to deviation, and our own contention that though this statement presupposes a background in which deviations from rules are generally met by hostile reactions, yet its characteristic use is not to predict this but to say that a person's case falls under such a rule. In fact, however, this difference is not a slight one. Indeed, until its importance is grasped, we cannot properly understand the whole distinctive style of human thought, speech, and action which is involved in the existence of rules and which constitutes the normative structure of society.

The following contrast again in terms of the 'internal' and 'external' aspect of rules may serve to mark what gives this distinction its great importance for the understanding not only of law but of the structure of any society. When a social group has certain rules of conduct, this fact affords an opportunity for many closely related yet different kinds of assertion; for it is possible to be concerned with the rules, either merely as an observer who does not himself accept them, or as a member of the group which accepts and uses them as guides to conduct. We may call these respectively the 'external' and the 'internal points of view'. Statements made from the external point of view may themselves be of different kinds. For the observer may, without accepting the rules himself, assert that the group accepts the rules, and thus may from outside refer to the way in which *they* are concerned with them from the internal point of view. But whatever the rules are, whether they are those of games, like chess or cricket, or moral or legal rules, we can if we choose occupy the position of an observer who does not even refer in this way to the internal point of view of the group. Such an observer is content merely to record the regularities of observable behaviour in which conformity with the rules partly consists and those further regularities, in the form of the hostile reaction, reproofs, or punishments, with which deviations from the rules are met. After a time the external observer may, on the basis of the regularities observed, correlate deviation with hostile reaction, and be able to predict with a fair measure of success, and to assess the chances that a deviation from the group's normal behaviour will meet with hostile reaction or punishment. Such knowledge may not only reveal much about the group, but might enable him to live among them without unpleasant consequences which would attend one who attempted to do so without such knowledge.

If, however, the observer really keeps austerely to this extreme external point of view and does not give any account of the manner in which members of the group who accept the rules view their own regular behaviour, his description of their life cannot be in terms of rules at all, and so not in the terms of the rule-dependent notions of obligation or duty. Instead, it will be in terms of observable regularities of conduct, predictions, probabilities, and signs. For such an observer, deviations by a member of the group from normal conduct will be a sign that hostile reaction is likely to follow, and nothing more. His view will be like the view of one who, having observed the working of a traffic signal in a busy street for some time, limits himself to saying that when the light turns red there is a high probability that the traffic will stop. He treats the light merely as a natural *sign that* people will behave in certain ways, as clouds are a *sign that* rain will come. In so doing he will miss out a whole dimension of the social life of those whom he is watching, since for them the red light is not merely a sign that others will stop: they look upon it as a *signal for* them to stop, and so a reason for stopping in conformity to rules which make stopping when the light is red a standard of behaviour and an obligation. To mention this is to bring into the account the way in which the group regards its own behaviour. It is to refer to the internal aspect of rules seen from their internal point of view.

The external point of view may very nearly reproduce the way in which the rules function in the lives of certain members of the group, namely those who reject its rules and are only concerned with them when and because they judge that unpleasant consequences are likely to follow violation. Their point of view will need for its expression, 'I was obliged to do it', 'I am likely to suffer for it if . . .', 'You will probably suffer for it if . . .', 'They will do that to you if . . .'. But they will not need forms of expression like 'I had an obligation' or 'You have an obligation' for these are required only by those who see their own and other persons' conduct from the internal point of view. What the external point of view, which limits itself to the observable regularities of behaviour, cannot reproduce is the way in which the rules function as rules in the lives of those who normally are the majority of society. These are the officials, lawyers, or private persons who use them, in one situation after another, as guides to the conduct of social life, as the basis for claims, demands, admissions, criticism, or punishment, viz., in all the familiar transactions of life according to rules. For them the violation of a rule is not merely a basis for the prediction that a hostile reaction will follow but a *reason* for hostility.

At any given moment the life of any society which lives by rules, legal or not, is likely to consist in a tension between those who, on the one hand, accept and voluntarily co-operate in maintaining the rules, and so see their own and other persons' behaviour in terms of the rules, and those who, on the other hand, reject the rules and attend to them only from the external point of view as a sign of possible punishment. One of the difficulties facing any legal theory anxious to do justice to the complexity of the facts is to remember the presence of both these points of view and not to define one of them out of existence. Perhaps all our criticisms of the predictive theory of obligation may be best summarized as the accusation that this is what it does to the internal aspect of obligatory rules.

3. THE ELEMENTS OF LAW

It is, of course, possible to imagine a society without a legislature, courts or officials of any kind. Indeed, there are many studies of primitive communities which not only claim that this possibility is realized but depict in detail the life of a society where the only means of social control is that general attitude of the group towards its own standard modes of behaviour in terms of which we have characterized rules of obligation. A social structure of this kind is often referred to as one of 'custom'; but we shall not use this term, because it often implies that the customary rules are very old and supported with less social pressure than other rules. To avoid these implications we shall refer to such a social structure as one of primary rules of obligation. If a society is to live by such primary rules alone, there are certain conditions which, granted a few of the most obvious truisms about human nature and the world we live in, must clearly be satisfied. The first of these conditions is that the rules must contain in some form restrictions on the free use of violence, theft, and deception to which human beings are tempted but which they must, in general, repress, if they are to coexist in close proximity to each other. Such rules are in fact always found in the primitive societies of which we have knowledge, together with a variety of others imposing on individuals various positive duties to perform services or make contributions to the common life. Secondly, though such a society may exhibit the tension, already described, between those who accept the rules and those who reject the rules except where fear of social pressure induces them to conform, it is plain that the latter cannot be more than a minority, if so loosely organized a society of persons, approximately equal in physical strength, is to endure: for otherwise those who reject the rules would have too little social pressure to fear. This too is confirmed by what we know of primitive communities where, though there are dissidents and malefactors, the majority live by the rules seen from the internal point of view.

More important for our present purpose is the following consideration. It is plain that only a small community closely knit by ties of kinship, common sentiment, and belief, and placed in a stable environment, could live successfully by such a régime of unofficial rules. In any other conditions such a simple form of social control must prove defective and will require supplementation in different ways. In the first place, the rules by which the group lives will not form a system, but will simply be a set of separate standards, without any identifying or common mark, except of course that they are the rules which a particular group of human beings accepts. They will in this respect resemble our own rules of etiquette. Hence if doubts arise as to what the rules are or as to the precise scope of some given rule, there will be no procedure for settling this doubt, either by reference to an authoritative text or to an official whose declarations on this point are authoritative. For, plainly, such a procedure and the acknowledgement of either authoritative text or persons involve the existence of rules of a type different from the rules of obligation or duty which *ex hypothesi* are all that the group has. This defect in the simple social structure of primary rules we may call its *uncertainty*.

A second defect is the *static* character of the rules. The only mode of change in the rules known to such a society will be the slow process of growth, whereby courses of conduct once thought optional become first habitual or usual, and then obligatory, and the converse process of decay, when deviations, once severely dealt with, are first tolerated and then pass unnoticed. There will be no means, in such a society, of deliberately adapting the rules to changing circumstances, either by eliminating old rules or introducing new ones: for, again, the possibility of doing this presupposes the existence of rules of a different type from the primary rules of obligation by which alone the society lives. In an extreme case the rules may be static in a more drastic sense. This, though never perhaps fully realized in any actual community, is worth considering because the remedy for it is something very characteristic of law. In this extreme case, not only would there be no way of deliberately changing the general rules, but the obligations which arise under the rules in particular cases could not be varied or modified by the deliberate choice of any individual. Each individual would simply have fixed obligations or duties to do or abstain from doing certain things. It might indeed very often be the case that others would benefit from the performance of these obligations; yet if there are only primary rules of obligation they would have no power to release those bound from performance or to transfer to others the benefits which would accrue from performance. For such operations of release or transfer create changes in the initial positions of individuals under the primary rules of obligation, and for these operations to be possible there must be rules of a sort different from the primary rules.

The third defect of this simple form of social life is the *inefficiency* of the diffuse social pressure by which the rules are maintained. Disputes as to whether an admitted rule has or has not been violated will always occur and will, in any but the smallest societies, continue interminably, if there is no agency specially empowered to ascertain finally, and authoritatively, the fact of violation. Lack of such final and authoritative determinations is to be distinguished from another weakness associated with it. This is the fact that punishments for violations of the rules, and other forms of social pressure involving physical effort or the use of force, are not administered by a special agency but are left to the individuals affected or to the group at large. It is obvious that the waste of time involved in the group's unorganized efforts to catch and punish offenders, and the smouldering vendettas which may result from self help in the absence of an official monopoly of 'sanctions', may be serious. The history of law does, however, strongly suggest that the lack of official agencies to determine authoritatively the fact of violation of the rules is a much more serious defect; for many societies have remedies for this defect long before the other.

The remedy for each of these three main defects in this simplest form of social structure consists in supplementing the *primary* rules of obligation with *secondary* rules which are rules of a different kind. The introduction of the remedy for each defect might, in itself, be considered a step from the pre-legal into the legal world; since each remedy brings with it many elements that permeate law: certainly all three remedies together are enough to convert the régime of primary rules into what is indisputably a legal system. We shall consider in turn each of these remedies and show why law may most illuminatingly be characterized as a union of primary rules of obligation with such secondary rules. Before we do this, however, the following general points should be noted. Though the remedies consist in the introduction of rules which are certainly different from each other, as well as from the primary rules of obligation which they supplement, they have important features in common and are connected in various ways. Thus they may all be said to be on a different level from the primary rules, for they are all *about* such rules; in the sense that while primary rules are concerned with the actions that individuals must or must not do, these secondary rules are all concerned with the primary rules themselves. They specify the ways in which the primary rules may be conclusively ascertained, introduced, eliminated, varied, and the fact of their violation conclusively determined.

The simplest form of remedy for the *uncertainty* of the régime of primary rules is the introduction of what we shall call a 'rule of recognition'. This will specify some feature or features possession of which by a suggested rule is taken as a conclusive affirmative indication that it is a rule of the group to be supported by the social pressure it exerts. The existence of such a rule of recognition may take any of a huge variety of forms, simple or complex. It may, as in the early law of many societies, be no more than that an authoritative list or text of the rules is to be found in a written document or carved on some public monument. No doubt as a matter of history this step from the pre-legal to the legal may be accomplished in distinguishable stages, of which the first is the mere reduction to writing of hitherto unwritten rules. This is not itself the crucial step, though it is a very important one: what is crucial is the acknowledgement of reference to the writing or inscription as *authoritative*, i.e. as the *proper* way of disposing of doubts as to the existence of the rule. Where there is such an acknowledgement there is a very simple form of secondary rule: a rule for conclusive identification of the primary rules of obligation.

In a developed legal system the rules of recognition are of course more complex; instead of identifying rules exclusively by reference to a text or list they do so by reference to some general characteristic possessed by the primary rules. This may be the fact of their having been enacted by a specific body, or their long customary practice, or their relation to judicial decisions. Moreover, where more than one of such general characteristics are treated as identifying criteria, provision may be made for their possible conflict by their arrangement in an

order of superiority, as by the common subordination of custom
or precedent to statute, the latter being a 'superior source' of
law. Such complexity may make the rules of recognition in a
modern legal system seem very different from the simple acceptance of an authoritative text: yet even in this simplest form,
such a rule brings with it many elements distinctive of law.
By providing an authoritative mark it introduces, although in
embryonic form, the idea of a legal system: for the rules are
now not just a discrete unconnected set but are, in a simple
way, unified. Further, in the simple operation of identifying a
given rule as possessing the required feature of being an item
on an authoritative list of rules we have the germ of the idea
of legal validity.

The remedy for the *static* quality of the régime of primary
rules consists in the introduction of what we shall call 'rules of
change'. The simplest form of such a rule is that which empowers
an individual or body of persons to introduce new primary rules
for the conduct of the life of the group, or of some class within
it, and to eliminate old rules. As we have already argued in
Chapter IV it is in terms of such a rule, and not in terms of
orders backed by threats, that the ideas of legislative enactment
and repeal are to be understood. Such rules of change may be
very simple or very complex: the powers conferred may be
unrestricted or limited in various ways: and the rules may,
besides specifying the persons who are to legislate, define in
more or less rigid terms the procedure to be followed in legislation. Plainly, there will be a very close connexion between the
rules of change and the rules of recognition: for where the
former exists the latter will necessarily incorporate a reference to
legislation as an identifying feature of the rules, though it need
not refer to all the details of procedure involved in legislation.
Usually some official certificate or official copy will, under the
rules of recognition, be taken as a sufficient proof of due enactment. Of course if there is a social structure so simple that the
only 'source of law' is legislation, the rule of recognition will
simply specify enactment as the unique identifying mark or
criterion of validity of the rules. This will be the case for example
in the imaginary kingdom of Rex I depicted in Chapter IV:
there the rule of recognition would simply be that whatever
Rex I enacts is law.

We have already described in some detail the rules which confer on individuals power to vary their initial positions under the primary rules. Without such private power-conferring rules society would lack some of the chief amenities which law confers upon it. For the operations which these rules make possible are the making of wills, contracts, transfers of property, and many other voluntarily created structures of rights and duties which typify life under law, though of course an elementary form of power-conferring rule also underlies the moral institution of a promise. The kinship of these rules with the rules of change involved in the notion of legislation is clear, and as recent theory such as Kelsen's has shown, many of the features which puzzle us in the institutions of contract or property are clarified by thinking of the operations of making a contract or transferring property as the exercise of limited legislative powers by individuals.

The third supplement to the simple régime of primary rules, intended to remedy the *inefficiency* of its diffused social pressure, consists of secondary rules empowering individuals to make authoritative determinations of the question whether, on a particular occasion, a primary rule has been broken. The minimal form of adjudication consists in such determinations, and we shall call the secondary rules which confer the power to make them 'rules of adjudication'. Besides identifying the individuals who are to adjudicate, such rules will also define the procedure to be followed. Like the other secondary rules these are on a different level from the primary rules: though they may be reinforced by further rules imposing duties on judges to adjudicate, they do not impose duties but confer judicial powers and a special status on judicial declarations about the breach of obligations. Again these rules, like the other secondary rules, define a group of important legal concepts: in this case the concepts of judge or court, jurisdiction and judgment. Besides these resemblances to the other secondary rules, rules of adjudication have intimate connexions with them. Indeed, a system which has rules of adjudication is necessarily also committed to a rule of recognition of an elementary and imperfect sort. This is so because, if courts are empowered to make authoritative determinations of the fact that a rule has been broken, these cannot avoid being taken as authoritative determinations of what the rules are. So the rule which confers jurisdiction will also be a rule of recognition, identifying the primary rules through the judgments of the courts and these judgments will become a 'source' of law. It is true that this form of rule of recognition, inseparable from the minimum form of jurisdiction, will be very imperfect. Unlike an authoritative text or a statute book, judgments may not be couched in general terms and their use as authoritative guides to the rules depends on a somewhat shaky inference from particular decisions, and the reliability of this must fluctuate both with the skill of the interpreter and the consistency of the judges.

It need hardly be said that in few legal systems are judicial powers confined to authoritative determinations of the fact of violation of the primary rules. Most systems have, after some delay, seen the advantages of further centralization of social pressure; and have partially prohibited the use of physical punishments or violent self help by private individuals. Instead they have supplemented the primary rules of obligation by further secondary rules, specifying or at least limiting the penalties for violation, and have conferred upon judges, where they have ascertained the fact of violation, the exclusive power to direct the application of penalties by other officials. These secondary rules provide the centralized official 'sanctions' of the system.

If we stand back and consider the structure which has resulted from the combination of primary rules of obligation with the secondary rules of recognition, change and adjudication, it is plain that we have here not only the heart of a legal system, but a most powerful tool for the analysis of much that has puzzled both the jurist and the political theorist.

Not only are the specifically legal concepts with which the lawyer is professionally concerned, such as those of obligation and rights, validity and source of law, legislation and jurisdiction, and sanction, best elucidated in terms of this combination of elements. The concepts (which bestride both law and political theory) of the state, of authority, and of an official require a similar analysis if the obscurity which still lingers about them is to be dissipated. The reason why an analysis in these terms of primary and secondary rules has this explanatory power is not

far to seek. Most of the obscurities and distortions surrounding
legal and political concepts arise from the fact that these
essentially involve reference to what we have called the internal
point of view: the view of those who do not merely record and
predict behaviour conforming to rules, but *use* the rules as
standards for the appraisal of their own and others' behaviour.
This requires more detailed attention in the analysis of legal
and political concepts than it has usually received. Under the
simple régime of primary rules the internal point of view is
manifested in its simplest form, in the use of those rules as the
basis of criticism, and as the justification of demands for conformity, social pressure, and punishment. Reference to this most
elementary manifestation of the internal point of view is required for the analysis of the basic concepts of obligation and
duty. With the addition to the system of secondary rules, the
range of what is said and done from the internal point of view
is much extended and diversified. With this extension comes a
whole set of new concepts and they demand a reference to the
internal point of view for their analysis. These include the
notions of legislation, jurisdiction, validity and, generally, of
legal powers, private and public. There is a constant pull
towards an analysis of these in the terms of ordinary or 'scientific', fact-stating or predictive discourse. But this can only
reproduce their external aspect: to do justice to their distinctive, internal aspect we need to see the different ways in which
the law-making operations of the legislator, the adjudication of
a court, the exercise of private or official powers, and other
'acts-in-the-law' are related to secondary rules.

In the next chapter we shall show how the ideas of the
validity of law and sources of law, and the truths latent among the
errors of the doctrines of sovereignty may be rephrased and
clarified in terms of rules of recognition. But we shall conclude
this chapter with a warning: though the combination of primary and secondary rules merits, because it explains many
aspects of law, the central place assigned to it, this cannot by
itself illuminate every problem. The union of primary and
secondary rules is at the centre of a legal system; but it is not
the whole, and as we move away from the centre we shall have
to accommodate, in ways indicated in later chapters, elements
of a different character.

VI

THE FOUNDATIONS OF A
LEGAL SYSTEM

I. RULE OF RECOGNITION AND LEGAL VALIDITY

ACCORDING to the theory criticized in Chapter IV the foundations of a legal system consist of the situation in which the
majority of a social group habitually obey the orders backed
by threats of the sovereign person or persons, who themselves
habitually obey no one. This social situation is, for this theory,
both a necessary and a sufficient condition of the existence of
law. We have already exhibited in some detail the incapacity of
this theory to account for some of the salient features of a
modern municipal legal system: yet nonetheless, as its hold
over the minds of many thinkers suggests, it does contain,
though in a blurred and misleading form, certain truths about
certain important aspects of law. These truths can, however,
only be clearly presented, and their importance rightly assessed,
in terms of the more complex social situation where a secondary
rule of recognition is accepted and used for the identification of
primary rules of obligation. It is this situation which deserves,
if anything does, to be called the foundations of a legal system.
In this chapter we shall discuss various elements of this situation which have received only partial or misleading expression
in the theory of sovereignty and elsewhere.

Wherever such a rule of recognition is accepted, both private
persons and officials are provided with authoritative criteria for
identifying primary rules of obligation. The criteria so provided
may, as we have seen, take any one or more of a variety of forms:
these include reference to an authoritative text; to legislative
enactment; to customary practice; to general declarations of
specified persons, or to past judicial decisions in particular
cases. In a very simple system like the world of Rex I depicted
in Chapter IV, where only what he enacts is law and no legal
limitations upon his legislative power are imposed by customary
rule or constitutional document, the sole criterion for identifying the law will be a simple reference to the fact of enactment by

Rex I. The existence of this simple form of rule of recognition
will be manifest in the general practice, on the part of officials
or private persons, of identifying the rules by this criterion. In
a modern legal system where there are a variety of 'sources' of
law, the rule of recognition is correspondingly more complex:
the criteria for identifying the law are multiple and commonly
include a written constitution, enactment by a legislature,
and judicial precedents. In most cases, provision is made for
possible conflict by ranking these criteria in an order of relative
subordination and primacy. It is in this way that in our system
'common law' is subordinate to 'statute'.

It is important to distinguish this relative *subordination* of one
criterion to another from *derivation*, since some spurious support
for the view that all law is essentially or 'really' (even if only
'tacitly') the product of legislation, has been gained from confusion of these two ideas. In our own system, custom and precedent are subordinate to legislation since customary and common law rules may be deprived of their status as law by statute.
Yet they owe their status of law, precarious as this may be, not
to a 'tacit' exercise of legislative power but to the acceptance of a
rule of recognition which accords them this independent though
subordinate place. Again, as in the simple case, the existence of
such a complex rule of recognition with this hierarchical ordering of distinct criteria is manifested in the general practice of
identifying the rules by such criteria.

In the day-to-day life of a legal system its rule of recognition
is very seldom expressly formulated as a rule; though occasionally, courts in England may announce in general terms the
relative place of one criterion of law in relation to another, as
when they assert the supremacy of Acts of Parliament over
other sources or suggested sources of law. For the most part
the rule of recognition is not stated, but its existence is *shown* in
the way in which particular rules are identified, either by courts
or other officials or private persons or their advisers. There is,
of course, a difference in the use made by courts of the criteria
provided by the rule and the use of them by others: for when
courts reach a particular conclusion on the footing that a
particular rule has been correctly identified as law, what they
say has a special authoritative status conferred on it by other
rules. In this respect, as in many others, the rule of recognition

of a legal system is like the scoring rule of a game. In the course of the game the general rule defining the activities which constitute scoring (runs, goals, &c.) is seldom formulated; instead it is *used* by officials and players in identifying the particular phases which count towards winning. Here too, the declarations of officials (umpire or scorer) have a special authoritative status attributed to them by other rules. Further, in both cases there is the possibility of a conflict between these authoritative applications of the rule and the general understanding of what the rule plainly requires according to its terms. This, as we shall see later, is a complication which must be catered for in any account of what it is for a system of rules of this sort to exist.

The use of unstated rules of recognition, by courts and others, in identifying particular rules of the system is characteristic of the internal point of view. Those who use them in this way thereby manifest their own acceptance of them as guiding rules and with this attitude there goes a characteristic vocabulary different from the natural expressions of the external point of view. Perhaps the simplest of these is the expression, 'It is the law that . . .', which we may find on the lips not only of judges, but of ordinary men living under a legal system, when they identify a given rule of the system. This, like the expression 'Out' or 'Goal', is the language of one assessing a situation by reference to rules which he in common with others acknowledges as appropriate for this purpose. This attitude of shared acceptance of rules is to be contrasted with that of an observer who records *ab extra* the fact that a social group accepts such rules but does not himself accept them. The natural expression of this external point of view is not 'It is the law that . . .' but 'In England they recognize as law . . . whatever the Queen in Parliament enacts. . . .' The first of these forms of expression we shall call an *internal statement* because it manifests the internal point of view and is naturally used by one who, accepting the rule of recognition and without stating the fact that it is accepted, applies the rule in recognizing some particular rule of the system as valid. The second form of expression we shall call an *external statement* because it is the natural language of an external observer of the system who, without himself accepting its rule of recognition, states the fact that others accept it.

If this use of an accepted rule of recognition in making

internal statements is understood and carefully distinguished from an external statement of fact that the rule is accepted, many obscurities concerning the notion of legal 'validity' disappear. For the word 'valid' is most frequently, though not always, used, in just such internal statements, applying to a particular rule of a legal system, an unstated but accepted rule of recognition. To say that a given rule is valid is to recognize it as passing all the tests provided by the rule of recognition and so as a rule of the system. We can indeed simply say that the statement that a particular rule is valid means that it satisfies all the criteria provided by the rule of recognition. This is incorrect only to the extent that it might obscure the internal character of such statements; for, like the cricketers' 'Out', these statements of validity normally apply to a particular case a rule of recognition accepted by the speaker and others, rather than expressly state that the rule is satisfied.

Some of the puzzles connected with the idea of legal validity are said to concern the relation between the validity and the 'efficacy' of law. If by 'efficacy' is meant that the fact that a rule of law which requires certain behaviour is obeyed more often than not, it is plain that there is no necessary connexion between the validity of any particular rule and *its* efficacy, unless the rule of recognition of the system includes among its criteria, as some do, the provision (sometimes referred to as a rule of obsolescence) that no rule is to count as a rule of the system if it has long ceased to be efficacious.

From the inefficacy of a particular rule, which may or may not count against its validity, we must distinguish a general disregard of the rules of the system. This may be so complete in character and so protracted that we should say, in the case of a new system, that it had never established itself as the legal system of a given group, or, in the case of a once-established system, that it had ceased to be the legal system of the group. In either case, the normal context or background for making any internal statement in terms of the rules of the system is absent. In such cases it would be generally *pointless* either to assess the rights and duties of particular persons by reference to the primary rules of a system or to assess the validity of any of its rules by reference to its rules of recognition. To insist on applying a system of rules which had either never actually been effective or had been discarded would, except in special circumstances mentioned below, be as futile as to assess the progress of a game by reference to a scoring rule which had never been accepted or had been discarded.

One who makes an internal statement concerning the validity of a particular rule of a system may be said to *presuppose* the truth of the external statement of fact that the system is generally efficacious. For the normal use of internal statements is in such a context of general efficacy. It would however be wrong to say that statements of validity 'mean' that the system is generally efficacious. For though it is normally pointless or idle to talk of the validity of a rule of a system which has never established itself or has been discarded, none the less it is not meaningless nor is it always pointless. One vivid way of teaching Roman Law is to speak *as if* the system were efficacious still and to discuss the validity of particular rules and solve problems in their terms; and one way of nursing hopes for the restoration of an old social order destroyed by revolution, and rejecting the new, is to cling to the criteria of legal validity of the old régime. This is implicitly done by the White Russian who still claims property under some rule of descent which was a valid rule of Tsarist Russia.

A grasp of the normal contextual connexion between the internal statement that a given rule of a system is valid and the external statement of fact that the system is generally efficacious, will help us see in its proper perspective the common theory that to assert the validity of a rule is to predict that it will be enforced by courts or some other official action taken. In many ways this theory is similar to the predictive analysis of obligation which we considered and rejected in the last chapter. In both cases alike the motive for advancing this predictive theory is the conviction that only thus can metaphysical interpretations be avoided: that either a statement that a rule is valid must ascribe some mysterious property which cannot be detected by empirical means or it must be a prediction of future behaviour of officials. In both cases also the plausibility of the theory is due to the same important fact: that the truth of the external statement of fact, which an observer might record, that the system is generally efficacious and likely to continue so, is normally presupposed by anyone who

accepts the rules and makes an internal statement of obligation or validity. The two are certainly very closely associated.
Finally, in both cases alike the mistake of the theory is the same:
it consists in neglecting the special character of the internal
statement and treating it as an external statement about official
action.

This mistake becomes immediately apparent when we consider how the judge's own statement that a particular rule is
valid functions in judicial decision; for, though here too, in
making such a statement, the judge presupposes but does not
state the general efficacy of the system, he plainly is not concerned to predict his own or others' official action. His statement that a rule is valid is an internal statement recognizing
that the rule satisfies the tests for identifying what is to
count as law in his court, and constitutes not a prophecy of but
part of the *reason* for his decision. There is indeed a more
plausible case for saying that a statement that a rule is valid is
a prediction when such a statement is made by a private person;
for in the case of conflict between unofficial statements of validity
or invalidity and that of a court in deciding a case, there is often
good sense in saying that the former must then be withdrawn.
Yet even here, as we shall see when we come in Chapter VII
to investigate the significance of such conflicts between official
declarations and the plain requirements of the rules, it may be
dogmatic to assume that it is withdrawn as a statement now
shown to be *wrong*, because it has falsely *predicted* what a court
would say. For there are more reasons for withdrawing statements than the fact that they are wrong, and also more ways of
being wrong than this allows.

The rule of recognition providing the criteria by which
the validity of other rules of the system is assessed is in an important sense, which we shall try to clarify, an *ultimate* rule: and
where, as is usual, there are several criteria ranked in order of
relative subordination and primacy one of them is *supreme*.
These ideas of the ultimacy of the rule of recognition and the
supremacy of one of its criteria merit some attention. It is
important to disentangle them from the theory, which we have
rejected, that somewhere in every legal system, even though it
lurks behind legal forms, there must be a sovereign legislative
power which is legally unlimited.

Of these two ideas, supreme criterion and ultimate rule, the first is the easiest to define. We may say that a criterion of legal validity or source of law is supreme if rules identified by reference to it are still recognized as rules of the system, even if they conflict with rules identified by reference to the other criteria, whereas rules identified by reference to the latter are not so recognized if they conflict with the rules identified by reference to the supreme criterion. A similar explanation in comparative terms can be given of the notions of 'superior' and 'subordinate' criteria which we have already used. It is plain that the notions of a superior and a supreme criterion merely refer to a *relative* place on a scale and do not import any notion of legally *unlimited* legislative power. Yet 'supreme' and 'unlimited' are easy to confuse—at least in legal theory. One reason for this is that in the simpler forms of legal system the ideas of ultimate rule of recognition, supreme criterion, and legally unlimited legislature seem to converge. For where there is a legislature subject to no constitutional limitations and competent by its enactment to deprive all other rules of law emanating from other sources of their status as law, it is part of the rule of recognition in such a system that enactment by that legislature is the supreme criterion of validity. This is, according to constitutional theory, the position in the United Kingdom. But even systems like that of the United States in which there is no such legally unlimited legislature may perfectly well contain an ultimate rule of recognition which provides a set of criteria of validity, one of which is supreme. This will be so, where the legislative competence of the ordinary legislature is limited by a constitution which contains no amending power, or places some clauses outside the scope of that power. Here there is no legally unlimited legislature, even in the widest interpretation of 'legislature'; but the system of course contains an ultimate rule of recognition and, in the clauses of its constitution, a supreme criterion of validity.

The sense in which the rule of recognition is the *ultimate* rule of a system is best understood if we pursue a very familiar chain of legal reasoning. If the question is raised whether some suggested rule is legally valid, we must, in order to answer the question, use a criterion of validity provided by some other rule. Is this purported by-law of the Oxfordshire County Council

valid? Yes: because it was made in exercise of the powers conferred, and in accordance with the procedure specified, by a
statutory order made by the Minister of Health. At this first
stage the statutory order provides the criteria in terms of which
the validity of the by-law is assessed. There may be no practical
need to go farther; but there is a standing possibility of doing
so. We may query the validity of the statutory order and assess
its validity in terms of the statute empowering the minister to
make such orders. Finally when the validity of the statute has
been queried and assessed by reference to the rule that what
the Queen in Parliament enacts is law, we are brought to a
stop in inquiries concerning validity: for we have reached a
rule which, like the intermediate statutory order and statute,
provides criteria for the assessment of the validity of other rules;
but it is also unlike them in that there is no rule providing
criteria for the assessment of its own legal validity.

There are, indeed, many questions which we can raise about
this ultimate rule. We can ask whether it is the practice of
courts, legislatures, officials, or private citizens in England
actually to use this rule as an ultimate rule of recognition. Or
has our process of legal reasoning been an idle game with the
criteria of validity of a system now discarded? We can ask
whether it is a satisfactory form of legal system which has such
a rule at its root. Does it produce more good than evil? Are
there prudential reasons for supporting it? Is there a moral
obligation to do so? These are plainly very important questions;
but, equally plainly, when we ask them about the rule of recognition, we are no longer attempting to answer the same kind
of question about it as those which we answered about other
rules with its aid. When we move from saying that a particular
enactment is valid, because it satisfies the rule that what the
Queen in Parliament enacts is law, to saying that in England
this last rule is used by courts, officials, and private persons as
the ultimate rule of recognition, we have moved from an internal statement of law asserting the validity of a rule of the
system to an external statement of fact which an observer of the
system might make even if he did not accept it. So too when we
move from the statement that a particular enactment is valid,
to the statement that the rule of recognition of the system is an
excellent one and the system based on it is one worthy of

support, we have moved from a statement of legal validity to a statement of value.

Some writers, who have emphasized the legal ultimacy of the rule of recognition, have expressed this by saying that, whereas the legal validity of other rules of the system can be demonstrated by reference to it, its own validity cannot be demonstrated but is 'assumed' or 'postulated' or is a 'hypothesis'. This may, however, be seriously misleading. Statements of legal validity made about particular rules in the day-to-day life of a legal system whether by judges, lawyers, or ordinary citizens do indeed carry with them certain presuppositions. They are internal statements of law expressing the point of view of those who accept the rule of recognition of the system and, as such, leave unstated much that could be stated in external statements of fact about the system. What is thus left unstated forms the normal background or context of statements of legal validity and is thus said to be 'presupposed' by them. But it is important to see precisely what these presupposed matters are, and not to obscure their character. They consist of two things. First, a person who seriously asserts the validity of some given rule of law, say a particular statute, himself makes use of a rule of recognition which he accepts as appropriate for identifying the law. Secondly, it is the case that this rule of recognition, in terms of which he assesses the validity of a particular statute, is not only accepted by him but is the rule of recognition actually accepted and employed in the general operation of the system. If the truth of this presupposition were doubted, it could be established by reference to actual practice: to the way in which courts identify what is to count as law, and to the general acceptance of or acquiescence in these identifications.

Neither of these two presuppositions are well described as 'assumptions' of a 'validity' which cannot be demonstrated. We only need the word 'validity', and commonly only use it, to answer questions which arise *within* a system of rules where the status of a rule as a member of the system depends on its satisfying certain criteria provided by the rule of recognition. No such question can arise as to the validity of the very rule of recognition which provides the criteria; it can neither be valid nor invalid but is simply accepted as appropriate for use in this way. To express this simple fact by saying darkly that its validity is 'assumed but cannot be demonstrated', is like saying that we assume, but can never demonstrate, that the standard metre bar in Paris which is the ultimate test of the correctness of all measurement in metres, is itself correct.

A more serious objection is that talk of the 'assumption' that the ultimate rule of recognition is valid conceals the essentially factual character of the second presupposition which lies behind the lawyers' statements of validity. No doubt the practice of judges, officials, and others, in which the actual existence of a rule of recognition consists, is a complex matter. As we shall see later, there are certainly situations in which questions as to the precise content and scope of this kind of rule, and even as to its existence, may not admit of a clear or determinate answer. None the less it is important to distinguish 'assuming the validity' from 'presupposing the existence' of such a rule; if only because failure to do this obscures what is meant by the assertion that such a rule *exists*.

In the simple system of primary rules of obligation sketched in the last chapter, the assertion that a given rule existed could only be an external statement of fact such as an observer who did not accept the rules might make and verify by ascertaining whether or not, as a matter of fact, a given mode of behaviour was generally accepted as a standard and was accompanied by those features which, as we have seen, distinguish a social rule from mere convergent habits. It is in this way also that we should now interpret and verify the assertion that in England a rule—though not a legal one—exists that we must bare the head on entering a church. If such rules as these are found to exist in the actual practice of a social group, there is no separate question of their validity to be discussed, though of course their value or desirability is open to question. Once their existence has been established as a fact we should only confuse matters by affirming or denying that they were valid or by saying that 'we assumed' but could not show their validity. Where, on the other hand, as in a mature legal system, we have a system of rules which includes a rule of recognition so that the status of a rule as a member of the system now depends on whether it satisfies certain criteria provided by the rule of recognition, this brings with it a new application of the word 'exist'. The statement that a rule exists may now no longer be what it was in the simple case of customary rules—an external statement of the *fact* that a certain mode of behaviour was generally accepted as a standard in practice. It may now be an internal statement applying an accepted but unstated rule of recognition and meaning (roughly) no more than 'valid given the system's criteria of validity'. In this respect, however, as in others a rule of recognition is unlike other rules of the system. The assertion that it exists can only be an external statement of fact. For whereas a subordinate rule of a system may be valid and in that sense 'exist' even if it is generally disregarded, the rule of recognition exists only as a complex, but normally concordant, practice of the courts, officials, and private persons in identifying the law by reference to certain criteria. Its existence is a matter of fact.

2. NEW QUESTIONS

Once we abandon the view that the foundations of a legal system consist in a habit of obedience to a legally unlimited sovereign and substitute for this the conception of an ultimate rule of recognition which provides a system of rules with its criteria of validity, a range of fascinating and important questions confronts us. They are relatively new questions; for they were veiled so long as jurisprudence and political theory were committed to the older ways of thought. They are also difficult questions, requiring for a full answer, on the one hand a grasp of some fundamental issues of constitutional law and on the other an appreciation of the characteristic manner in which legal forms may silently shift and change. We shall therefore investigate these questions only so far as they bear upon the wisdom or unwisdom of insisting, as we have done, that a central place should be assigned to the union of primary and secondary rules in the elucidation of the concept of law.

The first difficulty is that of classification; for the rule which, in the last resort, is used to identify the law escapes the conventional categories used for describing a legal system, though these are often taken to be exhaustive. Thus, English constitutional writers since Dicey have usually repeated the statement that the constitutional arrangements of the United Kingdom consist partly of laws strictly so called (statutes, orders in council, and rules embodied in precedents) and partly of

conventions which are mere usages, understandings or customs.
The latter include important rules such as that the Queen may
not refuse her consent to a bill duly passed by Peers and
Commons; there is, however, no legal duty on the Queen to
give her consent and such rules are called conventions because
the courts do not recognize them as imposing a legal duty.
Plainly the rule that what the Queen in Parliament enacts is
law does not fall into either of these categories. It is not a
convention, since the courts are most intimately concerned with
it and they use it in identifying the law; and it is not a rule on
the same level as the 'laws strictly so called' which it is used to
identify. Even if it were enacted by statute, this would not reduce
it to the level of a statute; for the legal status of such an enactment necessarily would depend on the fact that the rule existed
antecedently to and independently of the enactment. Moreover,
as we have shown in the last section, its existence, unlike that of
a statute, must consist in an actual practice.

This aspect of things extracts from some a cry of despair:
how can we show that the fundamental provisions of a constitution which are surely law are really law? Others reply with the
insistence that at the base of legal systems there is something
which is 'not law', which is 'pre-legal', 'meta-legal', or is just
'political fact'. This uneasiness is a sure sign that the categories
used for the description of this most important feature in any
system of law are too crude. The case for calling the rule of
recognition 'law' is that the rule providing criteria for the
identification of other rules of the system may well be thought a
defining feature of a legal system, and so itself worth calling
'law'; the case for calling it 'fact' is that to assert that such a
rule exists is indeed to make an external statement of an actual
fact concerning the manner in which the rules of an 'efficacious'
system are identified. Both these aspects claim attention but we
cannot do justice to them both by choosing one of the labels
'law' or 'fact'. Instead, we need to remember that the ultimate
rule of recognition may be regarded from two points of view:
one is expressed in the external statement of fact that the rule
exists in the actual practice of the system; the other is expressed in the internal statements of validity made by those
who use it in identifying the law.

A second set of questions arises out of the hidden complexity and vagueness of the assertion that a legal system *exists* in a given country or among a given social group. When we make this assertion we in fact refer in compressed, portmanteau form to a number of heterogeneous social facts, usually concomitant. The standard terminology of legal and political thought, developed in the shadow of a misleading theory, is apt to oversimplify and obscure the facts. Yet when we take off the spectacles constituted by this terminology and look at the facts, it becomes apparent that a legal system, like a human being, may at one stage be unborn, at a second not yet wholly independent of its mother, then enjoy a healthy independent existence, later decay and finally die. These half-way stages between birth and normal, independent existence and, again, between that and death, put out of joint our familiar ways of describing legal phenomena. They are worth our study because, baffling as they are, they throw into relief the full complexity of what we take for granted when, in the normal case, we make the confident and true assertion that in a given country a legal system exists.

One way of realizing this complexity is to see just where the simple, Austinian formula of a general habit of obedience to orders fails to reproduce or distorts the complex facts which constitute the minimum conditions which a society must satisfy if it is to have a legal system. We may allow that this formula does designate one necessary condition: namely, that where the laws impose obligations or duties these should be generally obeyed or at any rate not generally disobeyed. But, though essential, this only caters for what we may term the 'end product' of the legal system, where it makes its impact on the private citizen; whereas its day-to-day existence consists also in the official creation, the official identification, and the official use and application of law. The relationship with law involved here can be called 'obedience' only if that word is extended so far beyond its normal use as to cease to characterize informatively these operations. In no ordinary sense of 'obey' are legislators obeying rules when, in enacting laws, they conform to the rules conferring their legislative powers, except of course when the rules conferring such powers are reinforced by rules imposing a duty to follow them. Nor, in failing to conform with these rules do they 'disobey' a law, though they may fail to make one. Nor does the word

'obey' describe well what judges do when they apply the
system's rule of recognition and recognize a statute as valid
law and use it in the determination of disputes. We can
of course, if we wish, preserve the simple terminology of
'obedience' in face of the facts by many devices. One is to
express, e.g. the use made by judges of general criteria of validity in recognizing a statute, as a case of obedience to orders
given by the 'Founders of the Constitution', or (where there are
no 'Founders') as obedience to a 'depsychologized command'
i.e. a command without a commander. But this last should
perhaps have no more serious claims on our attention than the
notion of a nephew without an uncle. Alternatively we can
push out of sight the whole official side to law and forgo the
description of the use of rules made in legislation and adjudication, and instead, think of the whole official world as one person
(the 'sovereign') issuing orders, through various agents or
mouthpieces, which are habitually obeyed by the citizen. But
this is either no more than a convenient shorthand for complex
facts which still await description, or a disastrously confusing
piece of mythology.

It is natural to react from the failure of attempts to give an
account of what it is for a legal system to exist, in the agreeably
simple terms of the habitual obedience which is indeed characteristic of (though it does not always exhaustively describe)
the relationship of the ordinary citizen to law, by making the
opposite error. This consists in taking what is characteristic
(though again not exhaustive) of the official activities, especially
the judicial attitude or relationship to law, and treating this as
an adequate account of what must exist in a social group which
has a legal system. This amounts to replacing the simple conception that the bulk of society habitually obey the law with the
conception that they must generally share, accept, or regard as
binding the ultimate rule of recognition specifying the criteria
in terms of which the validity of laws are ultimately assessed.
Of course we can imagine, as we have done in Chapter III,
a simple society where knowledge and understanding of the
sources of law are widely diffused. There the 'constitution' was
so simple that no fiction would be involved in attributing
knowledge and acceptance of it to the ordinary citizen as well
as to the officials and lawyers. In the simple world of Rex I we

might well say that there was more than mere habitual obedience by the bulk of the population to his word. There it might well be the case that both they and the officials of the system 'accepted', in the same explicit, conscious way, a rule of recognition specifying Rex's word as the criterion of valid law for the whole society, though subjects and officials would have different roles to play and different relationships to the rules of law identified by this criterion. To insist that this state of affairs, imaginable in a simple society, always or usually exists in a complex modern state would be to insist on a fiction. Here surely the reality of the situation is that a great proportion of ordinary citizens—perhaps a majority—have no general conception of the legal structure or of its criteria of validity. The law which he obeys is something which he knows of only as 'the law'. He may obey it for a variety of different reasons and among them may often, though not always, be the knowledge that it will be best for him to do so. He will be aware of the general likely consequences of disobedience: that there are officials who may arrest him and others who will try him and send him to prison for breaking the law. So long as the laws which are valid by the system's tests of validity are obeyed by the bulk of the population this surely is all the evidence we need in order to establish that a given legal system exists.

But just because a legal system is a complex union of primary and secondary rules, this evidence is not all that is needed to describe the relationships to law involved in the existence of a legal system. It must be supplemented by a description of the relevant relationship of the officials of the system to the secondary rules which concern them as officials. Here what is crucial is that there should be a unified or shared official acceptance of the rule of recognition containing the system's criteria of validity. But it is just here that the simple notion of general obedience, which was adequate to characterize the indispensable minimum in the case of ordinary citizens, is inadequate. The point is not, or not merely, the 'linguistic' one that 'obedience' is not naturally used to refer to the way in which these secondary rules are respected as rules by courts and other officials. We could find, if necessary, some wider expression like 'follow', 'comply', or 'conform to' which would characterize both what ordinary citizens do in relation to law

when they report for military service and what judges do when
they identify a particular statute as law in their courts, on the
footing that what the Queen in Parliament enacts is law.
But these blanket terms would merely mask vital differences
which must be grasped if the minimum conditions involved in
the existence of the complex social phenomenon which we call a
legal system is to be understood.

What makes 'obedience' misleading as a description of what
legislators do in conforming to the rules conferring their powers,
and of what courts do in applying an accepted ultimate rule of
recognition, is that obeying a rule (or an order) *need* involve no
thought on the part of the person obeying that what he does is the
right thing both for himself and for others to do: he need have no
view of what he does as a fulfilment of a standard of behaviour
for others of the social group. He need not think of his conforming behaviour as 'right', 'correct', or 'obligatory'. His attitude, in
other words, need not have any of that critical character which
is involved whenever social rules are accepted and types of
conduct are treated as general standards. He need not, though
he may, share the internal point of view accepting the rules as
standards for all to whom they apply. Instead, he may think of
the rule only as something demanding action from *him* under
threat of penalty; he may obey it out of fear of the consequences, or from inertia, without thinking of himself or others
as having an obligation to do so and without being disposed to
criticize either himself or others for deviations. But this merely
personal concern with the rules, which is all the ordinary
citizen *may* have in obeying them, cannot characterize the
attitude of the courts to the rules with which they operate as
courts. This is most patently the case with the ultimate rule of
recognition in terms of which the validity of other rules is
assessed. This, if it is to exist at all, must be regarded from the
internal point of view as a public, common standard of correct
judicial decision, and not as something which each judge merely
obeys for his part only. Individual courts of the system though
they may, on occasion, deviate from these rules must, in general,
be critically concerned with such deviations as lapses from
standards, which are essentially common or public. This is not
merely a matter of the efficiency or health of the legal system,
but is logically a necessary condition of our ability to speak of

the existence of a single legal system. If only some judges acted 'for their part only' on the footing that what the Queen in Parliament enacts is law, and made no criticisms of those who did not respect this rule of recognition, the characteristic unity and continuity of a legal system would have disappeared. For this depends on the acceptance, at this crucial point, of common standards of legal validity. In the interval between these vagaries of judicial behaviour and the chaos which would ultimately ensue when the ordinary man was faced with contrary judicial orders, we would be at loss to describe the situation. We would be in the presence of a *lusus naturae* worth thinking about only because it sharpens our awareness of what is often too obvious to be noticed.

There are therefore two minimum conditions necessary and sufficient for the existence of a legal system. On the one hand those rules of behaviour which are valid according to the system's ultimate criteria of validity must be generally obeyed, and, on the other hand, its rules of recognition specifying the criteria of legal validity and its rules of change and adjudication must be effectively accepted as common public standards of official behaviour by its officials. The first condition is the only one which private citizens *need* satisfy: they may obey each 'for his part only' and from any motive whatever; though in a healthy society they will in fact often accept these rules as common standards of behaviour and acknowledge an obligation to obey them, or even trace this obligation to a more general obligation to respect the constitution. The second condition must also be satisfied by the officials of the system. They must regard these as common standards of official behaviour and appraise critically their own and each other's deviations as lapses. Of course it is also true that besides these there will be many primary rules which apply to officials in their merely personal capacity which they need only obey.

The assertion that a legal system exists is therefore a Janus-faced statement looking both towards obedience by ordinary citizens and to the acceptance by officials of secondary rules as critical common standards of official behaviour. We need not be surprised at this duality. It is merely the reflection of the composite character of a legal system as compared with a simpler decentralized pre-legal form of social structure which consists only of primary rules. In the simpler structure, since there are no officials, the rules must be widely accepted as setting critical standards for the behaviour of the group. If, there, the internal point of view is not widely disseminated there could not logically be any rules. But where there is a union of primary and secondary rules, which is, as we have argued, the most fruitful way of regarding a legal system, the acceptance of the rules as common standards for the group may be split off from the relatively passive matter of the ordinary individual acquiescing in the rules by obeying them for his part alone. In an extreme case the internal point of view with its characteristic normative use of legal language ('This is a valid rule') might be confined to the official world. In this more complex system, only officials might accept and use the system's criteria of legal validity. The society in which this was so might be deplorably sheeplike; the sheep might end in the slaughter-house. But there is little reason for thinking that it could not exist or for denying it the title of a legal system.

3. THE PATHOLOGY OF A LEGAL SYSTEM

Evidence for the existence of a legal system must therefore be drawn from two different sectors of social life. The normal, unproblematic case where we can say confidently that a legal system exists, is just one where it is clear that the two sectors are congruent in their respective typical concerns with the law. Crudely put, the facts are that the rules recognized as valid at the official level are generally obeyed. Sometimes, however, the official sector may be detached from the private sector, in the sense that there is no longer general obedience to the rules which are valid according to the criteria of validity in use in the courts. The variety of ways in which this may happen belongs to the pathology of legal systems; for they represent a breakdown in the complex congruent practice which is referred to when we make the external statement of fact that a legal system exists. There is here a partial failure of what is presupposed whenever, from within the particular system, we make internal statements of law. Such a breakdown may be the product of different disturbing factors. 'Revolution', where rival claims to govern are made from within the group, is only one case, and though this will always involve the breach of some of the laws of the existing system, it may entail only the legally unauthorized substitution of a new set of individuals as officials, and not a new constitution or legal system. Enemy occupation, where a rival claim to govern without authority under the existing system comes from without, is another case; and the simple breakdown of ordered legal control in the face of anarchy or banditry without political pretensions to govern is yet another.

In each of these cases there may be half-way stages during which the courts function, either on the territory or in exile, and still use the criteria of legal validity of the old once firmly established system; but these orders are ineffective in the territory. The stage at which it is right to say in such cases that the legal system has finally ceased to exist is a thing not susceptible of any exact determination. Plainly, if there is some considerable chance of a restoration or if the disturbance of the established system is an incident in a general war of which the issue is still uncertain, no unqualified assertion that it has ceased to exist would be warranted. This is so just because the statement that a legal system exists is of a sufficiently broad and general type to allow for interruptions; it is not verified or falsified by what happens in short spaces of time.

Of course difficult questions may arise after such interruptions have been succeeded by the resumption of normal relations between the courts and the population. A government returns from exile on the expulsion of occupying forces or the defeat of a rebel government; then questions arise as to what was or was not 'law' in the territory during the period of interruption. Here what is most important is to understand that this question may *not* be one of fact. If it were one of fact it would have to be settled by asking whether the interruption was so protracted and complete that the situation must be described as one in which the original system had ceased to exist and a new one was set up similar to the old, on the return from exile. Instead the question may be raised as one of international law, or it may, somewhat paradoxically, arise as a question of law within the very system of law existing since the restoration. In the latter case it might well be that the restored system included a retrospective law declaring the system to have been (or, more candidly, to be 'deemed' to have been) continuously the law of

the territory. This might be done even if the interruption were
so long as to make such a declaration seem quite at variance
with the conclusion that might have been reached had the
question been treated as a question of fact. In such a case there
is no reason why the declaration should not stand as a rule of
the restored system, determining the law which its courts must
apply to incidents and transactions occurring during the
period of interruption.

There is only a paradox here if we think of a legal system's
statements of law, concerning what are to be deemed to be
phases of its own past, present, or future existence, as rivals to
the factual statement about its existence, made from an external
point of view. Except for the apparent puzzle of self-reference
the legal status of a provision in an existing system concerning
the period during which it is to be considered to have existed,
is no different from a law of one system declaring that a certain
system is still in existence in another country, though the latter
is not likely to have many practical consequences. We are, in
fact, quite clear that the legal system in existence in the territory of the Soviet Union is not in fact that of the Tsarist régime.
But if a statute of the British Parliament declared that the law
of Tsarist Russia was still the law of Russian territory this would
indeed have meaning and legal effect as part of English law
referring to the U.S.S.R., but it would leave unaffected the
truth of the statement of fact contained in our last sentence.
The force and meaning of the statute would be merely to
determine the law to be applied in English courts, and so in
England, to cases with a Russian element.

The converse of the situation just described is to be seen in
the fascinating moments of transition during which a new
legal system emerges from the womb of an old one—sometimes
only after a Caesarian operation. The recent history of the
Commonwealth is an admirable field of study of this aspect of
the embryology of legal systems. The schematic, simplified outline of this development is as follows. At the beginning of a
period we may have a colony with a local legislature, judiciary,
and executive. This constitutional structure has been set up by
a statute of the United Kingdom Parliament, which retains
full legal competence to legislate for the colony; this includes
power to amend or repeal both the local laws and any of its

own statutes, including those referring to the constitution of the colony. At this stage the legal system of the colony is plainly a subordinate part of a wider system characterized by the ultimate rule of recognition that what the Queen in Parliament enacts is law for (*inter alia*) the colony. At the end of the period of development we find that the ultimate rule of recognition has shifted, for the legal competence of the Westminster Parliament to legislate for the former colony is no longer recognized in its courts. It is still true that much of the constitutional structure of the former colony is to be found in the original statute of the Westminster Parliament: but this is now only an historical fact, for it no longer owes its contemporary legal status in the territory to the authority of the Westminster Parliament. The legal system in the former colony has now a 'local root' in that the rule of recognition specifying the ultimate criteria of legal validity no longer refers to enactments of a legislature of another territory. The new rule rests simply on the fact that it is accepted and used as such a rule in the judicial and other official operations of a local system whose rules are generally obeyed. Hence, though the composition, mode of enactment, and structure of the local legislature may still be that prescribed in the original constitution, its enactments are valid now not because they are the exercise of powers granted by a valid statute of the Westminster Parliament. They are valid because, under the rule of recognition locally accepted, enactment by the local legislature is an ultimate criterion of validity.

This development may be achieved in many different ways. The parent legislature may, after a period in which it never in fact exercises its formal legislative authority over the colony except with its consent, finally retire from the scene by renouncing legislative power over the former colony. Here it is to be noted that there are theoretical doubts as to whether the courts in the United Kingdom would recognize the legal competence of the Westminster Parliament thus irrevocably to cut down its powers. The break away may, on the other hand, be achieved only by violence. But in either case we have at the end of this development two independent legal systems. This is a factual statement and not the less factual because it is one concerning the existence of legal systems. The main evidence for it is that in the former colony the ultimate rule of recognition now accepted and used includes, no longer among the criteria of validity, any reference to the operations of legislatures of other territories.

Again, however, and here Commonwealth history provides intriguing examples, it is possible that though in fact the legal system of the colony is now independent of its parent, the parent system may not recognize this fact. It may still be part of English law that the Westminster Parliament has retained, or can legally regain, power to legislate for the colony; and the domestic English courts may, if any cases involving a conflict between a Westminster statute and one of the local legislature comes before them, give effect to this view of the matter. In this case propositions of English law seem to conflict with fact. The law of the colony is *not* recognized in English courts as being what it is in fact: an independent legal system with its own local, ultimate rule of recognition. As a matter of fact there will be two legal systems, where English law will insist that there is only one But, just because one assertion is a statement of fact and the other a proposition of (English) law, the two do not logically conflict. To make the position clear we can, if we like, say that the statement of fact is true and the proposition of English law is 'correct in English law'. Similar distinctions between the factual assertion (or denial) that two independent legal systems exist, and propositions of law about the existence of a legal system, need to be borne in mind in considering the relationship between public international law and municipal law. Some very strange theories owe their only plausibility to a neglect of this distinction.

To complete this crude survey of the pathology and embryology of legal systems we should notice other forms of partial failure of the normal conditions, the congruence of which is asserted by the unqualified assertion that a legal system exists. The unity among officials, the existence of which is normally presupposed when internal statements of law are made within the system, may partly break down. It may be that, over certain constitutional issues and only over those, there is a division within the official world ultimately leading to a division among the judiciary. The beginning of such a split over the ultimate criteria to be used in identifying the law was seen in the constitutional troubles in South Africa in 1954, which came before the courts in *Harris* v. *Dönges*.[1] Here the legislature acted on a different view of its legal competence and powers from that taken by the courts, and enacted measures which the courts declared invalid. The response to this was the creation by the legislature of a special appellate 'court' to hear appeals from judgments of the ordinary courts which invalidated the enactments of the legislature. This court, in due course, heard such appeals and reversed the judgments of the ordinary courts; in turn, the ordinary courts declared the legislature creating the special courts invalid and their judgments a legal nullity. Had this process not been stopped (because the Government found it unwise to pursue this means of getting its way) we should have had an endless oscillation between two views of the competence of the legislature and so of the criteria of valid law. The normal conditions of official, and especially of judicial, harmony, under which alone it is possible to identify the system's rule of recognition, would have been suspended. Yet the great mass of legal operations not touching on this constitutional issue would go on as before. Till the population became divided and 'law and order' broke down it would be misleading to say that the original legal system had ceased to exist: for the expression 'the same legal system' is too broad and elastic to permit unified official consensus on *all* the original criteria of legal validity to be a necessary condition of the legal system remaining 'the same'. All we could do would be to describe the situation as we have done and note it as a sub-standard, abnormal case containing within it the threat that the legal system will dissolve.

This last case brings us to the borders of a wider topic which we discuss in the next chapter both in relation to the high constitutional matter of a legal system's ultimate criteria of validity and its 'ordinary' law. All rules involve recognizing or classifying particular cases as instances of general terms, and in the case of everything which we are prepared to call a rule it is possible to distinguish clear central cases, where it certainly applies and others where there are reasons for both asserting and denying that it applies. Nothing can eliminate this duality of a core of certainty and a penumbra of doubt when we are engaged in bringing particular situations under general rules. *NB.*

[1] [1952] 1 T.L.R. 1245.

This imparts to all rules a fringe of vagueness or 'open texture', and this may affect the rule of recognition specifying the ultimate criteria used in the identification of the law as much as a particular statute. This aspect of law is often held to show that any elucidation of the concept of law in terms of rules must be misleading. To insist on it in the face of the realities of the situation is often stigmatized as 'conceptualism' or 'formalism', and it is to the estimation of this charge that we shall now turn.

VII

FORMALISM AND RULE-SCEPTICISM

1. THE OPEN TEXTURE OF LAW

IN any large group general rules, standards, and principles must be the main instrument of social control, and not particular directions given to each individual separately. If it were not possible to communicate general standards of conduct, which multitudes of individuals could understand, without further direction, as requiring from them certain conduct when occasion arose, nothing that we now recognize as law could exist. Hence the law must predominantly, but by no means exclusively, refer to *classes* of person, and to *classes* of acts, things, and circumstances; and its successful operation over vast areas of social life depends on a widely diffused capacity to recognize particular acts, things, and circumstances as instances of the general classifications which the law makes.

Two principal devices, at first sight very different from each other, have been used for the communication of such general standards of conduct in advance of the successive occasions on which they are to be applied. One of them makes a maximal and the other a minimal use of general classifying words. The first is typified by what we call legislation and the second by precedent. We can see the distinguishing features of these in the following simple non-legal cases. One father before going to church says to his son, 'Every man and boy must take off his hat on entering a church.' Another baring his head as he enters the church says, 'Look: this is the right way to behave on such occasions.'

The communication or teaching of standards of conduct by example may take different forms, far more sophisticated than our simple case. Our case would more closely resemble the legal use of precedent, if instead of the child being told on the particular occasion to regard what his father did on entering the church as an example of the right thing to do, the father assumed that the child would regard him as an authority on proper behaviour, and would watch him in order to learn the way to behave. To approach further the legal use of precedent, we must suppose that the father is conceived by himself and others to subscribe to traditional standards of behaviour and not to be introducing new ones.

Communication by example in all its forms, though accompanied by some general verbal directions such as 'Do as I do', may leave open ranges of possibilities, and hence of doubt, as to what is intended even as to matters which the person seeking to communicate has himself clearly envisaged. How much of the performance must be imitated? Does it matter if the left hand is used, instead of the right, to remove the hat? That it is done slowly or smartly? That the hat is put under the seat? That it is not replaced on the head inside the church? These are all variants of general questions which the child might ask himself: 'In what ways must my conduct resemble his to be right?' 'What precisely is it about his conduct that is to be my guide?' In understanding the example, the child attends to some of its aspects rather than others. In so doing he is guided by common sense and knowledge of the general kind of things and purposes which adults think important, and by his appreciation of the general character of the occasion (going to church) and the kind of behaviour appropriate to it.

In contrast with the indeterminacies of examples, the communication of general standards by explicit general forms of language ('Every man must take off his hat on entering a church') seems clear, dependable, and certain. The features to be taken as general guides to conduct are here identified in words; they are verbally extricated, not left embedded with others in a concrete example. In order to know what to do on other occasions the child has no longer to guess what is intended, or what will be approved; he is not left to speculate as to the way in which his conduct must resemble the example if it is to be right. Instead, he has a verbal description which he can use to pick out what he must do in future and when he must do it. He has only to recognize instances of clear verbal terms, to 'subsume' particular facts under general classificatory heads and draw a simple syllogistic conclusion. He is not faced with the alternative of choosing at his peril or seeking further authoritative guidance. He has a rule which he can apply by himself to himself.

Much of the jurisprudence of this century has consisted of the progressive realization (and sometimes the exaggeration) of the important fact that the distinction between the uncertainties of communication by authoritative example (precedent), and the certainties of communication by authoritative general language (legislation) is far less firm than this naïve contrast suggests. Even when verbally formulated general rules are used, uncertainties as to the form of behaviour required by them may break out in particular concrete cases. Particular fact-situations do not await us already marked off from each other, and labelled as instances of the general rule, the application of which is in question; nor can the rule itself step forward to claim its own instances. In all fields of experience, not only that of rules, there is a limit, inherent in the nature of language, to the guidance which general language can provide. There will indeed be plain cases constantly recurring in similar contexts to which general expressions are clearly applicable ('If anything is a vehicle a motor-car is one') but there will also be cases where it is not clear whether they apply or not. ('Does "vehicle" used here include bicycles, airplanes, roller skates?') The latter are fact-situations, continually thrown up by nature or human invention, which possess only some of the features of the plain cases but others which they lack. Canons of 'interpretation' cannot eliminate, though they can diminish, these uncertainties; for these canons are themselves general rules for the use of language, and make use of general terms which themselves require interpretation. They cannot, any more than other rules, provide for their own interpretation. The plain case, where the general terms seem to need no interpretation and where the recognition of instances seems unproblematic or 'automatic', are only the familiar ones, constantly recurring in similar contexts, where there is general agreement in judgments as to the applicability of the classifying terms.

General terms would be useless to us as a medium of communication unless there were such familiar, generally unchallenged cases. But the variants on the familiar also call for classification under the general terms which at any given moment constitute part of our linguistic resources. Here something in the nature of a crisis in communication is precipitated: there are reasons both for and against our use of a general term, and no firm convention or general agreement dictates its use, or, on the other hand, its rejection by the person concerned to classify. If in such cases doubts are to be resolved, something in the nature of a choice between open alternatives must be made by whoever is to resolve them.

At this point, the authoritative general language in which a rule is expressed may guide only in an uncertain way much as an authoritative example does. The sense that the language of the rule will enable us simply to pick out easily recognizable instances, at this point gives way; subsumption and the drawing of a syllogistic conclusion no longer characterize the nerve of the reasoning involved in determining what is the right thing to do. Instead, the language of the rule seems now only to mark out an authoritative example, namely that constituted by the plain case. This may be used in much the same way as a precedent, though the language of the rule will limit the features demanding attention both more permanently and more closely than precedent does. Faced with the question whether the rule prohibiting the use of vehicles in the park is applicable to some combination of circumstances in which it appears indeterminate, all that the person called upon to answer can do is to consider (as does one who makes use of a precedent) whether the present case resembles the plain case 'sufficiently' in 'relevant' respects. The discretion thus left to him by language may be very wide; so that if he applies the rule, the conclusion, even though it may not be arbitrary or irrational, is in effect a choice. He chooses to add to a line of cases a new case because of resemblances which can reasonably be defended as both legally relevant and sufficiently close. In the case of legal rules, the criteria of relevance and closeness of resemblance depend on many complex factors running through the legal system and on the aims or purpose which may be attributed to the rule. To characterize these would be to characterize whatever is specific or peculiar in legal reasoning.

Whichever device, precedent or legislation, is chosen for the communication of standards of behaviour, these, however smoothly they work over the great mass of ordinary cases, will, at some point where their application is in question, prove indeterminate; they will have what has been termed an *open texture*. So far we have presented this, in the case of legislation, as a general feature of human language; uncertainty at the borderline is the price to be paid for the use of general classifying terms in any form of communication concerning matters of fact. Natural languages like English are when so used irreducibly open textured. It is, however, important to appreciate why, apart from this dependence on language as it actually is, with its characteristics of open texture, we should not cherish, even as an ideal, the conception of a rule so detailed that the question whether it applied or not to a particular case was always settled in advance, and never involved, at the point of actual application, a fresh choice between open alternatives. Put shortly, the reason is that the necessity for such choice is thrust upon us because we are men, not gods. It is a feature of the human predicament (and so of the legislative one) that we labour under two connected handicaps whenever we seek to regulate, unambiguously and in advance, some sphere of conduct by means of general standards to be used without further official direction on particular occasions. The first handicap is our relative ignorance of fact: the second is our relative indeterminacy of aim. If the world in which we live were characterized only by a finite number of features, and these together with all the modes in which they could combine were known to us, then provision could be made in advance for every possibility. We could make rules, the application of which to particular cases never called for a further choice. Everything could be known, and for everything, since it could be known, something could be done and specified in advance by rule. This would be a world fit for 'mechanical' jurisprudence.

Plainly this world is not our world; human legislators can have no such knowledge of all the possible combinations of circumstances which the future may bring. This inability to anticipate brings with it a relative indeterminacy of aim. When we are bold enough to frame some general rule of conduct (e.g. a rule that no vehicle may be taken into the park), the language used in this context fixes necessary conditions which anything must satisfy if it is to be within its scope, and certain clear examples of what is certainly within its scope may be present to our minds. They are the paradigm, clear cases (the motor-car, the bus, the motor-cycle); and our aim in legislating is so far determinate because we have made a certain choice.

We have initially settled the question that peace and quiet in the park is to be maintained at the cost, at any rate, of the exclusion of these things. On the other hand, until we have put the general aim of peace in the park into conjunction with those cases which we did not, or perhaps could not, initially envisage (perhaps a toy motor-car electrically propelled) our aim is, in this direction, indeterminate. We have not settled, because we have not anticipated, the question which will be raised by the unenvisaged case when it occurs: whether some degree of peace in the park is to be sacrificed to, or defended against, those children whose pleasure or interest it is to use these things. When the unenvisaged case does arise, we confront the issues at stake and can then settle the question by choosing between the competing interests in the way which best satisfies us. In doing so we shall have rendered more determinate our initial aim, and shall incidentally have settled a question as to the meaning, for the purposes of this rule, of a general word.

Different legal systems, or the same system at different times, may either ignore or acknowledge more or less explicitly such a need for the further exercise of choice in the application of general rules to particular cases. The vice known to legal theory as formalism or conceptualism consists in an attitude to verbally formulated rules which both seeks to disguise and to minimize the need for such choice, once the general rule has been laid down. One way of doing this is to freeze the meaning of the rule so that its general terms must have the same meaning in every case where its application is in question. To secure this we may fasten on certain features present in the plain case and insist that these are both necessary and sufficient to bring anything which has them within the scope of the rule, whatever other features it may have or lack, and whatever may be the social consequences of applying the rule in this way. To do this is to secure a measure of certainty or predictability at the cost of blindly prejudging what is to be done in a range of future cases, about whose composition we are ignorant. We shall thus indeed succeed in settling in advance, but also in the dark, issues which can only reasonably be settled when they arise and are identified. We shall be forced by this technique to include in the scope of a rule cases which we would wish to exclude in order to give effect to reasonable social aims, and which the open textured terms of our language would have allowed us to exclude, had we left them less rigidly defined. The rigidity of our classifications will thus war with our aims in having or maintaining the rule.

The consummation of this process is the jurists' 'heaven of concepts'; this is reached when a general term is given the same meaning not only in every application of a single rule, but whenever it appears in any rule in the legal system. No effort is then ever required or made to interpret the term in the light of the different issues at stake in its various recurrences.

In fact all systems, in different ways, compromise between two social needs: the need for certain rules which can, over great areas of conduct, safely be applied by private individuals to themselves without fresh official guidance or weighing up of social issues, and the need to leave open, for later settlement by an informed, official choice, issues which can only be properly appreciated and settled when they arise in a concrete case. In some legal systems at some periods it may be that too much is sacrificed to certainty, and that judicial interpretation of statutes or of precedent is too formal and so fails to respond to the similarities and differences between cases which are visible only when they are considered in the light of social aims. In other systems or at other periods it may seem that too much is treated by courts as perennially open or revisable in precedents, and too little respect paid to such limits as legislative language, despite its open texture, does after all provide. Legal theory has in this matter a curious history; for it is apt either to ignore or to exaggerate the indeterminacies of legal rules. To escape this oscillation between extremes we need to remind ourselves that human inability to anticipate the future, which is at the root of this indeterminacy, varies in degree in different fields of conduct, and that legal systems cater for this inability by a corresponding variety of techniques.

Sometimes the sphere to be legally controlled is recognized from the start as one in which the features of individual cases will vary so much in socially important but unpredictable respects, that uniform rules to be applied from case to case without further official direction cannot usefully be framed by the legislature in advance. Accordingly, to regulate such a sphere the legislature sets up very general standards and then delegates to an administrative, rule-making body acquainted with the varying types of case, the task of fashioning rules adapted to their special needs. Thus the legislature may require an industry to maintain certain standards: to charge only a *fair rate* or to provide *safe systems* of work. Instead of leaving the different enterprises to apply these vague standards to themselves, at the risk of being found to have violated them *ex post facto*, it may be found best to defer the use of sanctions for violations until the administrative body has by regulation specified what, for a given industry, is to count as a 'fair rate' or a 'safe system'. This rule-making power may be exercisable only after something like a judicial inquiry into the facts about the particular industry, and a hearing of arguments pro and con a given form of regulation.

Of course even with very general standards there will be plain indisputable examples of what does, or does not, satisfy them. Some extreme cases of what is, or is not, a 'fair rate' or a 'safe system' will always be identifiable *ab initio*. Thus at one end of the infinitely varied range of cases there will be a rate so high that it would hold the public up to ransom for a vital service, while yielding the entrepreneurs vast profits; at the other end there will be a rate so low that it fails to provide an incentive for running the enterprise. Both these in different ways would defeat any possible aim we could have in regulating rates. But these are only the extremes of a range of different factors and are not likely to be met in practice; between them fall the difficult real cases requiring attention. The anticipatable combinations of relevant factors are few, and this entails a relative indeterminacy in our initial aim of a fair rate or a safe system, and a need for further official choice. In these cases it is clear that the rule-making authority must exercise a discretion, and there is no possibility of treating the question raised by the various cases as if there were one uniquely correct answer to be found, as distinct from an answer which is a reasonable compromise between many conflicting interests.

A second similar technique is used where the sphere to be controlled is such that it is impossible to identify a class of specific actions to be uniformly done or foreborne and to make them the subject of a simple rule, yet the range of circumstances, though very varied, covers familiar features of common experience. Here common judgments of what is 'reasonable' can be used by the law. This technique leaves to individuals, subject to correction by a court, the task of weighing up and striking a reasonable balance between the social claims which arise in various unanticipatable forms. In this case they are required to conform to a variable standard *before* it has been officially defined, and they may learn from a court only *ex post facto* when they have violated it, what, in terms of specific actions or forbearances, is the standard required of them. Where the decisions of the court on such matters are regarded as precedents, their specification of the variable standard is very like the exercise of delegated rule-making power by an administrative body, though there are also obvious differences.

The most famous example of this technique in Anglo-American law is the use of the standard of due care in cases of negligence. Civil, and less frequently criminal, sanctions may be applied to those who fail to take reasonable care to avoid inflicting physical injuries on others. But what is reasonable or due care in a concrete situation? We can, of course, cite typical examples of due care: doing such things as stopping, looking, and listening where traffic is to be expected. But we are all well aware that the situations where care is demanded are hugely various and that many other actions are now required besides, or in place of, 'stop, look, and listen'; indeed these may not be enough and might be quite useless if looking would not help to avert the danger. What we are striving for in the application of standards of reasonable care is to ensure (1) that precautions will be taken which will avert substantial harm, yet (2) that the precautions are such that the burden of proper precautions does not involve too great a sacrifice of other respectable interests. Nothing much is sacrificed by stopping, looking, and listening unless of course a man bleeding to death is being driven to the hospital. But owing to the immense variety of possible cases where care is called for, we cannot *ab initio* foresee what combinations of circumstances will arise nor foresee what interests will have to be sacrificed or to what extent, if precaution against harm is to be taken. Hence it is that we are unable to consider, before particular cases arise, precisely what sacrifice or compromise of interests or values we wish to make in order to reduce the risk of harm. Again, our aim of securing people against harm is indeterminate till we put it in conjunction with, or test it against, possibilities which only experience will bring before us; when it does, then we have to face a decision which will, when made, render our aim *pro tanto* determinate.

Consideration of these two techniques throws into relief the characteristics of those wide areas of conduct which are successfully controlled *ab initio* by rule, requiring specific actions, with only a fringe of open texture, instead of a variable standard. They are characterized by the fact that certain distinguishable actions, events, or states of affairs are of such practical importance to us, as things either to avert or bring about, that very few concomitant circumstances incline us to regard them differently. The crudest example of this is the killing of a human being. We are in a position to make a rule against killing instead of laying down a variable standard ('due respect for human life'), although the circumstances in which human beings kill others are very various: this is so because very few factors appear to us to outweigh or make us revise our estimate of the importance of protecting life. Almost always killing, as it were, *dominates* the other factors by which it is accompanied, so when we rule it out in advance as 'killing', we are not blindly prejudging issues which require to be weighed against each other. Of course there are exceptions, factors which override this usually dominant one. There is killing in self-defence and other forms of justifiable homicide. But these are few and identifiable in relatively simple terms; they are admitted as exceptions to a general rule.

It is important to notice that the dominant status of some easily identifiable action, event, or state of affairs may be, in a sense, conventional or artificial, and not due to its 'natural' or 'intrinsic' importance to us as human beings. It does not matter which side of the road is prescribed by the rule of the road, nor (within limits) what formalities are prescribed for the execution of a conveyance; but it does matter very much that there should be an easily identifiable and uniform procedure, and so a clear right and wrong on these matters. When this has been introduced by law the importance of adhering to it is, with few exceptions, paramount; for relatively few attendant circumstances could outweigh it and those that do may be easily identifiable as exceptions and reduced to rule. The English law of real property very clearly illustrates this aspect of rules.

The communication of general rules by authoritative examples brings with it, as we have seen, indeterminacies of a more complex kind. The acknowledgement of precedent as a criterion of legal validity means different things in different systems, and in the same system at different times. Descriptions of the English 'theory' of precedent are, on certain points, still highly contentious: indeed even the key terms used in the theory, 'ratio decidendi', 'material facts', 'interpretation', have their own penumbra of uncertainty. We shall not offer any fresh general description, but merely attempt to characterize briefly, as we have in the case of statute, the area of open texture and the creative judicial activity within it.

Any honest description of the use of precedent in English law must allow a place for the following pairs of contrasting facts. *First*, there is no single method of determining the rule for which a given authoritative precedent is an authority. Notwithstanding this, in the vast majority of decided cases there is very little doubt. The head-note is usually correct enough. *Secondly*, there is no authoritative or uniquely correct formulation of any rule to be extracted from cases. On the other hand, there is often very general agreement, when the bearing of a precedent on a later case is in issue, that a given formulation is adequate. *Thirdly*, whatever authoritative status a rule extracted from precedent may have, it is compatible with the exercise by courts that are bound by it of the following two types of creative or legislative activity. On the one hand courts deciding a later case may reach an opposite decision to that in a precedent by narrowing the rule extracted from the precedent, and admitting some exception to it not before considered, or, if considered, left open. This process of 'distinguishing' the earlier case involves finding some legally relevant difference between it and the present case, and the class of such differences can never be exhaustively determined. On the other hand, in following an earlier precedent the courts may discard a restriction found in the rule as formulated from the earlier case, on the ground that it is not required by any rule established by statute or earlier precedent. To do this is to widen the rule. Notwithstanding these two forms of legislative activity, left open by the binding force of precedent, the result of the English system of precedent has been to produce, by its use, a body of rules of which a vast number, of both major and minor importance, are as determinate as any statutory rule. They can now only be altered by statute, as the courts themselves often declare in cases where the 'merits' seem to run counter to the requirements of the established precedents.

The open texture of law means that there are, indeed, areas of conduct where much must be left to be developed by courts or officials striking a balance, in the light of circumstances, between competing interests which vary in weight from case to case. None the less, the life of the law consists to a very large extent in the guidance both of officials and private individuals by determinate rules which, unlike the applications of variable standards, do *not* require from them a fresh judgment from case to case. This salient fact of social life remains true, even though uncertainties may break out as to the applicability of any rule (whether written or communicated by precedent) to a concrete case. Here at the margin of rules and in the fields left open by the theory of precedents, the courts perform a rule-producing function which administrative bodies perform centrally in the elaboration of variable standards. In a system where *stare decisis* is firmly acknowledged, this function of the courts is very like the exercise of delegated rule-making powers by an administrative body. In England this fact is often obscured by forms: for the courts often disclaim any such creative function and insist that the proper task of statutory interpretation and the use of precedent is, respectively, to search for the 'intention of the legislature' and the law that already exists.

2. VARIETIES OF RULE-SCEPTICISM

We have discussed at some length the open texture of law because it is important to see this feature in a just perspective. Failure to do justice to it will always provoke exaggerations which will obscure other features of law. In every legal system a large and important field is left open for the exercise of discretion by courts and other officials in rendering initially vague standards determinate, in resolving the uncertainties of statutes, or in developing and qualifying rules only broadly communicated by authoritative precedents. None the less these activities, important and insufficiently studied though they are, must not disguise the fact that both the framework within which they take place and their chief end-product is one of general rules. These are rules the application of which individuals can see for themselves in case after case, without further recourse to official direction or discretion.

It may seem strange that the contention that rules have a central place in the structure of a legal system could ever be seriously doubted. Yet 'rule-scepticism', or the claim that talk of rules is a myth, cloaking the truth that law consists simply of the decisions of courts and the prediction of them, can make a powerful appeal to a lawyer's candour. Stated in an unqualified general form, so as to embrace both secondary and primary rules, it is indeed quite incoherent; for the assertion that there are decisions of courts cannot consistently be combined with the denial that there are any rules at all. This is so because, as we have seen, the existence of a court entails the existence of secondary rules conferring jurisdiction on a changing succession of individuals and so making their decisions authoritative. In a community of people who understood the notions of a decision and a prediction of a decision, but not the notion of a rule, the idea of an *authoritative* decision would be lacking and with it the idea of a court. There would be nothing to distinguish the decision of a private person from that of a court. We might try to eke out, with the notion of 'habitual obedience', the deficiencies of predictability of decision as a foundation for the authoritative jurisdiction required in a court. But if we do this we shall find that the notion of a habit suffers, for this purpose, from all the inadequacies which came to light when in Chapter IV we considered it as a substitute for a rule conferring legislative powers.

In some more moderate versions of the theory it may be conceded that if there are to be courts there must be legal rules which constitute them, and these themselves cannot therefore be simply predictions of the decisions of courts. Little headway can, however, in fact be made with this concession alone. For it is an assertion characteristic of this type of theory that statutes are not law until applied by courts but only sources of law, and this is inconsistent with the assertion that the only rules that exist are those required to constitute courts. There must also be secondary rules conferring legislative powers on changing successions of individuals. For the theory does not deny that there are statutes; indeed it cites them as mere 'sources' of law, and only denies that statutes are law until applied by courts.

These objections though important and, against an incautious form of the theory, well taken, do not apply to it in all forms. It may well be that rule-scepticism was never intended as a denial of the existence of secondary rules conferring judicial or legislative power, and was never committed to the claim that these could be shown to be nothing more than decisions or predictions of decisions. Certainly, the examples on which this type of theory has most often relied are drawn from rules imposing duties or conferring rights or powers on private individuals. Yet, even if we suppose the denial that there are rules and the assertion that what are called rules are merely predictions of the decisions of courts to be limited in this way, there is one sense, at least, in which it is obviously false. For it cannot be doubted that at any rate in relation to some spheres of conduct in a modern state individuals do exhibit the whole range of conduct and attitudes which we have called the internal point of view. Laws function in their lives not merely as habits or the basis for predicting the decisions of courts or the actions of other officials, but as accepted legal standards of behaviour. That is, they not only do with tolerable regularity what the law requires of them, but they look upon it as a legal standard of conduct, refer to it in criticizing others, or in justifying demands, and in admitting criticism and demands made by others. In using legal rules in this normative way they no doubt assume that the courts and other officials will continue to decide and behave in certain regular and hence predictable ways, in accordance with the rules of the system; but it is surely an observable fact of social life that individuals do not confine themselves to the external point of view, recording and predicting the decisions of courts or the probable incidence of sanctions. Instead they continuously express in normative terms their shared acceptance of the law as a guide to conduct. We have considered at length in Chapter III the claim that nothing more is meant by normative terms such as 'obligation' than a prediction of official behaviour. If, as we have argued, that claim is false, legal rules function as such in social life: they are *used* as rules not as descriptions of habits or predictions. No doubt they are rules with an open texture and at the points where the texture is open, individuals can only predict how courts will decide and adjust their behaviour accordingly.

Rule-scepticism has a serious claim on our attention, but only as a theory of the function of rules in judicial decision. In this form, while conceding all the objections to which we have drawn attention, it amounts to the contention that, so far as the courts are concerned, there is nothing to circumscribe the area of open texture: so that it is false, if not senseless, to regard judges as themselves subject to rules or 'bound' to decide cases as they do. They may act with sufficient predictable regularity and uniformity to enable others, over long periods, to live by courts' decisions as rules. Judges may even experience feelings of compulsion when they decide as they do, and these feelings may be predictable too; but beyond this there is nothing which can be characterized as a rule which they observe. There is nothing which courts treat as standards of correct judicial behaviour, and so nothing in that behaviour which manifests the internal point of view characteristic of the acceptance of rules.

The theory in this form draws support from a variety of considerations of very different weight. The rule-sceptic is sometimes a disappointed absolutist; he has found that rules are not all they would be in a formalist's heaven, or in a world where men were like gods and could anticipate all possible combinations of fact, so that open-texture was not a necessary feature of rules. The sceptic's conception of what it is for a rule to exist, may thus be an unattainable ideal, and when he discovers that it is not attained by what are called rules, he expresses his disappointment by the denial that there are, or can be, any rules. Thus the fact that the rules, which judges claim bind them in deciding a case, have an open texture, or have exceptions not exhaustively specifiable in advance, and the fact that deviation from the rules will not draw down on the judge a physical sanction are often used to establish the sceptic's case. These facts are stressed to show that 'rules are important so far as they help you to predict what judges will do. That is all their importance except as pretty playthings.'[1]

[1] Llewellyn, *The Bramble Bush* (2nd edition), p. 9.

To argue in this way is to ignore what rules actually are in any sphere of real life. It suggests that we are faced with the dilemma: 'Either rules are what they would be in the formalist's heaven and they bind as fetters bind; or there are no rules, only predictable decisions or patterns of behaviour.' Yet surely this is a false dilemma. We promise to visit a friend the next day. When the day comes it turns out that keeping the promise would involve neglecting someone dangerously ill. The fact that this is accepted as an adequate reason for not keeping the promise surely does not mean that there is no rule requiring promises to be kept, only a certain regularity in keeping them. It does not follow from the fact that such rules have exceptions incapable of exhaustive statement, that in every situation we are left to our discretion and are never bound to keep a promise. A rule that ends with the word 'unless . . .' is still a rule.

Sometimes the existence of rules binding on courts is denied, because the question whether a person, in acting in a certain way, thereby manifested his acceptance of a rule requiring him so to act, is confused with psychological questions as to the processes of thought through which the person went before or in acting. Very often when a person accepts a rule as binding and as something he and others are not free to change, he may see what it requires in a given situation quite intuitively, and do that without first thinking of the rule and what it requires. When we move a piece in chess in accordance with the rules, or stop at a traffic light when it is red, our rule-complying behaviour is often a direct response to the situation, unmediated by calculation in terms of the rules. The evidence that such actions are genuine applications of the rule is their setting in certain circumstances. Some of these precede the particular action and others follow it: and some of them are stateable only in general and hypothetical terms. The most important of these factors which show that in acting we have applied a rule is that *if* our behaviour is challenged we are disposed to justify it by reference to the rule: and the genuineness of our acceptance of the rule may be manifested not only in our past and subsequent general acknowledgements of it and conformity to it, but in our criticism of our own and others' deviation from it. On such or similar evidence we may indeed conclude that if, before our 'unthinking' compliance with the rule, we had been asked to say what the right thing to do was and why, we would, if honest, have cited the rule in reply. It is this setting of our behaviour among such circumstances, and not its accompaniment by explicit thought of the rule, that is necessary to distinguish an action which is genuinely an observance of a rule from one that merely happens to coincide with it. It is thus that we would distinguish, as a compliance with an accepted rule, the adult chess-player's move from the action of the baby who merely pushed the piece into the right place.

This is not to say that pretence or 'window dressing' is not possible and sometimes successful. Tests for whether a person has merely pretended *ex post facto* that he acted on a rule are, like all empirical tests, inherently fallible but they are not inveterately so. It is possible that, in a given society, judges might always first reach their decisions intuitively or 'by hunches', and then merely choose from a catalogue of legal rules one which, they pretended, resembled the case in hand; they might then claim that this was the rule which they regarded as requiring their decision, although nothing else in their actions or words suggested that they regarded it as a rule binding on them. Some judicial decisions may be like this, but it is surely evident that for the most part decisions, like the chess-player's moves, are reached either by genuine effort to conform to rules consciously taken as guiding standards of decision or, if intuitively reached, are justified by rules which the judge was antecedently disposed to observe and whose relevance to the case in hand would generally be acknowledged.

The last but most interesting form of rule-scepticism does not rest either on the open character of legal rules or on the intuitive character of many decisions; but on the fact that the decision of a court has a unique position as something authoritative, and in the case of supreme tribunals, final. This form of the theory, to which we shall devote the next section, is implicit in Bishop Hoadly's famous phrase echoed so often by Gray in *The Nature and Sources of Law*, 'Nay whoever hath an absolute authority to interpret any written or spoken laws it is he who is the lawgiver to all intents and purposes and not the person who first wrote or spake them.'

3. FINALITY AND INFALLIBILITY IN JUDICIAL DECISION

A supreme tribunal has the last word in saying what the law is and, when it has said it, the statement that the court was 'wrong' has no consequences within the system: no one's rights or duties are thereby altered. The decision may, of course, be deprived of legal effect by legislation, but the very fact that resort to this is necessary demonstrates the empty character, so far as the law is concerned, of the statement that the court's decision was wrong. Consideration of these facts makes it seem pedantic to distinguish, in the case of a supreme tribunal's decisions, between their finality and infallibility. This leads to another form of the denial that courts in deciding are ever bound by rules: 'The law (or the constitution) is what the courts say it is.'

The most interesting and instructive feature of this form of the theory is its exploitation of the ambiguity of such statements as 'the law (or the constitution) is what the courts say it is', and the account which the theory must, to be consistent, give of the relation of non-official statements of law to the official statements of a court. To understand this ambiguity, we shall turn aside to consider its analogue in the case of a game. Many competitive games are played without an official scorer: notwithstanding their competing interests, the players succeed tolerably well in applying the scoring rule to particular cases; they usually agree in their judgments, and unresolved disputes may be few. Before the institution of an official scorer, a statement of the score made by a player represents, if he is honest, an effort to assess the progress of the game by reference to the particular scoring rule accepted in that game. Such statements of the score are internal statements applying the scoring rule, which though they presuppose that the players will, in general, abide by the rules and will object to their violation, are not statements or predictions of these facts.

Like the changes from a régime of custom to a mature system of law, the addition to the game of secondary rules providing for the institution of a scorer whose rulings are final, brings into the system a new kind of internal statement; for unlike the players' statements as to the score, the scorer's determinations are given, by secondary rules, a status which renders them unchallengeable. In *this* sense it is true that for the purposes of the game 'the score is what the scorer says it is'. But it is important to see that the scoring *rule* remains what it was before and it is the scorer's duty to apply it as best he can. 'The score is what the scorer says it is' would be false if it meant that there was no rule for scoring save what the scorer in his discretion chose to apply. There might indeed be a game with such a rule, and some amusement might be found in playing it if the scorer's discretion were exercised with some regularity; but it would be a different game. We may call such a game the game of 'scorer's discretion'.

It is plain that the advantages of quick and final settlement of disputes, which a scorer brings, are purchased at a price. The institution of a scorer may face the players with a predicament: the wish that the game should be regulated, as before, by the scoring rule and the wish for final authoritative decisions as to its application, where it is doubtful, may turn out to be conflicting aims. The scorer may make honest mistakes, be drunk or may wantonly violate his duty to apply the scoring rule to the best of his ability. He may for any of these reasons record a 'run' when the batsman has never moved. Provision may be made for correcting his rulings by appeal to a higher authority: but this must end somewhere in a final, authoritative judgment, which will be made by fallible human beings and so will carry with it the same risk of honest mistake, abuse, or violation. It is impossible to provide by rule for the correction of the breach of every rule.

The risk inherent in setting up an authority to make final authoritative applications of rules may materialize in any sphere. Those that might materialize in the humble sphere of a game are worth consideration, since they show, in a particularly clear fashion, that some of the inferences drawn by the rule-sceptic ignore certain distinctions which are necessary for the understanding of this form of authority wherever it is used. When an official scorer is established and his determinations of the score are made final, statements as to the score made by the players or other non-officials have no status within the game; they are irrelevant to its result. If they happen to coincide with the scorer's statement, well and good; if they conflict, they must be neglected in computing the result. But these very obvious facts would be distorted if the players' statements were classified as predictions of the scorer's rulings, and it would be absurd to explain the neglect of these statements, when they conflicted with the scorer's rulings, by saying that they were predictions of those rulings which had turned out to be false. The player, in making his own statements as to the score after the introduction of an official scorer, is doing what he did before: namely, assessing the progress of the game, as best he can, by reference to the scoring rule. This, too, is what the scorer himself, so long as he fulfils the duties of his position, is also doing. The difference between them is not that one is predicting what the other will say, but that the players' statements are unofficial applications of the scoring rule and hence have no significance in computing the result; whereas the scorer's statements are authoritative and final. It is important to observe that if the game played were 'scorer's discretion' then the relationship between unofficial and official statements would necessarily be different: the players' statements not only *would* be a prediction of the scorer's rulings but *could* be nothing else. For in that case 'the score is what the scorer says it is' would itself be the scoring *rule*; there would be no possibility of the players' statements being merely unofficial versions of what the scorer does officially. Then the scorer's rulings would be both final and infallible—or rather the question whether they were fallible or infallible would be meaningless; for there would be nothing for him to get 'right' or 'wrong'. But in an ordinary game 'the score is what the scorer says it is' is not the scoring rule: it is a rule providing for the authority and finality of his application of the scoring rule in particular cases.

The second lesson to be learnt from this example of authoritative decision touches more fundamental matters. We are able to distinguish a normal game from the game of 'scorer's discretion' simply because the scoring rule, though it has, like other rules, its area of open texture where the scorer has to exercise a choice, yet has a core of settled meaning. It is this which the scorer is not free to depart from, and which, so far as it goes, constitutes the standard of correct and incorrect scoring, both for the player, in making his unofficial statements as to the score, and for the scorer in his official rulings. It is this that makes it true to say that the scorer's rulings are, though final, not infallible. The same is true in law.

Up to a certain point, the fact that some rulings given by a scorer are plainly wrong is not inconsistent with the game continuing: they count as much as rulings which are obviously correct; but there is a limit to the extent to which tolerance of incorrect decisions is compatible with the continued existence of the same game, and this has an important legal analogue. The fact that isolated or exceptional official aberrations are tolerated does not mean that the game of cricket or baseball is no longer being played. On the other hand, if these aberrations are frequent, or if the scorer repudiates the scoring rule, there must come a point when either the players no longer accept the scorer's aberrant rulings or, if they do, the game has changed. It is no longer cricket or baseball but 'scorer's discretion'; for it is a defining feature of these other games that, in general, their results should be assessed in the way demanded by the plain meaning of the rule, whatever latitude its open texture may leave to the scorer. In some imaginable condition we should say that in truth the game being played was 'scorer's discretion' but the fact that in all games the scorer's rulings are final does not mean that that is what all games are.

These distinctions should be borne in mind when we are appraising the form of rule-scepticism that rests on the unique status of a court's decision as a final, authoritative statement of what the law is in a particular case. The open texture of law leaves to courts a law-creating power far wider and more important than that left to scorers, whose decisions are not used as law-making precedents. Whatever courts decide, both on matters lying within that part of the rule which seems plain to all, and those lying on its debatable border, stands till altered by legislation; and over the interpretation of that, courts will again have the same last authoritative voice. Nonetheless there still remains a distinction between a constitution which, after setting up a system of courts, provides that the law shall be whatever the supreme court thinks fit, and the actual constitution of the United States—or for that matter the constitution of any modern State. 'The constitution (or the law) is whatever the judges say it is', if interpreted as denying this distinction, is false. At any given moment judges, even those of a supreme court, are parts of a system the rules of which are determinate enough at the centre to supply standards of correct judicial decision. These are regarded by the courts as something which they are not free to disregard in the exercise of the authority to make those decisions which cannot be challenged within the system. Any individual judge coming to his office, like any scorer coming to his, finds a rule, such as the rule that the enactments of the Queen in Parliament are law, established as a tradition and accepted as the standard for the conduct of that office. This circumscribes, while allowing, the creative activity of its occupants. Such standards could not indeed continue to exist unless most of the judges of the time adhered to them, for their existence at any given time consists simply in the acceptance and use of them as standards of correct adjudication. But this does not make the judge who uses them the author of these standards, or in Hoadly's language the 'lawgiver' competent to decide as he pleases. The adherence of the judge is required to maintain the standards, but the judge does not make them.

It is, of course, possible that behind the shield of the rules which make judicial decisions final and authoritative, judges might combine in rejecting the existing rules and cease to regard even the clearest Acts of Parliament as imposing any limits on their decisions. If the majority of their rulings were of this character and were accepted this would amount to a transformation of the system parallel to the conversion of a game from cricket to 'scorer's discretion'. But the standing possibility of such transformations does not show that the system now is what it would be if the transformation took place. No rules can be guaranteed against breach or repudiation; for it is never psychologically or physically impossible for human beings to break or repudiate them; and if enough do so for long enough, then the rules will cease to exist. But the existence of rules at any given time does not require that there should be these impossible guarantees against destruction. To say that at a given time there is a rule requiring judges to accept as law Acts of Parliament or Acts of Congress entails first, that there is general compliance with this requirement and that deviation or repudiation on the part of individual judges is rare; secondly, that when or if it occurs it is or would be treated by a preponderant majority as a subject of serious criticism and as wrong, even though the result of the consequent decision in a particular case cannot, because of the rule as to the finality of decisions, be counteracted except by legislation which concedes its validity though not its correctness. It is logically possible that human beings might break all their promises: at first, perhaps, with the sense that this was the wrong thing to do, and then with no such sense. Then the rule which makes it obligatory to keep promises would cease to exist; this would, however, be a poor support for the view that no such rule exists at present and that promises are not really binding. The parallel argument in the case of judges, based on the possibility of their engineering the destruction of the present system, is no stronger.

Before we leave the topic of rule-scepticism we must say a last word about its positive contention that rules are the predictions of courts' decisions. It is plain and has often been remarked that whatever truth there may be in this, it can at best apply to the statements of law ventured by private individuals or their advisers. It cannot apply to the courts' own statements of a legal rule. These must either be, as some extremer 'Realists' claimed, a verbal covering for the exercise of an unfettered discretion, or they must be the formulation of rules genuinely regarded by the courts from the internal point of view as a standard of correct decision. On the other hand, predictions of judicial decisions have undeniably an important place in the law. When the area of open texture is reached, very often all we can profitably offer in answer to the question: 'What is the law on this matter?' is a guarded prediction of what the courts will do. Moreover, even where what the rules require is clear to all, the statement of it may often be made in the form of a prediction of the courts' decision. But it is important to notice that predominantly in the latter case, and to a varying degree in the former, the basis for such prediction is the knowledge that the courts regard legal rules not as predictions, but as standards to be followed in decision, determinate enough, in spite of their open texture, to limit, though not to exclude, their discretion. Hence, in many cases, predictions of what a court will do are like the prediction we might make that chess-players will move the bishop diagonally: they rest ultimately on an appreciation of the non-predictive aspect of rules, and of the internal point of view of the rules as standards accepted by those to whom the predictions relate. This is only a further aspect of the fact

already stressed in Chapter V that, though the existence of
rules in any social group renders predictions possible and often
reliable, it cannot be identified with them.

4. UNCERTAINTY IN THE RULE OF RECOGNITION

Formalism and rule-scepticism are the Scylla and Charybdis
of juristic theory; they are great exaggerations, salutary where
they correct each other, and the truth lies between them. Much
indeed that cannot be attempted here needs to be done to
characterize in informative detail this middle path, and to
show the varied types of reasoning which courts characteristically use in exercising the creative function left to them by the
open texture of law in statute or precedent. But we have said
enough in this chapter to enable us to resume, with profit, the
important topic deferred at the end of Chapter VI. This concerned the uncertainty, not of particular legal rules but of the
rule of recognition and so of the ultimate criteria used by courts in
identifying valid rules of law. The distinction between the uncertainty of a particular rule, and the uncertainty of the criterion
used in identifying it as a rule of the system, is not itself, in all
cases, a clear one. But it is clearest where the rules are statutory enactments with an authoritative text. The words of a
statute and what it requires in a particular case may be perfectly plain; yet there may be doubts as to whether the legislature has power to legislate in this way. Sometimes the resolution of these doubts requires only the interpretation of another
rule of law which conferred the legislative power, and the
validity of this may not be in doubt. This will be the case, for
example, where the validity of an enactment made by a subordinate authority is in question, because doubts arise as to the
meaning of the parent Act of Parliament defining the subordinate authority's legislative powers. This is merely a case of
the uncertainty or open texture of a particular statute and raises
no fundamental question.

To be distinguished from such ordinary questions are those
concerning the legal competence of the supreme legislature
itself. These concern the ultimate criteria of legal validity; and
they can arise even in a legal system like our own, in which
there is no written constitution specifying the competence of the
supreme legislature. In the overwhelming majority of cases the

formula 'Whatever the Queen in Parliament enacts is law' is an adequate expression of the rule as to the legal competence of Parliament, and is accepted as an ultimate criterion for the identification of law, however open the rules thus identified may be at their periphery. But doubts can arise as to its meaning or scope; we can ask what is meant by 'enacted by Parliament' and when doubts arise they may be settled by the courts. What inference is to be drawn as to the place of courts within a legal system from the fact that the ultimate rule of a legal system may thus be in doubt and that courts may resolve the doubt? Does it require some qualification of the thesis that the foundation of a legal system is an accepted rule of recognition specifying the criteria of legal validity?

To answer these questions we shall consider here some aspects of the English doctrine of the sovereignty of Parliament, though, of course, similar doubts can arise in relation to ultimate criteria of legal validity in any system. Under the influence of the Austinian doctrine that law is essentially the product of a legally untrammelled will, older constitutional theorists wrote as if it was a logical necesssity that there should be a legislature which was sovereign, in the sense that it is free, at every moment of its existence as a continuing body, not only from legal limitations imposed *ab extra*, but also from its own prior legislation. That Parliament is sovereign in this sense may now be regarded as established, and the principle that no earlier Parliament can preclude its 'successors' from repealing its legislation constitutes part of the ultimate rule of recognition used by the courts in identifying valid rules of law. It is, however, important to see that no necessity of logic, still less of nature, dictates that there should be such a Parliament; it is only one arrangement among others, equally conceivable, which has come to be accepted with us as the criterion of legal validity. Among these others is another principle which might equally well, perhaps better, deserve the name of 'sovereignty'. This is the principle that Parliament should *not* be incapable of limiting irrevocably the legislative competence of its successors but, on the contrary, should have this wider self-limiting power. Parliament would then at least once in its history be capable of exercising an even larger sphere of legislative competence than the accepted established doctrine allows to it.

The requirement that at every moment of its existence Parliament should be free from legal limitations including even those imposed by itself is, after all, only one interpretation of the ambiguous idea of legal omnipotence. It in effect makes a choice between a *continuing* omnipotence in all matters not affecting the legislative competence of successive parliaments, and an unrestricted *self-embracing* omnipotence the exercise of which can only be enjoyed once. These two conceptions of omnipotence have their parallel in two conceptions of an omnipotent God: on the one hand, a God who at every moment of His existence enjoys the same powers and so is incapable of cutting down those powers, and, on the other, a God whose powers include the power to destroy for the future his omnipotence. Which form of omnipotence—continuing or self-embracing—our Parliament enjoys is an empirical question concerning the form of rule which is accepted as the ultimate criterion in identifying the law. Though it is a question about a rule lying at the base of a legal system, it is still a question of fact to which at any given moment of time, on some points at least, there may be a quite determinate answer. Thus it is clear that the presently accepted rule is one of continuing sovereignty, so that Parliament cannot protect its statutes from repeal.

Yet, as with every other rule, the fact that the rule of parliamentary sovereignty is determinate at this point does not mean that it is so at all points. Questions can be raised about it to which at present there is no answer which is clearly right or wrong. These can be settled only by a choice, made by someone to whose choices in this matter authority is eventually accorded. Such indeterminacies in the rule of parliamentary sovereignty present themselves in the following way. It is conceded under the present rule that Parliament cannot by statute irrevocably withdraw any topic from the scope of future legislation by Parliament; but a distinction may be drawn between an enactment simply purporting to do that and one which, while leaving it still open to Parliament to legislate on any topic, purports to alter the 'manner and form' of legislation. The latter may, for example, require that on certain issues no legislation shall be effective unless it is passed by a majority of the two Houses sitting together, or unless it is confirmed by a plebiscite. It may 'entrench' such a provision by the stipulation that the provision itself can be repealed only by the same special process. Such a partial alteration in the legislative process may well be consistent with the present rule that Parliament cannot irrevocably bind its successors; for what it does is not so much to *bind* successors, as to eliminate them *quoad* certain issues and transfer their legislative powers over these issues to the new special body. So it may be said that, in relation to these special issues, Parliament has not 'bound' or 'fettered' Parliament or diminished its continuing omnipotence, but has 'redefined' Parliament and what must be done to legislate.

Plainly, if this device were valid, Parliament could achieve by its use very much the same results as those which the accepted doctrine, that Parliament cannot bind its successors, seems to put beyond its power. For though, indeed, the difference between circumscribing the area over which Parliament can legislate, and merely changing the manner and form of legislation, is clear enough in some cases, in effect these categories shade into each other. A statute which, after fixing a minimum wage for engineers, provided that no bill concerning engineers' pay should have effect as law unless confirmed by resolution of the Engineers' Union and went on to entrench this provision, might indeed secure all that, in practice, could be done by a statute which fixed the wage 'for ever', and then crudely prohibited its repeal altogether. Yet an argument, which lawyers would recognize as having some force, can be made to show that although the latter would be ineffective under the present rule of continuing parliamentary sovereignty, the former would not. The steps of the argument consist of a succession of contentions as to what Parliament can do, each of which would command less assent than its predecessor though having some analogy with it. None of them can be ruled out as wrong or accepted with confidence as right; for we are in the area of open texture of the system's most fundamental rule. Here at any moment a question may arise to which there is no answer—only answers.

Thus it might be conceded that Parliament might irrevocably alter the present constitution of Parliament by abolishing the House of Lords altogether, and so going beyond the Parliament Acts of 1911 and 1949 which dispensed with its consent to certain legislation and which some authorities prefer to interpret as a mere revocable delegation of some of Parliament's powers to the Queen and Commons. It might also be conceded, as Dicey asserted,[1] that Parliament could destroy itself totally, by an Act declaring its powers at an end and repealing the legislation providing for the election of future Parliaments. If so, Parliament might validly accompany this legislative suicide by an Act transferring all its powers to some other body, say the Manchester Corporation. If it can do this, cannot it effectually do something less? Can it not put an end to its powers to legislate on certain matters and transfer these to a new composite entity which includes itself and some further body? On this footing may not section 4 of the Statute of Westminster, providing for the consent of a Dominion to any legislation affecting it, actually have done this in relation to Parliament's powers to legislate for a Dominion? The contention that this can effectively be repealed without the consent of the Dominion may not only, as Lord Sankey said, be 'theory' which 'has no relation to realities'. It may be bad theory—or at least no better than the opposite one. Finally, if Parliament can be reconstituted in these ways by its own action, why cannot it reconstitute itself by providing that the Engineers' Union shall be a necessary consenting element in certain types of legislation?

It is quite possible that some of the questionable propositions which constitute the doubtful, but not obviously mistaken, steps in this argument, will one day be endorsed or rejected by a court called on to decide the matter. Then we shall have an answer to the questions which they raise, and that answer, so long as the system exists, will have a unique authoritative status among the answers which might be given. The courts will have made determinate at this point the ultimate rule by which valid law is identified. Here 'the constitution is what the judges say it is' does *not* mean merely that particular decisions of supreme tribunals cannot be challenged. At first sight the spectacle seems paradoxical: here are courts exercising creative powers which settle the ultimate criteria by which the validity of the very laws, which confer upon them jurisdiction as judges, must itself be tested. How can a constitution confer authority to say what the constitution is? But the paradox vanishes if we remember that though every rule may be doubtful at some

---

[1] *The Law of the Constitution* (10th edn.), p. 68 n.

points, it is indeed a necessary condition of a legal system existing, that not every rule is open to doubt on all points. The possibility of courts having authority at any given time to decide these limiting questions concerning the ultimate criteria of validity, depends merely on the fact that, at that time, the application of those criteria to a vast area of law, including the rules which confer that authority, raises no doubts, though their precise scope and ambit do.

This answer, however, may to some seem too short a way with the question. It may appear to characterize very inadequately the activity of courts on the fringes of the fundamental rules which specify the criteria of legal validity; this may be because it assimilates the activity too closely to ordinary cases where courts exercise a creative choice in interpreting a particular statute which has proved indeterminate. It is clear that such ordinary cases must arise in any system, and so it seems obviously to be part, even if only an implied part, of the rules on which courts act that courts have jurisdiction to settle them by choosing between the alternatives which the statute leaves open, even if they prefer to disguise this choice as a discovery. But, at least in the absence of a written constitution, questions concerning the fundamental criteria of validity often seem *not* to have this previously envisageable quality, which makes it natural to say that, when they arise, the courts already have, under the existing rules, a clear authority to settle questions of this sort.

One form of 'formalist' error may perhaps just be that of thinking that every step taken by a court is covered by some general rule conferring in advance the authority to take it, so that its creative powers are *always* a form of delegated legislative power. The truth may be that, when courts settle previously unenvisaged questions concerning the most fundamental constitutional rules, they *get* their authority to decide them accepted after the questions have arisen and the decision has been given. Here all that succeeds is success. It is conceivable that the constitutional question at issue may divide society too fundamentally to permit of its disposition by a judicial decision. The issues in South Africa concerning the entrenched clauses of the South Africa Act, 1909, at one time threatened to be too divisive for legal settlement. But where less vital social issues

are concerned, a very surprising piece of judicial law-making
concerning the very sources of law may be calmly 'swallowed'.
Where this is so, it will often in *retrospect* be said, and may
genuinely appear, that there always was an 'inherent' power in
the courts to do what they have done. Yet this may be a pious
fiction, if the only evidence for it is the success of what has been
done.

   The manipulation by English courts of the rules concerning the binding force of precedent is perhaps most honestly
described in this last way as a successful bid to take powers and
use them. Here power acquires authority *ex post facto* from
success. Thus before the decision of the Court of Criminal
Appeal in *Rex* v. *Taylor*[1] the question whether that court had
authority to rule that it was not bound by its own precedents
on matters concerning the liberty of the subject might have
appeared entirely open. But the ruling was made and is now
followed as law. The statement that the court always had an
inherent power to rule in this way would surely only be a way
of making the situation look more tidy than it really is. Here,
at the fringe of these very fundamental things, we should welcome the rule-sceptic, as long as he does not forget that it is at
the fringe that he is welcome; and does not blind us to the
fact that what makes possible these striking developments by
courts of the most fundamental rules is, in great measure, the
prestige gathered by courts from their unquestionably rule-
governed operations over the vast, central areas of the law.

[1] [1950] 2 K.B. 368.

VIII

JUSTICE AND MORALITY

We have found it necessary, in order to elucidate features distinctive of law as a means of social control, to introduce elements which cannot be constructed out of the ideas of an order, a threat, obedience, habits, and generality. Too much that is characteristic of law is distorted by the effort to explain it in these simple terms. Thus we found it necessary to distinguish from the idea of a general habit that of a social rule, and to emphasize the internal aspect of rules manifested in their use as guiding and critical standards of conduct. We then distinguished among rules between primary rules of obligation and secondary rules of recognition, change, and adjudication. The main theme of this book is that so many of the distinctive operations of the law, and so many of the ideas which constitute the framework of legal thought, require for their elucidation reference to one or both of these two types of rule, that their union may be justly regarded as the 'essence' of law, though they may not always be found together wherever the word 'law' is correctly used. Our justification for assigning to the union of primary and secondary rules this central place is not that they will there do the work of a dictionary, but that they have great explanatory power.

We must now turn our attention to the claim which, in the perennial discussion of the 'essence' or the 'nature' or 'the definition' of law, has been most frequently opposed to the simple imperative theory which we have found inadequate. This is the general contention that between law and morality there is a connexion which is in some sense 'necessary', and that it is this which deserves to be taken as central, in any attempt to analyse or elucidate the notion of law. Advocates of this view might not be concerned to dispute our criticisms of the simple imperative theory. They might even concede that it was a useful advance; and that the union of primary and secondary rules was indeed more important than orders backed by threats as a starting-point for the understanding of law. Their argument would, however, be that this is not enough: that even these elements are of subordinate importance, and that until the 'necessary' relationship with morality is made explicit and its central importance seen, the mists which have so long clouded the understanding of law cannot be dissipated. From this point of view the questionable or challengeable cases of law would not merely be the law of primitive societies or international law, which have been considered doubtful because of their lack of a legislature, courts with compulsory jurisdiction, and centrally organized sanctions. Far more questionable from this point of view is the title to be treated as law of those municipal systems which exhibit the full complement of *juge, gendarme et legislateur* but fail to conform to certain fundamental requirements of justice or morality. In the words of St. Augustine[1] 'What are states without justice but robber-bands enlarged?'

The claim that between law and morality there is a necessary connexion has many important variants, not all of them conspicuous for their clarity. There are many possible interpretations of the key terms 'necessary' and 'morality' and these have not always been distinguished and separately considered by either advocates or critics. The clearest, perhaps, because it is the most extreme form of expression of this point of view, is that associated with the Thomist tradition of Natural Law. This comprises a twofold contention: first that there are certain principles of true morality or justice, discoverable by human reason without the aid of revelation even though they have a divine origin; secondly that man-made laws which conflict with these principles are not valid law. 'Lex iniusta non est lex.' Other variants of this general point of view take a different view of both the status of principles of morality and of the consequences of conflict between law and morality. Some conceive morality not as immutable principles of conduct or as discoverable by reason, but as expressions of human attitudes to conduct which may vary from society to society or from individual to individual. Theories of this form usually also hold that conflict between law and even the most fundamental requirements of morality is not sufficient to deprive a rule of its status as law; they interpret the 'necessary' connexion between law and morality in a different way. They claim that for a legal

[1] *Confessions*, iv.·

system to exist there must be a widely diffused, though not necessarily universal, recognition of a moral obligation to obey the law, even though this may be overriden in particular cases by a stronger moral obligation not to obey particular morally iniquitous laws.

The full assessment of the different varieties of theory asserting a necessary connexion between law and morals would take us far into moral philosophy. But something less than this may provide any thoughtful reader with enough to form a reasoned view of the truth and importance of such claims. For this pur- * pose what is most needed is a separation and identification of some long-entangled issues, which we consider in this chapter and the next. The first of these issues concerns the distinction within the general sphere of morality of the specific idea of justice and the special features which account for its peculiarly intimate connexion with law. The second concerns the characteristics which distinguish moral rules and principles not only from legal rules but from all other forms of social rule or standards of conduct. These two issues are the subject of this chapter; the third, which is the subject of the next, concerns the many different senses and ways in which legal rules and morals may be said to be related.

1. PRINCIPLES OF JUSTICE

The terms most frequently used by lawyers in the praise or condemnation of law or its administration are the words 'just' and 'unjust' and very often they write as if the ideas of justice and morality were coextensive. There are indeed very good reasons why justice should have a most prominent place in the criticism of legal arrangements; yet it is important to see that it is a distinct segment of morality, and that laws and the administration of laws may have or lack excellences of different kinds. Very little reflection on some common types of moral judgment is enough to show this special character of justice. A man guilty of gross cruelty to his child would often be judged to have done something morally *wrong*, *bad*, or even *wicked* or to have disregarded his moral *obligation* or duty to his child. But it would be strange to criticize his conduct as *unjust*. This is not because the word 'unjust' is too weak in condemnatory force, but because the point of moral criticism in terms of justice or injustice is usually different from, and more specific than, the other types of general moral criticism which are appropriate in this particular case and are expressed by words like 'wrong', 'bad', or 'wicked'. 'Unjust' would become appropriate if the man had arbitrarily selected one of his children for severer punishment than those given to others guilty of the same fault, or if he had punished the child for some offence without taking steps to see that he really was the wrongdoer. Similarly, when we turn from the criticism of individual conduct to the criticism of law, we might express our approval of a law requiring parents to send their children to school, by saying that it was a good law and our disapproval of a law forbidding the criticism of the Government, as by calling it a bad law. Such criticisms would not normally be couched in terms of 'justice' and 'injustice'. 'Just', on the other hand, would be the appropriate expression of approval of a law distributing the burden of taxation according to wealth; so 'unjust' would be appropriate for the expression of disapproval of a law which forbade coloured people to use the public means of transport or the parks. That just and un-just are more specific forms of moral criticism than good and bad or right and wrong, is plain from the fact that we might intelligibly claim that a law was good because it was just, or that it was bad because it was unjust, but not that it was just because good, or unjust because bad.

The distinctive features of justice and their special connexion with law begin to emerge if it is observed that most of the criticisms made in terms of just and unjust could almost equally well be conveyed by the words 'fair' and 'unfair'. Fairness is plainly not coextensive with morality in general; references to it are mainly relevant in two situations in social life. One is when we are concerned not with a single individual's conduct but with the way in which *classes* of individuals are treated, when some burden or benefit falls to be distributed among them. Hence what is typically fair or unfair is a 'share'. The second situation is when some injury has been done and compensation or redress is claimed. These are not the only contexts where appraisals in terms of justice or fairness are made. We speak not only of distributions or compensations as just or fair but also of a judge as just or unjust; a trial as fair or unfair; and a person as justly or unjustly convicted. These are derivative applications of the notion of justice which are explicable once the primary application of justice to matters of distribution and compensation is understood.

The general principle latent in these diverse applications of the idea of justice is that individuals are entitled in respect of each other to a certain relative position of equality or inequality. This is something to be respected in the vicissitudes of social life when burdens or benefits fall to be distributed; it is also something to be restored when it is disturbed. Hence justice is traditionally thought of as maintaining or restoring a *balance* or *proportion*, and its leading precept is often formulated as 'Treat like cases alike'; though we need to add to the latter 'and treat different cases differently'. So when, in the name of justice, we protest against a law forbidding coloured people the use of the public parks, the point of such criticism is that such a law is bad, because in distributing the benefits of public amenities among the population it discriminates between persons who are, in all relevant respects, alike. Conversely, if a law is praised as just because it withdraws from some special section some privilege or immunity, e.g. in taxation, the guiding thought is that there is no such relevant difference between the privileged class and the rest of the community as to entitle them to the special treatment. These simple examples are, however, enough to show that, though 'Treat like cases alike and different cases differently' is a central element in the idea of justice, it is by itself incomplete and, until supplemented, cannot afford any determinate guide to conduct. This is so because any set of human beings will resemble each other in some respects and differ from each other in others and, until it is established what resemblance and differences are relevant, 'Treat like cases alike' must remain an empty form. To fill it we must know when, for the purposes in hand, cases are to be regarded as alike and what differences are relevant. Without this further supplement we cannot proceed to criticize laws or other social arrangements as unjust. It is not unjust for the law when it forbids homicide to treat the red-haired murderers in the same way as others; indeed it would be as unjust if it treated them differently, as it would be if it refused to treat differently the sane and the insane.

There is therefore a certain complexity in the structure of the idea of justice. We may say that it consists of two parts: a uniform or constant feature, summarized in the precept 'Treat like cases alike' and a shifting or varying criterion used in determining when, for any given purpose, cases are alike or different. In this respect justice is like the notions of what is genuine, or tall, or warm, which contain an implicit reference to a standard which varies with the classification of the thing to which they are applied. A tall child may be the same height as a short man, a warm winter the same temperature as a cold summer, and a fake diamond may be a genuine antique. But justice is far more complicated than these notions because the shifting standard of relevant resemblance between different cases incorporated in it not only varies with the type of subject to which it is applied, but may often be open to challenge even in relation to a single type of subject.

In certain cases, indeed, the resemblances and differences between human beings which are relevant for the criticism of legal arrangements as just or unjust are quite obvious. This is pre-eminently the case when we are concerned not with the justice or injustice of the *law* but of its *application* in particular cases. For here the relevant resemblances and differences between individuals, to which the person who administers the law must attend, are determined by the law itself. To say that the law against murder is justly applied is to say that it is impartially applied to all those and only those who are alike in having done what the law forbids; no prejudice or interest has deflected the administrator from treating them 'equally'. Consistently with this the procedural standards such as '*audi alteram partem*' 'let no one be a judge in his own cause' are thought of as requirements of justice, and in England and America are often referred to as principles of Natural Justice. This is so because they are guarantees of impartiality or objectivity, designed to secure that the law is applied to all those and only to those who are alike in the relevant respect marked out by the law itself.

The connexion between this aspect of justice and the very notion of proceeding by rule is obviously very close. Indeed, it might be said that to apply a law justly to different cases is simply to take seriously the assertion that what is to be applied in different cases is the same general rule, without prejudice, interest, or caprice. This close connexion between justice in the administration of the law and the very notion of a rule has tempted some famous thinkers to identify justice with conformity to law. Yet plainly this is an error unless 'law' is given some specially wide meaning; for such an account of justice leaves unexplained the fact that criticism in the name of justice is not confined to the administration of the law in particular cases, but the laws themselves are often criticized as just or unjust. Indeed there is no absurdity in conceding that an unjust law forbidding the access of coloured persons to the parks has been justly administered, in that only persons genuinely guilty of breaking the law were punished under it and then only after a fair trial.

When we turn from the justice or injustice of the administration of the law to the criticism of the law itself in these terms, it is plain that the law itself cannot now determine what resemblances and differences among individuals the law must recognize if its rules are to treat like cases alike and so be just. Here accordingly there is much room for doubt and dispute. Fundamental differences, in general moral and political outlook, may lead to irreconcilable differences and disagreement as to what characteristics of human beings are to be taken as relevant for the criticism of law as unjust. Thus, when in the previous example we stigmatized as unjust a law forbidding coloured people access to the parks, this was on the footing that, at least in the distribution of such amenities, differences of colour are irrelevant. Certainly in the modern world, the fact that human beings, of whatever colour, are capable of thought, feeling, and self-control, would be generally though not universally accepted as constituting crucial resemblances between them to which the law should attend. Hence, in most civilized countries there is a great measure of agreement that both the criminal law (conceived not only as restricting liberty but as providing protection from various sorts of harm) and the civil law (conceived as offering redress for harm), would be unjust if in the distribution of these burdens and benefits they discriminated between persons, by reference to such characteristics as colour or religious belief. And if, instead of these well-known *foci* of human prejudice, the law discriminated by reference to such obvious irrelevancies as height, weight, or beauty it would be both unjust and ludicrous. If murderers belonging to the established church were exempt from capital punishment, if only members of the peerage could sue for libel, if assaults on coloured persons were punished less severely than those on whites, the laws would in most modern communities be con-demned as unjust on the footing that *prima facie* human beings should be treated alike and these privileges and immunities rested on no relevant ground.

Indeed so deeply embedded in modern man is the principle that *prima facie* human beings are entitled to be treated alike that almost universally where the laws do discriminate by reference to such matters as colour and race, lip service at least is still widely paid to this principle. If such discriminations are attacked they are often defended by the assertion that the class discriminated against lack, or have not yet developed, certain essential human attributes; or it may be said that, regrettable though it is, the demands of justice requiring their equal treat-ment must be overridden in order to preserve something held to be of greater value, which would be jeopardized if such discriminations were not made. Yet though lip service is now general, it is certainly possible to conceive of a morality which did not resort to these often disingenuous devices to justify discrimination and inequalities, but openly rejected the prin-ciple that *prima facie* human beings were to be treated alike. Instead, human beings might be thought of as falling naturally and unalterably into certain classes, so that some were naturally fitted to be free and others to be their slaves or, as Aristotle expressed it, the living instruments of others. Here the sense of *prima facie* equality among men would be absent. Something of this view is to be found in Aristotle and Plato, though even there, there is more than a hint that any full defence of slavery would involve showing that those enslaved lacked the capacity for independent existence or differed from the free in their capacity to realize some ideal of the good life.

It is therefore clear that the criteria of relevant resemblances and differences may often vary with the fundamental moral outlook of a given person or society. Where this is so, assess-ments of the justice or injustice of the law may be met with counter-assertions inspired by a different morality. But some-

times a consideration of the object which the law in question is
admittedly designed to realize may make clear the resemblances
and differences which a just law should recognize and they
may then be scarcely open to dispute. If a law provides for the
relief of poverty then the requirement of the principle that
'Like cases be treated alike' would surely involve attention to
the *need* of different claimants for relief. A similar criterion of
need is implicitly recognized when the burden of taxation is
adjusted by a graded income tax to the wealth of the individuals
taxed. Sometimes what is relevant are the *capacities* of persons
for a specific function with which the exercise of the law in
question may be concerned. Laws which exclude from the
franchise, or withhold the power to make wills or contracts
from children, or the insane, are regarded as just because such
persons lack the capacity, which sane adults are presumed to
have, to make a rational use of these facilities. Such discriminations are made on grounds which are obviously relevant,
whereas discriminations in these matters between the sexes or
between persons of different colour are not; though of course it
has been argued in defence of the subjection of women, or
coloured people, that women or coloured people lack the white
male's capacity for rational thought and decision. To argue
thus is of course to admit that equal capacity for a particular
function is the criterion of justice in the case of such law,
though in the absence of any evidence that such capacity is
lacking in women or coloured persons, again only lip service
is paid to this principle.

So far we have considered the justice or injustice of laws
which may be viewed as *distributing* among individuals burdens
and benefits. Some of the benefits are tangible, like poor relief,
or food rations; others are intangible, like the protection from
bodily harm given by the criminal law, or the facilities afforded
by laws relating to testamentary or contractual capacity, or the
right to vote. From distribution in this wide sense, we must
distinguish *compensation* for injury done by one person to another.
Here the connexion between what is just and the central precept of justice 'Treat like cases alike and different cases differently' is certainly less direct. Yet it is not too indirect to be
traced and may be seen in the following way. The laws which
provide for the compensation by one person of another for

torts or civil injuries might be considered unjust for two different reasons. They might, on the one hand, establish unfair privileges or immunities. This would be so if only peers could sue for libel, or if no white person were liable to a coloured person for trespass or assault. Such laws would violate, in a straightforward way, principles of fair distribution of the rights and duties of compensation. But such laws might also be unjust in a quite different way: for while making no unfair discriminations they might fail altogether to provide a remedy for certain types of injury inflicted by one person on another, even though morally compensation would be thought due. In this matter the law might be unjust while treating all alike.

The vice of such laws would then not be the maldistribution, but the refusal to all alike, of compensation for injuries which it was morally wrong to inflict on others. The crudest case of such unjust refusal of redress would be a system in which no one could obtain damages for physical harm wantonly inflicted. It is worth observing that *this* injustice would still remain even if the criminal law prohibited such assaults under penalty. Few instances of anything so crude can be found, but the failure of English law to provide compensation for invasions of privacy, often found profitable by advertisers, has often been criticized in this way. Failure to provide compensation where morally it is held due is, however, also the gravamen of the charge of injustice against technicalities of the law of tort or contract which permit 'unjust enrichment' at the expense of another by some action considered morally wrong.

The connexion between the justice and injustice of the compensation for injury, and the principle 'Treat like cases alike and different cases differently', lies in the fact that outside the law there is a moral conviction that those with whom the law is concerned have a right to mutual forbearance from certain kinds of harmful conduct. Such a structure of reciprocal rights and obligations proscribing at least the grosser sorts of harm, constitutes the basis, though not the whole, of the morality of every social group. Its effect is to create among individuals a moral and, in a sense, an artificial equality to offset the inequalities of nature. For when the moral code forbids one man to rob or use violence on another even when superior strength or cunning would enable him to do so with impunity, the strong and cunning are put on a level with the weak and simple. Their cases are made morally alike. Hence the strong man who disregards morality and takes advantage of his strength to injure another is conceived as upsetting this equilibrium, or order of equality, established by morals; justice then requires that this moral *status quo* should as far as possible be restored by the wrongdoer. In simple cases of theft this would simply involve giving back the thing taken; and compensation for other injuries is an extension of this primitive notion. One who has physically injured another either intentionally or through negligence is thought of as having taken something from his victim; and though he has not literally done this, the figure is not too far fetched: for he has profited at his victim's expense, even if it is only by indulging his wish to injure him or not sacrificing his ease to the duty of taking adequate precautions. Thus when laws provide compensation where justice demands it, they recognize indirectly the principle 'Treat like cases alike' by providing for the restoration, after disturbance, of the moral *status quo* in which victim and wrongdoer are on a footing of equality and so alike. Again, it is conceivable that there might be a moral outlook which did not put individuals on a footing of reciprocal equality in these matters. The moral code might forbid Barbarians to assault Greeks but allow Greeks to assault Barbarians. In such cases a Barbarian may be thought morally bound to compensate a Greek for injuries done though entitled to no such compensation himself. The moral order here would be one of inequality in which victim and wrongdoer were treated differently. For such an outlook, repellent though it may be to us, the law would be just only if it reflected this difference and treated different cases differently.

In this brief outline of justice we have considered only some of its simpler applications in order to show the specific form of excellence attributed to laws which are appraised as just. Not only is this distinct from other values which laws may have or lack, but sometimes the demands of justice may conflict with other values. This may occur, when a court, in sentencing a particular offender for a crime which has become prevalent, passes a severer sentence than that passed in other similar cases, and avowedly does this 'as a warning'. There is here a sacrifice of the principle 'Treat like cases alike' to the general security or welfare of society. In civil cases, a similar conflict between justice and the general good is resolved in favour of the latter, when the law provides no remedy for some moral wrong because to enforce compensation in such cases might involve great difficulties of proof, or overburden the courts, or unduly hamper enterprise. There is a limit to the amount of law enforcement which any society can afford, even when moral wrong has been done. Conversely the law, in the name of the general welfare of society, may enforce compensation from one who has injured another, even where morally, as a matter of justice, it might not be thought due. This is often said to be the case when liability in tort is strict, i.e. independent of the intention to injure or failure to take care. This form of liability is sometimes defended on the ground that it is in the interest of 'society' that those accidentally injured should be compensated; and it is claimed that the easiest way of doing this is to place the burden on those whose activities, however carefully controlled, result in such accidents. They commonly have deep pockets and opportunities to insure. When this defence is made, there is in it an implicit appeal to the general welfare of society which, though it may be morally acceptable and sometimes even called 'social justice', differs from the primary forms of justice which are concerned simply to redress, as far as possible, the status quo as between two individuals.

An important juncture point between ideas of justice and social good or welfare should be noticed. Very few social changes or laws are agreeable to or advance the welfare of all individuals alike. Only laws which provide for the most elementary needs, such as police protection or roads, come near to this. In most cases the law provides benefits for one class of the population only at the cost of depriving others of what they prefer. Provision for the poor can be made only out of the goods of others; compulsory school education for all may mean not only loss of liberty for those who wish to educate their children privately, but may be financed only at the cost of reducing or sacrificing capital investment in industry or old-age pensions or free medical services. When a choice has been made between such competing alternatives it may be defended -as proper on the ground that it was for the 'public good' or the 'common good'. It is not clear what these phrases mean, since there seems to be no scale by which contributions of the various alternatives to the common good can be measured and the greater identified. It is, however, clear that a choice, made without prior consideration of the interests of all sections of the community would be open to criticism as merely partisan and unjust. It would, however, be rescued from *this* imputation if the claims of all had been impartially considered before legislation, even though in the result the claims of one section were subordinated to those of others.

Some might indeed argue that all that in fact could be meant by the claim that a choice between the competing claims of different classes or interests was made 'for the common good', was that the claims of all had been thus impartially surveyed before decision. Whether this is true or not, it seems clear that justice in this sense is at least a necessary condition to be satisfied by any legislative choice which purports to be for the common good. We have here a further aspect of distributive justice, differing from those simple forms which we have discussed. For here what is justly 'distributed' is not some specific benefit among a class of claimants to it, but impartial attention to and consideration of competing claims to different benefits.

2. MORAL AND LEGAL OBLIGATION

Justice constitutes one segment of morality primarily concerned not with individual conduct but with the ways in which *classes* of individuals are treated. It is this which gives justice its special relevance in the criticism of law and of other public or social institutions. It is the most public and the most legal of the virtues. But principles of justice do not exhaust the idea of morality; and not all criticism of law made on moral grounds is made in the name of justice. Laws may be condemned as morally bad simply because they require men to do particular actions which morality forbids individuals to do, or because they require men to abstain from doing those which are morally obligatory.

It is therefore necessary to characterize, in general terms, those principles, rules, and standards relating to the conduct of individuals which belong to morality and make conduct morally obligatory. Two related difficulties confront us here. The first is that the word 'morality' and all other associated or nearly synonymous terms like 'ethics', have their own considerable area of vagueness or 'open texture'. There are certain forms of principle or rule which some would rank as moral and which others would not. Secondly, even where there is agreement on this point and certain rules or principles are accepted as indisputably belonging to morality, there may still be great philosophical disagreement as to their *status* or relation to the rest of human knowledge and experience. Are they immutable principles which constitute part of the fabric of the Universe, not made by man, but awaiting discovery by the human intellect? Or are they expressions of changing human attitudes, choices, demands, or feelings? These are crude formulations of two extremes in moral philosophy. Between them lie many complicated and subtle variants, which philosophers have developed in the effort to elucidate the nature of morality.

In what follows we shall seek to evade these philosophical difficulties. We shall later[1] identify under the heads of 'Importance', 'Immunity from deliberate change', 'Voluntary character of moral offences', and 'Forms of moral pressure' four cardinal features which are constantly found together in those principles, rules, and standards of conduct which are most commonly accounted 'moral'. These four features reflect different aspects of a characteristic and important function which such standards perform in social life or in the life of individuals. This alone would justify us in marking off whatever has these four features for separate consideration, and above all, for contrast and comparison with law. Moreover, the claim that morality has these four features is neutral between rival philosophical theories as to its *status* or 'fundamental' character. Certainly most, if not all, philosophers would agree that these four features were necessary in any moral rule or principle, though they would offer very different interpretations or explanations of the fact that morality possesses them. It may indeed be objected that these features though necessary are *only* necessary and not sufficient to distinguish morality from certain rules or principles of conduct which would be excluded from morality by a more stringent test. We shall refer to the facts on which such objections are based but we shall

[1] Below, p. 169.

adhere to the wider sense of 'morality'. Our justification for this
is both that this accords with much usage and that what the
word in this wide sense designates, performs an important,
distinguishable function in social and individual life.

We shall consider first the social phenomenon often referred
to as '*the* morality' of a given society or the 'accepted' or 'conventional' morality of an actual social group. These phrases
refer to standards of conduct which are widely shared in a
particular society, and are to be contrasted with the moral
principles or moral ideals which may govern an individual's
life, but which he does not share with any considerable number
of those with whom he lives. The basic element in the shared
or accepted morality of a social group consists of rules of the
kind which we have already described in Chapter V when we
were concerned to elucidate the general idea of obligation,
and which we there called primary rules of obligation. These
rules are distinguished from others both by the serious social
pressure by which they are supported, and by the considerable
sacrifice of individual interest or inclination which compliance
with them involves. In the same chapter we also drew a picture
of a society at a stage in which such rules were the only means
of social control. We noticed that at that stage there might
be nothing corresponding to the clear distinction made, in
more developed societies, between legal and moral rules. Possibly some embryonic form of this distinction might be present
if there were some rules which were primarily maintained
by threats of punishment for disobedience, and others maintained by appeals to presumed respect for the rules or to feelings
of guilt or remorse. When this early stage is passed, and the
step from the pre-legal into the legal world is taken, so that the
means of social control now includes a system of rules containing rules of recognition, adjudication, and change, this
contrast between legal and other rules hardens into something definite. The primary rules of obligation identified
through the official system are now set apart from other rules,
which continue to exist side by side with those officially recognized. In fact in our own, and indeed in all communities which
reach this stage, there are many types of social rule and standard lying outside the legal system; only some of these are
usually thought and spoken of as moral, though certain legal

theorists have used the word 'moral' to designate all non-legal rules.

Such non-legal rules may be distinguished and classified in many different ways. Some are rules of very limited scope concerning only a particular sphere of conduct (e.g. dress) or activities for which there are only intermittent opportunities, deliberately created (ceremonies and games). Some rules are conceived as applying to the social group in general; others to special sub-groups within it, either marked off by certain characteristics as a distinct social class, or by their own choice to meet or combine for limited purposes. Some rules are considered to be binding by virtue of agreement and may allow for voluntary withdrawal: others are thought not to have their origin in agreement or any other form of deliberate choice. Some rules when broken may meet with no more than an assertion or reminder of the 'right' thing to do (e.g. etiquette or rules of correct speech), others with serious blame or contempt or more or less protracted exclusion from the association concerned. Though no precise scale could be constructed, a conception of the relative importance attributed to these different types of rules is reflected both in the measure of sacrifice of private interest which they demand, and the weight of social pressure for conformity.

In all societies which have developed a legal system there are, among its non-legal rules, some to which supreme importance is attached, and which in spite of crucial differences have many similarities to its law. Very often the vocabulary of 'rights,' 'obligations', and 'duties' used to express the requirements of legal rules is used with the addition of 'moral', to express the acts or forbearances required by these rules. In all communities there is a partial overlap in content between legal and moral obligation; though the requirements of legal rules are more specific and are hedged round with more detailed exceptions than their moral counterparts. Characteristically, moral obligation and duty, like many legal rules, concern what is to be done or not to be done in circumstances constantly recurring in the life of the group, rather than in rare or intermittent activities on deliberately selected occasions. What such rules require are either forbearances, or actions which are simple in the sense that no special skill or intellect is required for their performance. Moral obligations, like most legal obligations, are within the capacity of any normal adult. Compliance with these moral rules, as with legal rules, is taken as a matter of course, so that while breach attracts serious censure, conformity to moral obligation, again, like obedience to the law, is not a matter for praise except when marked by exceptional conscientiousness, endurance, or resistance to special temptation. Various classifications of moral obligations and duties may be made. Some belong to relatively distinct, enduring functions or roles, which not all members of society occupy. Such are the duties of a father or husband to care for his family. On the other hand, there are both general obligations which all normal adults are conceived as having throughout life (e.g. to abstain from violence) and special obligations which any such member may incur by entering into special relations with others (e.g. obligations to keep promises or return services rendered).

The obligations and duties recognized in moral rules of this most fundamental kind may vary from society to society or within a single society at different times. Some of them may reflect quite erroneous or even superstitious beliefs as to what is required for the health or safety of the group; in one society it may be a wife's duty to throw herself on her husband's funeral pyre, and in another, suicide may be an offence against common morality. There is a diversity among moral codes which may spring either from the peculiar but real needs of a given society, or from superstition or ignorance. Yet the social morality of societies which have reached the stage where this can be distinguished from its law, always includes certain obligations and duties, requiring the sacrifice of private inclination or interest which is essential to the survival of any society, so long as men and the world in which they live retain some of their most familiar and obvious characteristics. Among such rules obviously required for social life are those forbidding, or at least restricting, the free use of violence, rules requiring certain forms of honesty and truthfulness in dealings with others, and rules forbidding the destruction of tangible things or their seizure from others. If conformity with these most elementary rules were not thought a matter of course among any group of individuals, living in close proximity to each other, we should be doubtful of the description of the group as a society, and certain that it could not endure for long.

Moral and legal rules of obligation and duty have therefore certain striking similarities enough to show that their common vocabulary is no accident. These may be summarized as follows. They are alike in that they are conceived as binding independently of the consent of the individual bound and are supported by serious social pressure for conformity; compliance with both legal and moral obligations is regarded not as a matter for praise but as a minimum contribution to social life to be taken as a matter of course. Further both law and morals include rules governing the behaviour of individuals in situations constantly recurring throughout life rather than special activities or occasions, and though both may include much that is peculiar to the real or fancied needs of a particular society, both make demands which must obviously be satisfied by any group of human beings who are to succeed in living together. Hence some forms of prohibition of violence to person or property, and some requirements of honesty and truthfulness will be found in both alike. Yet, in spite of these similarities, it has seemed obvious to many that there are certain characteristics which law and morals cannot share, though in the history of jurisprudence these have proved most difficult to formulate.

The most famous attempt to convey in summary fashion their essential difference is the theory which asserts that, while legal rules only require 'external' behaviour and are indifferent to the motives, intentions, or other 'internal' accompaniments of conduct, morals on the other hand do not require any specific external actions but only a good will or proper intentions or motive. This really amounts to the surprising assertion that legal and moral rules properly understood could not ever have the same content; and though it does contain a hint of the truth it is, as it stands, profoundly misleading. It is in fact an inference, though a mistaken one, from certain important characteristics of morals, and particularly from certain differences between moral blame and legal punishment. If someone does something forbidden by moral rules or fails to do what they require, the fact that he did so unintentionally and in spite of every care is an excuse from *moral* blame; whereas a legal system or custom may have rules of 'strict liability' under which those who have broken the rules unintentionally and

without 'fault' may be liable to punishment. So it is indeed
true that while the notion of 'strict liability' in morals comes as
near to being a contradiction in terms as anything in this
sphere, it is something which may be merely open to criticism when found in a legal system. But this does not mean
that morals require only good intention, will, or motives.
Indeed to argue thus is, as we show later, to confuse the idea of
an *excuse* with that of a *justification* for conduct.

Nonetheless there is something of importance caricatured in
this confused argument; the vague sense that the difference
between law and morals is connected with a contrast between
the 'internality' of the one and the 'externality' of the other is
too recurrent a theme in speculation about law and morals to
be altogether baseless. Rather than dismiss it, we shall treat it
as a compendious statement of four cardinal related features
which collectively serve to distinguish morality not only from
legal rules but from other forms of social rule.

(i) *Importance*. To say that an essential feature of *any* moral
rule or standard is that it is regarded as something of great
importance to maintain may appear both truistic and vague.
Yet this feature cannot be omitted in any faithful account of
the morality of any social group or individual, nor can it be
made more precise. It is manifested in many ways: first, in the
simple fact that moral standards are maintained against the
drive of strong passions which they restrict, and at the cost
of sacrificing considerable personal interest; secondly, in the
serious forms of social pressure exerted not only to obtain conformity in individual cases, but to secure that moral standards
are taught or communicated as a matter of course to all in
society; thirdly, in the general recognition that, if moral standards were not generally accepted, far-reaching and distaste-
ful changes in the life of individuals would occur. In contrast
with morals, the rules of deportment, manners, dress, and
some, though not all, rules of law, occupy a relatively low
place in the scale of serious importance. They may be tiresome
to follow, but they do not demand great sacrifice: no great
pressure is exerted to obtain conformity and no great alterations
in other areas of social life would follow if they were not observed or changed. Much of the importance thus ascribed to the
maintenance of moral rules may be very simply explained on

agreeably rationalistic lines; for even though they demand
sacrifice of private interests on the part of the person bound,
compliance with them secures vital interests which all share
alike. It does so either by directly protecting persons from
obvious harm or by maintaining the fabric of a tolerable,
orderly society. But though the rationality of much social
morality, as a protection from obvious harms, may be defended
in this way, this simple utilitarian approach is not always
possible; nor, where it is, should it be taken to represent the
point of view of those who live by a morality. After all, a most
prominent part of the morality of any society consists of rules
concerning sexual behaviour, and it is far from clear that the
importance attached to them is connected with the belief that
the conduct they forbid is harmful to others; nor could such
rules always be shown in fact to have this justification. Even in
a modern society which has ceased to look on its morality as
divinely ordained, calculations of harmfulness to others do not
account for the importance attached to moral regulation of
sexual behaviour such as the common veto on homosexuality.
Sexual functions and feelings are matter of such moment and
emotional concern to all, that deviations from the accepted or
normal forms of their expression easily become invested with an
intrinsic 'pudor' or importance. They are abhorred, not out
of conviction of their social harmfulness but simply as 'un-
natural' or in themselves repugnant. Yet it would be absurd to
deny the title of morality to emphatic social vetoes of this
sort; indeed, sexual morality is perhaps the most prominent
aspect of what plain men think morality to be. Of course
the fact that society may view its own morality in this 'non-
utilitarian' way does not mean that its rules are immune from
criticism or condemnation, where their maintenance is judged
useless or purchased at the cost of great suffering.

Legal rules, as we have seen, may correspond with moral
rules in the sense of requiring or forbidding the same behaviour.
Those that do so are no doubt felt to be as important as their
moral counterparts. Yet importance is not essential to the
status of all legal rules as it is to that of morals. A legal rule
may be generally thought quite unimportant to maintain;
indeed it may generally be agreed that it should be repealed:
yet it remains a legal rule until it is repealed. It would, on the

other hand, be absurd to think of a rule as part of the morality of a society even though no one thought it any longer important or worth maintaining. Old customs and traditions now maintained merely for old time's sake may, indeed, once have had the status of moral rules, but their status as part of morality has evaporated together with the importance attached to their observance and breach.

(ii) *Immunity from deliberate change*. It is characteristic of a legal system that new legal rules can be introduced and old ones changed or repealed by deliberate enactment, even though some laws may be protected from change by a written constitution limiting the competence of the supreme legislature. By contrast moral rules or principles *cannot* be brought into being or changed or eliminated in this way. To assert that this 'cannot' be is not, however, to deny that some conceivable state of affairs is actually the case, as the assertion that human beings 'cannot' alter the climate would be. Instead this assertion points to the following facts. It is perfectly good sense to say such things as 'As from 1 January 1960 it will be a criminal offence to do so-and-so' or 'As from 1 January 1960 it will be no longer illegal to do so-and-so' and to support such statements by reference to laws which have been enacted or repealed. By contrast such statements as 'As from tomorrow it will no longer be immoral to do so-and-so' or 'On 1 January last it became immoral to do so-and-so' and attempts to support these by reference to deliberate enactment would be astonishing paradoxes, if not senseless. For it is inconsistent with the part played by morality in the lives of individuals that moral rules, principles, or standards should be regarded, as laws are, as things capable of creation or change by deliberate act. Standards of conduct cannot be endowed with, or deprived of, moral status by human *fiat*, though the daily use of such concepts as enactment and repeal shows that the same is not true of law.

Much moral philosophy is devoted to the explanation of this feature of morality, and to the elucidation of the sense that morality is something 'there' to be recognized, not made by deliberate human choice. But the fact itself as distinct from its explanation is not a peculiarity of moral rules. This is why this feature of morality, though exceedingly important, cannot serve by itself to distinguish morality from all other forms of social

norms. For in this respect, though not in others, any social
tradition is like morals: tradition too is incapable of enactment
or repeal by human *fiat*. The story, perhaps apocryphal, that
the headmaster of a new English public school announced
that, as from the beginning of the next term, it would be a
tradition of the school that senior boys should wear a certain
dress, depends for its comic effect wholly on the logical incompatibility of the notion of a tradition with that of deliberate
enactment and choice. Rules acquire and lose the status of
traditions by growing, being practised, ceasing to be practised,
and decaying; and rules brought into being or eliminated
otherwise than by these slow, involuntary processes could not
thereby acquire or lose the status of tradition.

The fact that morals and traditions cannot be directly
changed, as laws may be, by legislative enactment must not be
mistaken for immunity from other forms of change. Indeed
though a moral rule or tradition cannot be repealed or changed
by deliberate choice or enactment, the enactment or repeal of
laws may well be among the causes of a change or decay of some
moral standard or some tradition. If a traditional practice such
as the celebrations on Guy Fawkes night is forbidden by law and
punished, the practice may cease and the tradition may disappear. Conversely, if the laws require military service from
certain classes, this may ultimately develop a tradition among
them which may well outlive the law. So too legal enactments
may set standards of honesty and humanity, which ultimately
alter and raise the current morality; conversely legal repression
of practices thought morally obligatory may, in the end, cause
the sense of their importance and so their status as morality to
be lost; yet, very often, the law loses such battles with ingrained
morality, and the moral rule continues in full vigour side by side
with laws which forbid what it enjoins.

These modes of change of tradition and morality in which
the law may be a causal factor must be distinguished from
legislative change or repeal. For though the acquisition or loss
of *legal* status due to enactment may indeed be spoken of as the
enacted statute's 'legal effect' this is not a contingent causal
change, as the statute's eventual effect on morals and tradition
is. This difference may be simply seen in the fact that while
it is always possible to doubt whether a clear, valid, legal enact-

ment will lead to a change in morals, no similar doubts could be entertained as to whether a clear, valid, legal enactment has changed the law.

The incompatibility of the idea of morality or tradition with that of change by deliberate enactment, must also be distinguished from the immunity conferred on certain laws in some systems by the restrictive clauses of a constitution. Such immunity is not a necessary element in the status of a law as a law, for this immunity may be removed by constitutional amendment. Unlike such legal immunity from legislative change, the incapacity of morals or tradition for similar modes of change is not something which varies from community to community or from time to time. It is incorporated in the meaning of these terms; the idea of a moral legislature with competence to make and change morals, as legal enactments make and change law, is repugnant to the whole notion of morality. When we come to consider international law we shall find it important to distinguish the mere *de facto* absence of a legislature, which may be regarded as a defect of the system, from the fundamental inconsistency which, as we have stressed here, is latent in the idea that moral rules or standards could be made or repealed by legislation.

(iii) *Voluntary character of moral offences*. The old conception that morals are exclusively concerned with what is 'internal' while law is concerned only with 'external' behaviour is in part a misstatement of the two features already discussed. But it is most often treated as a reference to certain prominent characteristics of moral responsibility and moral blame. If a person whose action, judged *ab extra*, has offended against moral rules or principles, succeeds in establishing that he did this unintentionally and in spite of every precaution that it was possible for him to take, he is excused from moral responsibility, and to blame him in these circumstances would itself be considered morally objectionable. Moral blame is therefore excluded because he has done all that he could do. In any developed legal system the same is true up to a point; for the general requirement of *mens rea* is an element in criminal responsibility designed to secure that those who offend without carelessness, unwittingly, or in conditions in which they lacked the bodily or mental capacity to conform to the law, should be excused.

A legal system would be open to serious moral condemnation if this were not so, at any rate in cases of serious crimes carrying severe punishments.

Nonetheless admission of such excuses in all legal systems is qualified in many different ways. The real or alleged difficulties of proof of psychological facts may lead a legal system to refuse to investigate the actual mental states or capacities of particular individuals, and, instead, to use 'objective tests', whereby the individual charged with an offence is taken to have the capacities for control or ability to take precautions that a normal or 'reasonable' man would have. Some systems may refuse to consider 'volitional' as distinct from 'cognitive' disabilities; if so they confine the range of excuses to lack of intention or defects of knowledge. Again, the legal system may, for certain types of offence, impose 'strict liability' and make responsibility independent of *mens rea* altogether, except perhaps for the minimum requirement that the accused must possess normal muscular control.

It is therefore clear that legal responsibility is not necessarily excluded by the demonstration that an accused person could not have kept the law which he has broken; by contrast, in morals 'I could not help it' is always an excuse, and moral obligation would be altogether different from what it is if the moral 'ought' did not in this sense imply 'can'. Yet it is important to see that 'I could not help it' is only an excuse (though a good one), and to <u>distinguish excuse from justification</u>; for, as we have said, the claim that morals do not require external behaviour rests on a confusion of these two ideas. If good intentions were a justification for doing what moral rules forbid, there would be nothing to deplore in the action of a man who had accidentally and in spite of every care killed another. We should look upon it as we now look upon a man's killing another, when this is required as a necessary measure of self defence. The latter is *justified* because killing, in such circumstances, is a kind of conduct which the system is not concerned to prevent and may even encourage, though it is of course an exception to a general prohibition of killing. Where someone is *excused* because he offended unintentionally, the underlying moral conception is not that this action is of a kind which it is the policy of the law to permit or even welcome; it is that when we investigate the mental condition of the particular offender, we find that he lacked the normal capacity to conform to the law's requirements. Hence this aspect of the 'internality' of morals does not mean that morals is not a form of control of outward conduct; but only that it is a necessary condition for moral responsibility that the individual must have a certain type of control over his conduct. Even in morals there is a difference between 'He did not do the wrong thing' and 'He could not help doing what he did'.

(iv) *The form of moral pressure.* A further distinguishing feature of morality is the characteristic form of moral pressure which is exerted in its support. This feature is closely related to the last and like it has powerfully contributed to the vague sense that moral is concerned with what is 'internal'. The facts which have led to this interpretation of morality are these. If it were the case that whenever someone was about to break a rule of conduct, *only* threats of physical punishment or unpleasant consequences were used in argument to dissuade him, then it would be impossible to regard such a rule as a part of the morality of the society, though this would not be any objection to treating it as part of its law. Indeed the typical form of legal pressure may well be said to consist in such threats. With morals on the other hand the typical form of pressure consists in appeals to the respect for the rules, as things important in themselves, which is presumed to be shared by those addressed. So moral pressure is characteristically, though not exclusively, exerted not by threats or by appeals to fear or interest, but by reminders of the moral character of the action contemplated and of the demands of morality. 'That would be a lie', 'That would be to break your promise'. In the background there are indeed the 'internal' moral analogues of fear of punishment; for it is assumed that protests will awaken in those addressed a sense of shame or guilt: they may be 'punished' by their own conscience. Of course sometimes such distinctively moral appeals are accompanied by threats of physical punishment, or by appeals to ordinary personal interest; deviations from the moral code meet with many different forms of hostile social reaction, ranging from relatively informal expressions of contempt to severance of social relations or ostracism. But emphatic reminders of what the rules demand, appeals to conscience, and reliance on the operation of guilt and remorse, are the characteristic and most prominent forms of pressure used for the support of social morality. That it should be supported in just these ways is a simple consequence of the acceptance of moral rules and standards, as things which it is supremely and obviously important to maintain. Standards not supported in these ways could not have the place in social and personal life distinctive of moral obligation.

3. MORAL IDEALS AND SOCIAL CRITICISM

Moral obligation and duty are the bedrock of social morality but they are not the whole. Before we examine other forms we shall, however, consider an objection to the way in which we have characterized moral obligation. The fourfold criteria which in the last section we used to distinguish it from other forms of social standard or rule (importance, immunity from deliberate change, the voluntary character of moral offences, and the special form of moral pressure) are in a sense *formal* criteria. They make no direct reference to any necessary content which rules or standards must have in order to be moral, nor even to any purpose which they must serve in social life. We have, indeed, insisted that in all moral codes there will be found some form of prohibition of the use of violence, to persons or things, and requirements of truthfulness, fair dealing, and respect for promises. These things, granted only certain very obvious truisms about human nature and the character of the physical world, can be seen in fact to be essential if human beings are to live continuously together in close proximity; and it therefore would be extraordinary if rules providing for them were not everywhere endowed with the moral importance and status which we have described. It seems clear that the sacrifice of personal interest which such rules *demand* is the price which must be paid in a world such as ours for living with others, and the protection they *afford* is the minimum which, for beings such as ourselves, makes living with others worth while. These simple facts constitute, as we argue in the next chapter, a core of indisputable truth in the doctrines of Natural Law.

Many moralists would wish to bring into the definition of morality as a further criterion beyond the four which we have offered, this connexion, which seems so clear, between morality

and human needs and interests. They would stipulate that
nothing is to be recognized as part of morality unless it could
survive rational criticism in terms of human interests, and so be
shown to advance them (perhaps even in some fair or equal
way), in the society whose rules they are. Some might even go
further, and refuse to recognize as moral any principle or rule
of conduct, unless the benefits of the forbearances and actions
it required were extended, beyond the boundaries of a particular society, to all who were themselves willing and able to respect such rules. We have, however, intentionally taken a
broader view of morality, so as to include in it all social rules
and standards which, in the actual practice of a society,
exhibit the four features we have mentioned. Some of these
would survive criticism in the light of these further suggested
tests; others would not but might be condemned as irrational
or unenlightened or even barbarous. We have done this not
merely because the weight of usage of the word 'moral' favours
this broader meaning, but because to take the narrower restricted view, which would exclude these, would force us to
divide in a very unrealistic manner elements in a social structure which function in an identical manner, in the lives of those
who live by it. Moral prohibitions of conduct, which may not in
fact harm others, are not only regarded with precisely the same
instinctive respect as those that do; they enter together with the
requirements of more rationally defensible rules into social
estimates of character; and, with them, form part of the generally
accepted picture of the life which individuals are expected and
indeed are assumed to live.

It is, however, both true and important that morality includes much more than the *obligations* and *duties* which are
recognized in the actual practice of social groups. Obligation
and duty are only the bedrock of morality, even of social
morality, and there are forms of morality which extend beyond
the accepted shared morality of particular societies. Two
further aspects of morality require attention here. First, even
within the morality of a particular society, there exist side by side
with the structure of mandatory moral obligations and duties
and the relatively clear rules that define them, certain moral
ideals. The realization of these is not taken, as duty is, as a matter
of course, but as an achievement deserving praise. The hero and

the saint are extreme types of those who do *more* than their duty. What they do is not like obligation or duty, something which can be demanded of them, and failure to do it is not regarded as wrong or a matter for censure. On a humbler scale than the saint or hero, are those who are recognized in a society as deserving praise for the moral virtues which they manifest in daily life such as bravery, charity, benevolence, patience, or chastity. The connexion between such socially recognized ideals and virtues and the primary mandatory forms of social obligation and duty is fairly clear. Many moral virtues are qualities consisting in the ability and disposition to carry forward beyond the limited extent which duty demands, the kind of concern for others' interests or sacrifice of personal interest which it does demand. Benevolence and charity are examples of this. Other moral virtues like temperance, patience, bravery, or conscientiousness are in a sense ancillary: they are qualities of character shown in exceptional devotion to duty or in the pursuit of substantive moral ideals in the face of special temptation or danger.

The further reaches of morality take us in different ways beyond the confines of the obligations and ideals recognized in particular social groups to the principles and ideals used in the moral criticism of society itself; yet even here important connexions remain with the primordial social form of morality. It is always possible, when we come to examine the accepted morality either of our own or some other society, that we shall find much to criticize; it may, in the light of currently available knowledge, appear unnecessarily repressive, cruel, superstitious, or unenlightened. It may cramp human liberty, especially in the discussion and practice of religion or in experimentation with different forms of human life, even when only negligible benefits are thereby secured for others. Above all, a given society's morality may extend its protections from harm to its own members only, or even only to certain classes, leaving a slave or helot class at the mercy of their masters' whims. Implicit in this type of criticism which (even though it might be rejected) would certainly be accorded recognition as 'moral' criticism, is the assumption that the arrangements of society, including its accepted morality, must satisfy two formal conditions, one of rationality and the other of generality. Thus it is implied in such criticism first that social arrangements should not rest on beliefs which can be shown to be mistaken, and secondly that the protections from harm, which morality characteristically affords through the actions and forbearances it demands, should be extended at least to all men who are able and willing themselves to observe such restrictions. Thus such moral criticism of society as that enshrined in watchwords like liberty, fraternity, equality, and the pursuit of happiness draws its moral character from the fact that it invites reform, either in the name of some value or combination of values already recognized (though perhaps to an inadequate extent) in all actual social moralities or in the name of a version of these, refined and extended so as to meet the two demands of rationality and generality.

Of course it does not follow from the fact that criticism of the accepted morality or other social arrangements in the name of liberty or equality is itself recognized as *moral* criticism that the rejection of it in the names of other values may not also be moral. The denunciation of restriction on liberty might be met by the claim that the sacrifice of liberty to social or economic equality or security was itself justified. Such differences of weight or emphasis placed on different moral values may prove irreconcilable. They may amount to radically different ideal conceptions of society and form the moral basis of opposed political parties. One of the great justifications of democracy is that it permits experimentation and a revisable choice between such alternatives.

Finally, not all extensions of morality beyond the obligations and ideals generally recognized in a given society need take the form of social criticism. It is important to remember that morality has its private aspect, shown in the individual's recognition of ideals which he need not either share with others or regard as a source of criticism of others, still less of society as a whole. Lives may be ruled by dedication to the pursuit of heroic, romantic, aesthetic or scholarly ideals or, less agreeably, to mortification of the flesh. Here too, it could be argued that if we speak of morality, we do so because the values thus pursued by individuals are at least analogous to some of those recognized in the morality of their own society. But the analogy is surely not one of content, but one of form and function. For such ideals play, in the life of individuals, the same part as morality does in a society. They are ranked as supremely important, so that their pursuit is felt as duty to which other interests or desires are to be sacrificed; though conversions are possible the notion that such ideals could be adopted, changed, or eliminated by a deliberate choice is chimerical; and, finally, deviations from such ideals are 'punished' by the same conscience, guilt, and remorse as that to which social morality makes its primary appeal.

IX

LAWS AND MORALS

1. NATURAL LAW AND LEGAL POSITIVISM

THERE are many different types of relation between law and morals and there is nothing which can be profitably singled out for study as *the* relation between them. Instead it is important to distinguish some of the many different things which may be meant by the assertion or denial that law and morals are related. Sometimes what is asserted is a kind of connexion which few if any have ever denied; but its indisputable existence may be wrongly accepted as a sign of some more doubtful connexion, or even mistaken for it. Thus, it cannot seriously be disputed that the development of law, at all times and places, has in fact been profoundly influenced both by the conventional morality and ideals of particular social groups, and also by forms of enlightened moral criticism urged by individuals, whose moral horizon has transcended the morality currently accepted. But it is possible to take this truth illicitly, as a warrant for a different proposition: namely that a legal system *must* exhibit some specific conformity with morality or justice, or *must* rest on a widely diffused conviction that there is a moral obligation to obey it. Again, though this proposition may, in some sense, be true, it does not follow from it that the criteria of legal validity of particular laws used in a legal system must include, tacitly if not explicitly, a reference to morality or justice.

Many other questions besides these may be said to concern the relations between law and morals. In this chapter we shall discuss only two of them, though both will involve some consideration of many others. The first is a question which may still be illuminatingly described as the issue between Natural Law and Legal Positivism, though each of these titles has come to be used for a range of different theses about law and morals. Here we shall take Legal Positivism to mean the simple contention that it is in no sense a necessary truth that laws reproduce or satisfy certain demands of morality, though in fact they have often done so. But just because those who have taken this view have either been silent or differed very much concerning the nature of morality, it is necessary to consider two very different forms in which Legal Positivism has been rejected. One of these is expressed most clearly in the classical theories of Natural Law: that there are certain principles of human conduct, awaiting discovery by human reason, with which manmade law must conform if it is to be valid. The other takes a different, less rationalist view of morality, and offers a different account of the ways in which legal validity is connected with moral value. We shall consider the first of these in this section and the next.

In the vast literature from Plato to the present day which is dedicated to the assertion, and also to the denial, of the proposition that the ways in which men ought to behave may be discovered by human reason, the disputants on one side seem to say to those on the other, 'You are blind if you cannot see this' only to receive in reply, 'You have been dreaming.' This is so, because the claim that there are true principles of right conduct, rationally discoverable, has not usually been advanced as a separate doctrine but was originally presented, and for long defended, as part of a general conception of nature, inanimate and living. This outlook is, in many ways, antithetic to the general conception of nature which constitutes the framework of modern secular thought. Hence it is that, to its critics, Natural Law theory has seemed to spring from deep and old confusions from which modern thought has triumphantly freed itself; while to its advocates, the critics appear merely to insist on surface trivialities, ignoring profounder truths.

Thus many modern critics have thought that the claim that laws of proper conduct may be discovered by human reason rested on a simple ambiguity of the word 'law', and that when this ambiguity was exposed Natural Law received its deathblow. It is in this way that John Stuart Mill dealt with Montesquieu, who in the first chapter of the *Esprit des Lois* naïvely inquires why it is that, while inanimate things such as the stars and also animals obey 'the law of their nature', man does not do so but falls into sin. This, Mill thought, revealed the perennial confusion between laws which formulate the course or regularities of nature, and laws which require men to behave in

certain ways. The former, which can be discovered by observation and reasoning, may be called 'descriptive' and it is for the
scientist thus to discover them; the latter cannot be so established, for they are not statements or descriptions of facts, but
are 'prescriptions' or demands that men shall behave in certain
ways. The answer therefore to Montesquieu's question is simple:
prescriptive laws may be broken and yet remain laws, because
that merely means that human beings do not do what they are
told to do; but it is meaningless to say of the laws of nature,
discovered by science, either that they can or cannot be broken.
If the stars behave in ways contrary to the scientific laws which
purport to describe their regular movements, these are not
broken but they lose their title to be called 'laws' and must be
reformulated. To these differences in the sense of 'law', there
correspond systematic differences in the associated vocabulary of words like 'must', 'bound to', 'ought', and 'should'.
So, on this view, belief in Natural Law is reducible to a very
simple fallacy: a failure to perceive the very different senses
which those law-impregnated words can bear. It is as if the
believer had failed to perceive the very different meaning of
such words in 'You are bound to report for military service'
and 'It is bound to freeze if the wind goes round to the north'.

Critics like Bentham and Mill, who most fiercely attacked
Natural Law, often attributed their opponents' confusion
between these distinct senses of law, to the survival of the belief
that the observed regularities of nature were prescribed or
decreed by a Divine Governor of the Universe. On such a
theocratic view, the only difference between the law of gravity
and the Ten Commandments—God's law for Man—was, as
Blackstone asserted, the relatively minor one that men, alone
of created things, were endowed with reason and free will;
and so unlike things, could discover and disobey the divine
prescriptions. Natural Law has, however, not always been
associated with belief in a Divine Governor or Lawgiver of the
universe, and even where it has been, its characteristic tenets
have not been logically dependent on that belief. Both the
relevant sense of the word 'natural', which enters into Natural
Law, and its general outlook minimizing the difference, so
obvious and so important to modern minds, between prescriptive and descriptive laws, have their roots in Greek thought

which was, for this purpose, quite secular. Indeed, the continued reassertion of some form of Natural Law doctrine is due in part to the fact that its appeal is independent of both divine and human authority, and to the fact that despite a terminology, and much metaphysics, which few could now accept, it contains certain elementary truths of importance for the understanding of both morality and law. These we shall endeavour to disentangle from their metaphysical setting and restate here in simpler terms.

For modern secular thought the world of inanimate and living things, animals, and men is a scene of recurrent kinds of events and changes which exemplify certain regular connexions. Some at least of these, human beings have discovered and formulated as laws of nature. To understand nature is, in this modern view, to bring to bear on some part of it, knowledge of these regularities. The structure of great scientific theories does not of course mirror in any simple way observable fact, events, or changes; often, indeed, a great part of such theories consists of abstract mathematical formulations with no direct counterpart in observable fact. Their connexion with observable events and changes lies in the fact that, from these abstract formulations, generalizations may be deduced which do refer to, and may be confirmed or falsified by, observable events. A scientific theory's claim to forward our understanding of nature is therefore, in the last resort, dependent on its power to predict what will occur, which is based on generalizations of what regularly occurs. The law of gravity and the second law of thermodynamics are, for modern thought, laws of nature and more than mere mathematical constructions in virtue of the information they yield concerning the regularities of observable phenomena.

The doctrine of Natural Law is part of an older conception of nature in which the observable world is not merely a scene of such regularities, and knowledge of nature is not merely a knowledge of them. Instead, on this older outlook every nameable kind of existing thing, human, animate, and inanimate, is conceived not only as tending to maintain itself in existence but as proceeding towards a definite optimum state which is the specific good—or the end (τέλος, finis) appropriate for it.

This is the teleological conception of nature as containing in
itself levels of excellence which things realize. The stages by
which a thing of any given kind progresses to its specific or
proper end are regular, and may be formulated in generalizations describing the thing's characteristic mode of change, or
action, or development; to that extent the teleological view of
nature overlaps with modern thought. The difference is that
on the teleological view, the events regularly befalling things
are not thought of *merely* as occurring regularly, and the questions whether they *do* occur regularly and whether they *should*
occur or whether it is *good* that they occur are not regarded as
separate questions. On the contrary (except for some rare
monstrosities ascribed to 'chance') what generally occurs can
both be explained and evaluated as good or what ought to
occur, by exhibiting it as a step towards the proper end or goal
of the thing concerned. The laws of a thing's development
therefore should show both how it should and how it does
regularly behave or change.

This mode of thinking about nature seems strange when
stated abstractly. It may appear less fantastic if we recall some
of the ways in which even now we refer at least to living things,
for a teleological view is still reflected in common ways of
describing their development. Thus in the case of an acorn,
growth into an oak is something which is not only regularly
achieved by acorns, but is distinguished unlike its decay (which
is also regular) as an optimum state of maturity in the light of
which the intermediate stages are both explained and judged
as good or bad, and the 'functions' of its various parts and struc-
tural changes identified. The normal growth of leaves is
required if it is to obtain the moisture necessary for 'full' or
'proper' development, and it is the 'function' of leaves to supply
this. Hence we think and speak of this growth as what 'ought
naturally to occur'. In the case of the action or movements of
inanimate things, such ways of talking seem much less plausible
unless they are artefacts designed by human beings for a purpose. The notion that a stone on falling to the ground is realizing
some appropriate 'end' or returning to its 'proper place', like a
horse galloping home to a stable, is now somewhat comic.

Indeed, one of the difficulties in understanding a teleological
view of nature is that just as it minimized the differences between

statements of what regularly happens and statements of what
ought to happen, so too it minimizes the difference, so important in modern thought, between human beings *with* a purpose
of their own which they consciously strive to realize and other
living or inanimate things. For in the teleological view of the
world, man, like other things, is thought of as tending towards
a specific optimum state or end which is set for him and the fact,
that he, unlike other things, may do this consciously, is not
conceived as a radical difference between him and the rest of
nature. This specific human end or good is in part, like that of
other living things, a condition of biological maturity and
developed physical powers; but it also includes, as its distinctively human element, a development and excellence of mind
and character manifested in thought and conduct. Unlike
other things, man is able by reasoning and reflection to discover what the attainment of this excellence of mind and
character involves and to desire it. Yet even so, on this teleological view, this optimum state is not man's good or end because he desires it; rather he desires it because it is already his
natural end.

Again, much of this teleological point of view survives in
some of the ways in which we think and speak of human beings.
It is latent in our identification of certain things as human *needs*
which it is *good* to satisfy and of certain things done to or
suffered *by* human beings as *harm* or *injury*. Thus, though it is
true that some men may refuse to eat or rest because they wish
to die, we think of eating and resting as something more than
things which men regularly do or just happen to desire. Food
and rest are human needs, even if some refuse them when they
are needed. Hence we say not only that it is natural for all men
to eat and sleep, but that all men ought to eat and rest sometimes, or that it is naturally good to do these things. The force
of the word 'naturally', in such judgments of human conduct,
is to differentiate them both from judgments which reflect mere
conventions or human prescriptions ('You ought to take off
your hat'), the content of which cannot be discovered by
thought or reflection, and also from judgments which merely
indicate what is required for achieving some particular objective, which at a given time one man may happen to have and
another may not. The same outlook is present in our concep-

tion of the *functions* of bodily organs and the line we draw between these and mere causal properties. We say it is the function of the heart to circulate the blood, but not that it is the function of a cancerous growth to cause death.

These crude examples designed to illustrate teleological elements still alive in ordinary thought about human action, are drawn from the lowly sphere of biological fact which man shares with other animals. It will be rightly observed that what makes sense of this mode of thought and expression is something entirely obvious: it is the tacit assumption that the proper end of human activity is survival, and this rests on the simple contingent fact that most men most of the time wish to continue in existence. The actions which we speak of as those which are naturally good to do, are those which are required for survival; the notions of a human need, of harm, and of the *function* of bodily organs or changes rests on the same simple fact. Certainly if we stop here, we shall have only a very attenuated version of Natural Law: for the classical exponents of this outlook conceived of survival (*perseverare in esse suo*) as merely the lowest stratum in a much more complex and far more debatable concept of the human end or good for man. Aristotle included in it the disinterested cultivation of the human intellect, and Aquinas the knowledge of God, and both these represent values which may be and have been challenged. Yet other thinkers, Hobbes and Hume among them, have been willing to lower their sights: they have seen in the modest aim of survival the central indisputable element which gives empirical good sense to the terminology of Natural Law. 'Human nature cannot by any means subsist without the association of individuals: and that association never could have place were no regard paid to the laws of equity and justice.'[1]

This simple thought has in fact very much to do with the characteristics of both law and morals, and it can be disentangled from more disputable parts of the general teleological outlook in which the end or good for man appears as a specific way of life about which, in fact, men may profoundly disagree. Moreover, we can, in referring to survival, discard, as too metaphysical for modern minds, the notion that this is something antecedently fixed which men necessarily desire because

N.B.

---

[1] Hume, *Treatise of Human Nature*, iii. ii, 'Of Justice and Injustice'.

it is their proper goal or end. Instead we may hold it to be a
mere contingent fact which could be otherwise, that in general
men do desire to live, and that we may mean nothing more by
calling survival a human goal or end than that men do desire
it. Yet even if we think of it in this common-sense way, survival
has still a special status in relation to human conduct and in
our thought about it, which parallels the prominence and the
necessity ascribed to it in the orthodox formulations of Natural
Law. For it is not merely that an overwhelming majority of
men do wish to live, even at the cost of hideous misery, but that
this is reflected in whole structures of our thought and language,
in terms of which we describe the world and each other. We
could not subtract the general wish to live and leave intact
concepts like danger and safety, harm and benefit, need and
function, disease and cure; for these are ways of simultaneously describing and appraising things by reference to the
contribution they make to survival which is accepted as an
aim.

   There are, however, simpler, less philosophical, considerations than these which show acceptance of survival as an aim
to be necessary, in a sense more directly relevant to the discussion of human law and morals. We are committed to it as
something presupposed by the terms of the discussion; for our
concern is with social arrangements for continued existence,
not with those of a suicide club. We wish to know whether,
among these social arrangements, there are some which may
illuminatingly be ranked as natural laws discoverable by reason,
and what their relation is to human law and morality. To
raise this or any other question concerning _how_ men should live
together, we must assume that their aim, generally speaking,
is to live. From this point the argument is a simple one. Reflection on some very obvious generalizations—indeed truisms—
concerning human nature and the world in which men live,
show that as long as these hold good, there are certain rules of
conduct which any social organization must contain if it is to
be viable. Such rules do in fact constitute a common element
in the law and conventional morality of all societies which have
progressed to the point where these are distinguished as different
forms of social control. With them are found, both in law and
morals, much that is peculiar to a particular society and much

that may seem arbitrary or a mere matter of choice. Such uni⌐
versally recognized principles of conduct which have a basis in
elementary truths concerning human beings, their natural
environment, and aims, may be considered the *minimum content*   N3
of Natural Law, in contrast with the more grandiose and more
challengeable constructions which have often been proffered⌐
under that name. In the next section we shall consider, in the
form of five truisms, the salient characteristics of human nature
upon which this modest but important minimum rests.

2. THE MINIMUM CONTENT OF NATURAL LAW

⌐   In considering the simple truisms which we set forth here,
and their connexion with law and morals, it is important to
observe that in each case the facts mentioned afford a *reason
why*, given survival as an aim, law and morals should include
⌐a specific content. The general form of the argument is simply
that without such a content laws and morals could not forward
the minimum purpose of survival which men have in associating
with each other. In the absence of this content men, as they
are, would have no reason for obeying voluntarily any rules;
and without a minimum of co-operation given voluntarily by
those who find that it is in their interest to submit to and
maintain the rules, coercion of others who would not voluntarily conform would be impossible. It is important to stress
the distinctively rational connexion between natural facts and
the content of legal and moral rules in this approach, because it is both possible and important to inquire into quite
different forms of connexion between natural facts and legal or
moral rules. Thus, the still young sciences of psychology and
sociology may discover or may even have discovered that, unless
certain physical, psychological, or economic conditions are
satisfied, e.g. unless young children are fed and nurtured in
certain ways within the family, no system of laws or code of
morals can be established, or that only those laws can function
successfully which conform to a certain type. Connexions of this
sort between natural conditions and systems of rules are not
mediated by *reasons*; for they do not relate the existence of
certain rules to the conscious aims or purpose of those whose rules
they are. Being fed in infancy in a certain way may well be shown
to be a necessary condition or even a *cause* of a population

developing or maintaining a moral or legal code, but it is not a *reason* for their doing so. Such causal connexions do not of course conflict with the connexions which rest on purposes or conscious aims; they may indeed be considered more important or fundamental than the latter, since they may actually explain why human beings have those conscious aims or purposes which Natural Law takes as its starting-points. Causal explanations of this type do not rest on truisms nor are they mediated by conscious aims or purposes: they are for sociology or psychology like other sciences to establish by the methods of generalization and theory, resting on observation and, where possible, on experiment. Such connexions therefore are of a different kind from those which relate the content of certain legal and moral rules to the facts stated in the following truisms.

(i) *Human vulnerability*. The common requirements of law and morality consist for the most part not of active services to be rendered but of forbearances, which are usually formulated in negative form as prohibitions. Of these the most important for social life are those that restrict the use of violence in killing or inflicting bodily harm. The basic character of such rules may be brought out in a question: If there were not these rules what point could there be for beings such as ourselves in having rules of *any* other kind? The force of this rhetorical question rests on the fact that men are both occasionally prone to, and normally vulnerable to, bodily attack. Yet though this is a truism it is not a necessary truth; for things might have been, and might one day be, otherwise. There are species of animals whose physical structure (including exoskeletons or a carapace) renders them virtually immune from attack by other members of their species and animals who have no organs enabling them to attack. If men were to lose their vulnerability to each other there would vanish one obvious reason for the most characteristic provision of law and morals: *Thou shalt not kill*.

(ii) *Approximate equality*. Men differ from each other in physical strength, agility, and even more in intellectual capacity. Nonetheless it is a fact of quite major importance for the understanding of different forms of law and morality, that no individual is so much more powerful than others, that he is able, without co-operation, to dominate or subdue them for more than a short period. Even the strongest must sleep at times and, when asleep, loses temporarily his superiority. This fact of approximate equality, more than any other, makes obvious the necessity for a system of mutual forbearance and compromise which is the base of both legal and moral obligation. Social life with its rules requiring such forbearances is irksome at times; but it is at any rate less nasty, less brutish, and less short than unrestrained aggression for beings thus approximately equal. It is, of course, entirely consistent with this and an equal truism that when such a system of forbearance is established there will always be some who will wish to exploit it, by simultaneously living within its shelter and breaking its restrictions. This, indeed is, as we later show, one of the natural facts which makes the step from merely moral to organized, legal forms of control a necessary one. Again, things might have been otherwise. Instead of being approximately equal there might have been some men immensely stronger than others and better able to dispense with rest, either because some were in these ways far above the present average, or because most were far below it. Such exceptional men might have much to gain by aggression and little to gain from mutual forbearance or compromise with others. But we need not have recourse to the fantasy of giants among pygmies to see the cardinal importance of the fact of approximate equality: for it is illustrated better by the facts of international life, where there are (or were) vast disparities in strength and vulnerability between the states. This inequality, as we shall later see, between the units of international law is one of the things that has imparted to it a character so different from municipal law and limited the extent to which it is capable of operating as an organized coercive system.

(iii) _Limited altruism._ Men are not devils dominated by a wish to exterminate each other, and the demonstration that, given only the modest aim of survival, the basic rules of law and morals are necessities, must not be identified with the false view that men are predominantly selfish and have no disinterested interest in the survival and welfare of their fellows. But if men are not devils, neither are they angels; and the fact that they are a mean between these two extremes is something which makes a system of mutual forbearances both necessary and possible. With angels, never tempted to harm others, rules requiring forbearances would not be necessary. With devils prepared to destroy, reckless of the cost to themselves, they would be impossible. As things are, human altruism is limited in range and intermittent, and the tendencies to aggression are frequent enough to be fatal to social life if not controlled.

(iv) *Limited resources*. It is a merely contingent fact that human beings need food, clothes, and shelter; that these do not exist at hand in limitless abundance; but are scarce, have to be grown or won from nature, or have to be constructed by human toil. These facts alone make indispensable some minimal form of the institution of property (though not necessarily individual property), and the distinctive kind of rule which requires respect for it. The simplest forms of property are to be seen in rules excluding persons generally other than the 'owner' from entry on, or the use of land, or from taking or using material things. If crops are to grow, land must be secure from indiscriminate entry, and food must, in the intervals between its growth or capture and consumption, be secure from being taken by others. At all times and places life itself depends on these minimal forbearances. Again, in this respect, things might have been otherwise than they are. The human organism might have been constructed like plants, capable of extracting food from air, or what it needs might have grown without cultivation, in limitless abundance.

The rules which we have so far discussed are *static* rules, in the sense that the obligations they impose and the incidence of these obligations are not variable by individuals. But the division of labour, which all but the smallest groups must develop to obtain adequate supplies, brings with it the need for rules which are *dynamic* in the sense that they enable individuals to create obligations and to vary their incidence. Among these are rules enabling men to transfer, exchange, or sell their products; for these transactions involve the capacity to alter the incidence of those initial rights and obligations which define the simplest form of property. The same inescapable division of labour, and perennial need for co-operation, are also factors which make other forms of dynamic or obligation-creating rule necessary in social life. These secure the recognition of promises as a source of obligation. By this device individuals are enabled by words, spoken or written, to make themselves liable to blame or punishment for failure to act in certain stipulated ways. Where altruism is not unlimited, a standing procedure providing for such self-binding operations is required in order to create a minimum form of confidence in the future behaviour of others, and to ensure the predictability necessary for co-operation. This is most obviously needed where what is to be exchanged or jointly planned are mutual services, or wherever goods which are to be exchanged or sold are not simultaneously or immediately available.

(v) *Limited understanding and strength of will*. The facts that make rules respecting persons, property, and promises necessary in social life are simple and their mutual benefits are obvious. Most men are capable of seeing them and of sacrificing the immediate short-term interests which conformity to such rules demands. They may indeed obey, from a variety of motives: some from prudential calculation that the sacrifices are worth the gains, some from a disinterested interest in the welfare of others, and some because they look upon the rules as worthy of respect in themselves and find their ideals in devotion to them. On the other hand, neither understanding of long-term interest, nor the strength or goodness of will, upon which the efficacy of these different motives towards obedience depends, are shared by all men alike. All are tempted at times to prefer their own immediate interests and, in the absence of a special organization for their detection and punishment, many would succumb to the temptation. No doubt the advantages of mutual forbearance are so palpable that the number and strength of those who would co-operate voluntarily in a coercive system will normally be greater than any likely combination of malefactors. Yet, except in very small closely-knit societies, submission to the system of restraints would be folly if there were no organization for the coercion of those who would then try to obtain the advantages of the system without submitting to its obligations. 'Sanctions' are therefore required not as the normal motive for obedience, but as a *guarantee* that those who would voluntarily obey shall not be sacrificed to those who would not. To obey, without this, would be to risk going to the wall. Given this standing danger, what reason demands is *voluntary* co-operation in a *coercive* system.

It is to be observed that the same natural fact of approximate equality between men is of crucial importance in the efficacy of organized sanctions. If some men were vastly more powerful than others, and so not dependent on their forbearance, the strength of the malefactors might exceed that of the supporters of law and order. Given such inequalities, the use of sanctions could not be successful and would involve dangers at least as great as those which they were designed to suppress. In these circumstances instead of social life being based on a system of mutual forbearances, with force used only intermittently against a minority of malefactors, the only viable system would be one in which the weak submitted to the strong on the best terms they could make and lived under their 'protection'. This, because of the scarcity of resources, would lead to a number of conflicting power centres, each grouped round its 'strong man': these might intermittently war with each other, though the natural sanction, never negligible, of the risk of defeat might ensure an uneasy peace. Rules of a sort might then be accepted for the regulation of issues over which the 'powers' were unwilling to fight. Again we need not think in fanciful terms of pygmies and giants in order to understand the simple logistics of approximate equality and its importance for law. The international scene, where the units concerned have differed vastly in strength, affords illustration enough. For centuries the disparities between states have resulted in a system where organized sanctions have been impossible, and law has been confined to matters which did not affect 'vital' issues. How far atomic weapons, when available to all, will redress the balance of unequal power, and bring forms of control more closely resembling municipal criminal law, remains to be seen.

The simple truisms we have discussed not only disclose the core of good sense in the doctrine of Natural Law. They are of vital importance for the understanding of law and morals, and they explain why the definition of the basic forms of these in purely formal terms, without reference to any specific content or social needs, has proved so inadequate. Perhaps the major benefit to jurisprudence from this outlook is the escape it affords from certain misleading dichotomies which often obscure the discussion of the characteristics of law. Thus, for example, the traditional question whether every legal system *must* provide for sanctions can be presented in a fresh and clearer ✓ light, when we command the view of things presented by this simple version of Natural Law. We shall no longer have to choose between two unsuitable alternatives which are often taken as exhaustive: on the one hand that of saying that this is required by 'the' meaning of the words 'law' or 'legal system', and on the other that of saying that it is 'just a fact' that most legal systems do provide for sanctions. Neither of these alternatives is satisfactory. There are no settled principles forbidding the use of the word 'law' of systems where there are no centrally organized sanctions, and there is good reason (though no compulsion) for using the expression 'international law' of a system, which has none. On the other hand we do need to distinguish the place that sanctions must have within a municipal system, if it is to serve the minimum purposes of beings constituted as men are. We can say, given the setting of natural ✶ facts and aims, which make sanctions both possible and necessary in a municipal system, that this is a *natural necessity*; and some such phrase is needed also to convey the status of the minimum forms of protection for persons, property, and promises which are similarly indispensable features of municipal law. It is in this form that we should reply to the positivist thesis that 'law may have any content'. For it is a truth of some importance that for the adequate description not only of law but of many other social institutions, a place must be reserved, besides definitions and ordinary statements of fact, for a third category of statements: those the truth of which is contingent on human beings and the world they live in retaining the salient characteristics which they have.

3. LEGAL VALIDITY AND MORAL VALUE

The protections and benefits provided by the system of mutual forbearances which underlies both law and morals may, in different societies, be extended to very different ranges of persons. It is true that the denial of these elementary protections to any class of human beings, willing to accept the corresponding restrictions, would offend the principles of morality and justice to which all modern states pay, at any rate, lip service. Their professed moral outlook is, in general, permeated by the conception that in these fundamentals at least, human beings are entitled to be treated alike and that differences of treatment require more to justify them than just an appeal to the interests of others.

Yet it is plain that neither the law nor the accepted morality of societies need extend their minimal protections and benefits to all within their scope, and often they have not done so. In slave-owning societies the sense that the slaves are human beings, not mere objects to be used, may be lost by the dominant group, who may yet remain morally most sensitive to each other's claims and interests. Huckleberry Finn, when asked if the explosion of a steamboat boiler had hurt anyone, replied, 'No'm: killed a nigger.' Aunt Sally's comment 'Well it's lucky because sometimes people do get hurt' sums up a whole morality which has often prevailed among men. Where it does prevail, as Huck found to his cost, to extend to slaves the concern for others which is natural between members of the dominant group may well be looked on as a grave moral offence, bringing with it all the sequelae of moral guilt. Nazi Germany and South Africa offer parallels unpleasantly near to us in time.

Though the law of some societies has occasionally been in advance of the accepted morality, normally law follows morality and even the homicide of a slave may be regarded only as a waste of public resources or as an offence against the master whose property he is. Even where slavery is not officially recognized, discriminations on grounds of race, colour, or creed may produce a legal system and a social morality which does not recognize that all men are entitled to a minimum of protection from others.

These painful facts of human history are enough to show that, though a society to be viable must offer *some* of its members a system of mutual forbearances, it need not, unfortunately, offer them to all. It is true, as we have already emphasized in discussing the need for and the possibility of sanctions, that if a system of rules is to be imposed by force on any, there must be a sufficient number who accept it voluntarily. Without their voluntary co-operation, thus creating *authority*, the coercive power of law and government cannot be established. But coercive power, thus established on its basis of authority, may be used in two principal ways. It may be exerted only against malefactors who, though they are afforded the protection of the

rules, yet selfishly break them. On the other hand, it may be
used to subdue and maintain, in a position of permanent inferiority, a subject group whose size, relatively to the master
group, may be large or small, depending on the means of
coercion, solidarity, and discipline available to the latter, and
the helplessness or inability to organize of the former. For those
thus oppressed there may be nothing in the system to command
their loyalty but only things to fear. They are its victims, not its
beneficiaries.

In the earlier chapters of this book we stressed the fact that
the existence of a legal system is a social phenomenon which
always presents two aspects, to both of which we must attend if
our view of it is to be realistic. It involves the attitudes and
behaviour involved in the voluntary acceptance of rules and
also the simpler attitudes and behaviour involved in mere
obedience or acquiescence.

Hence a society with law contains those who look upon its
rules from the internal point of view as accepted standards of
behaviour, and not merely as reliable predictions of what will
befall them, at the hands of officials, if they disobey. But it also
comprises those upon whom, either because they are malefactors or mere helpless victims of the system, these legal
standards have to be imposed by force or threat of force; they
are concerned with the rules merely as a source of possible
punishment. The balance between these two components will
be determined by many different factors. If the system is fair
and caters genuinely for the vital interests of all those from whom
it demands obedience, it may gain and retain the allegiance
of most for most of the time, and will accordingly be stable.
On the other hand it may be a narrow and exclusive system run
in the interests of the dominant group, and it may be made
continually more repressive and unstable with the latent threat
of upheaval. Between these two extremes various combinations
of these attitudes to law are to be found, often in the same individual.

Reflection on this aspect of things reveals a sobering truth:
the step from the simple form of society, where primary rules
of obligation are the only means of social control, into the legal
world with its centrally organized legislature, courts, officials,
and sanctions brings its solid gains at a certain cost. The gains

are those of adaptability to change, certainty, and efficiency, and these are immense; the cost is the risk that the centrally organized power may well be used for the oppression of numbers with whose support it can dispense, in a way that the simpler régime of primary rules could not. Because this risk has materialized and may do so again, the claim that there is some further way in which law *must* conform to morals beyond that which we have exhibited as the minimum content of Natural Law, needs very careful scrutiny. Many such assertions either fail to make clear the sense in which the connexion between law and morals is alleged to be necessary; or upon examination they turn out to mean something which is both true and important, but which it is most confusing to present as a necessary connexion between law and morals. We shall end this chapter by examining six forms of this claim.

(i) *Power and authority*. It is often said that a legal system must rest on a sense of moral obligation or on the conviction of the moral value of the system, since it does not and cannot rest on mere power of man over man. We have ourselves stressed, in the earlier chapters of this book, the inadequacy of orders backed by threats and habits of obedience for the understanding of the foundations of a legal system and the idea of legal validity. Not only do these require for their elucidation the notion of an accepted rule of recognition, as we have argued at length in Chapter VI, but, as we have seen in this chapter, a necessary condition of the existence of coercive power is that some at least must voluntarily co-operate in the system and accept its rules. In this sense it is true that the coercive power of law presupposes its accepted authority. But the dichotomy of 'law based merely on power' and 'law which is accepted as morally binding' is not exhaustive. Not only may vast numbers be coerced by laws which they do not regard as morally binding, but it is not even true that those who do accept the system voluntarily, must conceive of themselves as morally bound to do so, though the system will be most stable when they do so. In fact, their allegiance to the system may be based on many different considerations: calculations of long-term interest; disinterested interest in others; an unreflecting inherited or traditional attitude; or the mere wish to do as others do. There is indeed no reason why those who accept the authority of the system should not examine their conscience and decide that, morally, they ought not to accept it, yet for a variety of reasons continue to do so.

These commonplaces may have become obscured by the general use of the same vocabulary to express both the legal and the moral obligations which men acknowledge. Those who accept the authority of a legal system look upon it from the internal point of view, and express their sense of its requirements in internal statements couched in the normative language which is common to both law and morals: 'I (You) ought', 'I (he) must', 'I (they) have an obligation'. Yet they are not thereby committed to a *moral* judgment that it is morally right to do what the law requires. No doubt if nothing else is said, there is a presumption that any one who speaks in these ways of his or others' legal obligations, does not think that there is any moral or other reason against fulfilling them. This, however, does not show that nothing can be acknowledged as legally obligatory unless it is accepted as morally obligatory. The presumption which we have mentioned rests on the fact that it will often be pointless to acknowledge or point out a legal obligation, if the speaker has conclusive reasons, moral or otherwise, to urge against fulfilling it.

(ii) *The influence of morality on law*. The law of every modern state shows at a thousand points the influence of both the accepted social morality and wider moral ideals. These influences enter into law either abruptly and avowedly through legislation, or silently and piecemeal through the judicial process. In some systems, as in the United States, the ultimate criteria of legal validity explicitly incorporate principles of justice or substantive moral values; in other systems, as in England, where there are no formal restrictions on the competence of the supreme legislature, its legislation may yet no less scrupulously conform to justice or morality. The further ways in which law mirrors morality are myriad, and still insufficiently studied: statutes may be a mere legal shell and demand by their express terms to be filled out with the aid of moral principles; the range of enforceable contracts may be limited by reference to conceptions of morality and fairness; liability for both civil and criminal wrongs may be adjusted to prevailing views of moral responsibility. No 'positivist' could deny that these are facts, or that the stability of legal systems depends in part upon such types of correspondence with morals. If this is what is meant by the ⌐ necessary connexion of law and morals, its existence should be ⌐ conceded.

(iii) _Interpretation._ Laws require interpretation if they are to be applied to concrete cases, and once the myths which obscure the nature of the judicial processes are dispelled by realistic study, it is patent, as we have shown in Chapter VI, that the open texture of law leaves a vast field for a creative activity which some call legislative. Neither in interpreting statutes nor precedents are judges confined to the alternatives of blind, arbitrary choice, or 'mechanical' deduction from rules with predetermined meaning. Very often their choice is guided by an assumption that the purpose of the rules which they are interpreting is a reasonable one, so that the rules are not intended to work injustice or offend settled moral principles. ⌐Judicial decision, especially on matters of high constitutional import, often involves a choice between moral values, and not merely the application of some single outstanding moral principle; for it is folly to believe that where the meaning of the law is in doubt, morality always has a clear answer to offer. At this point judges may again make a choice which is neither arbitrary nor mechanical; and here often display characteristic judicial virtues, the special appropriateness of which to legal decision explains why some feel reluctant to call such judicial activity 'legislative'. These virtues are: impartiality and neutrality in surveying the alternatives; consideration for the interest of all who will be affected; and a concern to deploy some acceptable general principle as a reasoned basis for decision. No doubt because a plurality of such principles is always possible it cannot be _demonstrated_ that a decision is uniquely correct: but it may be made acceptable as the reasoned product of informed impartial choice. In all this we have the 'weighing' and 'balancing' characteristic of the effort to do justice between competing interests.

Few would deny the importance of these elements, which may well be called 'moral', in rendering decisions acceptable; and the loose and changing tradition or canons of interpretation, which in most systems govern interpretation, often vaguely incorporate them. Yet if these facts are tendered as evidence of

the *necessary* connexion of law and morals, we need to remember
that the same principles have been honoured nearly as much
in the breach as in the observance. For, from Austin to the
present day, reminders that such elements *should* guide decision
have come, in the main, from critics who have found that
judicial law-making has often been blind to social values,
'automatic', or inadequately reasoned.

(iv) *The criticism of law.* Sometimes the claim that there is a
necessary connexion between law and morality comes to no
more than the assertion that a *good* legal system must conform
at certain points, such as those already mentioned in the last
paragraph, to the requirements of justice and morality. Some
may regard this as an obvious truism; but it is not a tautology,
and in fact, in the criticism of law, there may be disagreement
both as to the appropriate moral standards and as to the required points of conformity. Does the morality, with which law
must conform if it is to be good, mean the accepted morality of
the group whose law it is, even though this may rest on superstition or may withhold its benefits and protection from slaves or
subject classes? Or does morality mean standards which are
enlightened in the sense that they rest on rational beliefs as to
matters of fact, and accept all human beings as entitled to
equal consideration and respect?

No doubt the contention that a legal system must treat all
human beings within its scope as entitled to certain basic
protections and freedoms, is now generally accepted as a statement of an ideal of obvious relevance in the criticism of law.
Even where practice departs from it, lip service to this ideal is
usually forthcoming. It may even be the case that a morality
which does not take this view of the right of all men to equal
consideration, can be shown by philosophy to be involved in
some inner contradiction, dogmatism, or irrationality. If so,
the enlightened morality which recognizes these rights has
special credentials as the true morality, and is not just one among
many possible moralities. These are claims which cannot be
investigated here, but even if they are conceded, they cannot
alter, and should not obscure, the fact that municipal legal
systems, with their characteristic structure of primary and
secondary rules, have long endured though they have flouted
these principles of justice. What, if anything, is to be gained

from denying that iniquitous rules are law, we consider
below.

(v) _Principles of legality and justice._ It may be said that the
distinction between a good legal system which conforms at
certain points to morality and justice, and a legal system which
does not, is a fallacious one, because a minimum of justice is
necessarily realized whenever human behaviour is controlled
by general rules publicly announced and judicially applied.
Indeed we have already pointed out,[1] in analysing the idea of
justice, that its simplest form (justice in the application of the
law) consists in no more than taking seriously the notion that
what is to be applied to a multiplicity of different persons is the
same general rule, undeflected by prejudice, interest, or caprice.
This impartiality is what the procedural standards known to
English and American lawyers as principles of 'Natural Justice'
are designed to secure. Hence, though the most odious laws may
be justly applied, we have, in the bare notion of applying a
general rule of law, the germ at least of justice.

Further aspects of this minimum form of justice which might
well be called 'natural' emerge if we study what is in fact involved in any method of social control—rules of games as well
as law—which consists primarily of general standards of conduct communicated to classes of persons, who are then expected
to understand and conform to the rules without further official
direction. If social control of this sort is to function, the rules
must satisfy certain conditions: they must be intelligible and
within the capacity of most to obey, and in general they must
not be retrospective, though exceptionally they may be. This
means that, for the most part, those who are eventually
punished for breach of the rules will have had the ability and
opportunity to obey. Plainly these features of control by rule
are closely related to the requirements of justice which lawyers
term principles of legality. Indeed one critic of positivism has
seen in these aspects of control by rules, something amounting
to a necessary connexion between law and morality, and suggested that they be called 'the inner morality of law'. Again, if
this is what the necessary connexion of law and morality means,
we may accept it. It is unfortunately compatible with very
great iniquity.

[1] p. 156 above.

(vi) _Legal validity and resistance to law_. However incautiously they may have formulated their general outlook, few legal theorists classed as positivists would have been concerned to deny the forms of connexion between law and morals discussed under the last five headings. What then was the concern of the great battle-cries of legal positivism: 'The existence of law is one thing; its merit or demerit another';[1] 'The law of a State is not an ideal but something which actually exists . . . it is not that which ought to be, but that which is';[2] 'Legal norms may have any kind of content'?[3]

What these thinkers were, in the main, concerned to promote was clarity and honesty in the formulation of the theoretical and moral issues raised by the existence of particular laws which were morally iniquitous but were enacted in proper form, clear in meaning, and satisfied all the acknowledged criteria of validity of a system. Their view was that, in thinking about such laws, both the theorist and the unfortunate official or private citizen who was called on to apply or obey them, could only be confused by an invitation to refuse the title of 'law' or 'valid' to them. They thought that, to confront these problems, simpler, more candid resources were available, which would bring into focus far better, every relevant intellectual and moral consideration: we should say, 'This is law; but it is too iniquitous to be applied or obeyed.'

The opposed point of view is one which appears attractive when, after revolution or major upheavals, the Courts of a system have to consider their attitude to the moral iniquities committed in legal form by private citizens or officials under an earlier régime. Their punishment may be felt socially desirable, and yet, to procure it by frankly retrospective legislation, making criminal what was permitted or even required by the law of the earlier régime, may be difficult, itself morally odious, or perhaps not possible. In these circumstances it may seem natural to exploit the moral implications latent in the vocabulary of the law and especially in words like _ius_, _recht_, _diritto_, _droit_ which are laden with the theory of Natural Law. It may then appear tempting to say that enactments which en-

---

[1] Austin, _The Province of Jurisprudence Defined_, Lecture V, pp. 184–5.
[2] Gray, _The Nature and Sources of the Law_, S. 213.
[3] Kelsen, _General Theory of Law and State_, p. 113.

joined or permitted iniquity should not be recognized as valid, or have the quality of law, even if the system in which they were enacted acknowledged no restriction upon the legislative competence of its legislature. It is in this form that Natural Law arguments were revived in Germany after the last war in response to the acute social problems left by the iniquities of Nazi rule and its defeat. Should informers who, for selfish ends, procured the imprisonment of others for offences against monstrous statutes passed during the Nazi régime, be punished? Was it possible to convict them in the courts of post-war Germany on the footing that such statutes violated the Natural Law and were therefore void so that the victims' imprisonment for breach of such statutes was in fact unlawful, and procuring it was itself an offence?[1] Simple as the issue looks between those who would accept and those who would repudiate the view that morally iniquitous rules cannot be law, the disputants seem often very unclear as to its general character. It is true that we are here concerned with alternative ways of formulating a moral decision not to apply, obey, or allow others to plead in their defence morally iniquitous rules: yet the issue is ill presented as a verbal one. Neither side to the dispute would be content if they were told, 'Yes: you are right, the correct way in English (or in German) of putting that sort of point is to say what you have said.' So, though the positivist might point to a weight of English usage, showing that there is no contradiction in asserting that a rule of law is too iniquitous to be obeyed, and that it does not follow from the proposition that a rule is too iniquitous to obey that it is not a valid rule of law, their opponents would hardly regard this as disposing of the case.

Plainly we cannot grapple adequately with this issue if we see it as one concerning the proprieties of linguistic usage. For what really is at stake is the comparative merit of a wider and a narrower concept or way of classifying rules, which belong to a system of rules generally effective in social life. If we are to make a reasoned choice between these concepts, it must be because one is superior to the other in the way in which it will

[1] See the judgment of 27 July 1945, Oberlandesgericht Bamberg, 5 *Süddeutsche Juristen-Zeitung*, 207: discussed at length in H. L. A. Hart, 'Legal Positivism and the Separation of Law and Morals', in *Harvard L. Rev.* lxxi (1958), 598, and in L. Fuller, 'Positivism and Fidelity to Law', ibid., p. 630. But note corrected account of this judgment *infra*, pp. 254–5.

assist our theoretical inquiries, or advance and clarify our moral deliberations, or both.

The wider of these two rival concepts of law includes the narrower. If we adopt the wider concept, this will lead us in theoretical inquiries to group and consider together as 'law' all rules which are valid by the formal tests of a system of primary and secondary rules, even though some of them offend against a society's own morality or against what we may hold to be an enlightened or true morality. If we adopt the narrower con- ✱ cept we shall exclude from 'law' such morally offensive rules. It seems clear that <u>nothing is to be gained in the theoretical or</u> NB . <u>scientific study of law as a social phenomenon by adopting the</u> <u>narrower concept: it would lead us to exclude certain rules even</u> <u>though they exhibit all the other complex characteristics of</u> <u>law.</u> Nothing, surely, but confusion could follow from a pro- posal to leave the study of such rules to another discipline, and certainly no history or other form of legal study has found it profitable to do this. If we adopt the wider concept of law, we ⌐ can accommodate within it the study of whatever special   NB features morally iniquitous laws have, and the reaction of society ⌐ to them. Hence the use of the narrower concept here must inevitably split, in a confusing way, our effort to understand both the development and potentialities of the specific method of social control to be seen in a system of primary and second- ary rules. Study of its use involves study of its abuse.

What then of the practical merits of the narrower concept of law in moral deliberation? In what way is it better, when faced with morally iniquitous demands, to think 'This is in no sense law' rather than 'This is law but too iniquitous to obey or apply'? Would this make men more clear-headed or readier to disobey when morality demands it? Would it lead to better ways of disposing of the problems such as the Nazi régime left behind? No doubt ideas have their influence; but it scarcely seems that an effort to train and educate men in the use of a narrower concept of legal validity, in which there is no place for valid but morally iniquitous laws, is likely to lead to a stiffening of resis- tance to evil, in the face of threats of organized power, or a clearer realization of what is morally at stake when obedience is demanded. So long as human beings can gain sufficient co-operation from some to enable them to dominate others, they will use the forms of law as one of their instruments. Wicked men will enact wicked rules which others will enforce. What surely is most needed in order to make men clear sighted in confronting the official abuse of power, is that they should preserve the sense that the certification of something as legally valid is not conclusive of the question of obedience, and that, however great the aura of majesty or authority which the official system may have, its demands must in the end be submitted to a moral scrutiny. This sense, that there is something outside the official system, by reference to which in the last resort the individual must solve his problems of obedience, is surely more likely to be kept alive among those who are accustomed to think that rules of law may be iniquitous, than among those who think that nothing iniquitous can anywhere have the status of law.

But perhaps a stronger reason for preferring the wider concept of law, which will enable us to think and say, 'This is law but iniquitous', is that to withhold legal recognition from iniquitous rules may grossly oversimplify the variety of moral issues to which they give rise. Older writers who, like Bentham and Austin, insisted on the distinction between what law is and what it ought to be, did so partly because they thought that unless men kept these separate they might, without counting the cost to society, make hasty judgments that laws were invalid and ought not to be obeyed. But besides this danger of anarchy, which they may well have overrated, there is another form of oversimplification. If we narrow our point of view and think only of the person who is called upon to *obey* evil rules, we may regard it as a matter of indifference whether or not he thinks that he is faced with a valid rule of 'law' so long as he sees its moral iniquity and does what morality requires. But besides the moral question of obedience (Am I to do this evil thing?) there is Socrates' question of submission: Am I to submit to punishment for disobedience or make my escape? There is also the question which confronted the post-war German courts, 'Are we to punish those who did evil things when they were permitted by evil rules then in force?' These questions raise very different problems of morality and justice, which we need to consider independently of each other: they cannot be solved by a refusal, made once and for all, to recognize evil laws as

valid for any purpose. This is too crude a way with delicate and ⌐
complex moral issues.

A concept of law which allows the invalidity of law to be
distinguished from its immorality, enables us to see the complexity and variety of these separate issues; whereas a narrow
concept of law which denies legal validity to iniquitous rules
may blind us to them. It may be conceded that the German
informers, who for selfish ends procured the punishment of
others under monstrous laws, did what morality forbad; yet
morality may also demand that the state should punish only
those who, in doing evil, did what the state at the time forbad.
This is the principle of *nulla poena sine lege*. If inroads have to be
made on this principle in order to avert something held to be a
greater evil than its sacrifice, it is vital that the issues at stake be
clearly identified. A case of retroactive punishment should not
be made to look like an ordinary case of punishment for an act
illegal at the time. At least it can be claimed for the simple
positivist doctrine that morally iniquitous rules may still be law,
that this offers no disguise for the choice between evils which,
in extreme circumstances, may have to be made.

X

INTERNATIONAL LAW

I. SOURCES OF DOUBT

THE idea of a union of primary and secondary rules to which so important a place has been assigned in this book may be regarded as a mean between juristic extremes. For legal theory has sought the key to the understanding of law sometimes in the simple idea of an order backed by threats and sometimes in the complex idea of morality. With both of these law has certainly many affinities and connexions; yet, as we have seen, there is a perennial danger of exaggerating these and of obscuring the special features which distinguish law from other means of social control. It is a virtue of the idea which we have taken as central that it permits us to see the multiple relationships between law, coercion, and morality for what they are, and to consider afresh in what, if any, sense these are necessary.

Though the idea of the union of primary and secondary rules has these virtues, and though it would accord with usage to treat the existence of this characteristic union of rules as a sufficient condition for the application of the expression 'legal system', we have not claimed that the word 'law' must be defined in its terms. It is because we make no such claim to identify or regulate in this way the use of words like 'law' or 'legal', that this book is offered as an elucidation of the *concept* of law, rather than a definition of 'law' which might naturally be expected to provide a rule or rules for the use of these expressions. Consistently with this aim, we investigated, in the last chapter, the claim made in the German cases, that the title of valid law should be withheld from certain rules on account of their moral iniquity, even though they belonged to an existing system of primary and secondary rules. In the end we rejected this claim; but we did so, not because it conflicted with the view that rules belonging to such a system must be called 'law', nor because it conflicted with the weight of usage. Instead we criticized the attempt to narrow the class of valid laws by the extrusion of what was morally iniquitous, on the ground that to do this did not advance or clarify either theoretical inquiries or moral deliberation. For these purposes, the broader concept which is consistent with so much usage and which would permit us to regard rules however morally iniquitous as law, proved on examination to be adequate.

International law presents us with the converse case. For, though it is consistent with the usage of the last 150 years to use the expression 'law' here, the absence of an international legislature, courts with compulsory jurisdiction, and centrally organized sanctions have inspired misgivings, at any rate in the breasts of legal theorists. The absence of these institutions means that the rules for states resemble that simple form of social structure, consisting only of primary rules of obligation, which, when we find it among societies of individuals, we are accustomed to contrast with a developed legal system. It is indeed arguable, as we shall show, that international law not only lacks the secondary rules of change and adjudication which provide for legislature and courts, but also a unifying rule of recognition specifying 'sources' of law and providing general criteria for the identification of its rules. These differences are indeed striking and the question 'Is international law really law?' can hardly be put aside. But in this case also, we shall neither dismiss the doubts, which many feel, with a simple reminder of the existing usage; nor shall we simply confirm them on the footing that the existence of a union of primary and secondary rules is a necessary as well as a sufficient condition for the proper use of the expression 'legal system'. Instead we shall inquire into the detailed character of the doubts which have been felt, and, as in the German case, we shall ask whether the common wider usage that speaks of 'international law' is likely to obstruct any practical or theoretical aim.

Though we shall devote to it only a single chapter some writers have proposed an even shorter treatment for this question concerning the character of international law. To them it has seemed that the question 'Is international law really law?' has only arisen or survived, because a trivial question about the meaning of words has been mistaken for a serious question about the nature of things: since the facts which differentiate international law from municipal law are clear and well known, the only question to be settled is whether we should observe the existing convention or depart from it; and this is a matter for each person to settle for himself. But this short way with the question is surely too short. It is true that among the reasons which have led theorists to hesitate over the extension of the word 'law' to international law, a too simple, and indeed absurd view, of what justifies the application of the same word to many different things has played some part. The variety of types of principle which commonly guide the extension of general classifying terms has too often been ignored in jurisprudence. Nonetheless, the sources of doubt about international law are deeper, and more interesting than these mistaken views about the use of words. Moreover, the two alternatives offered by this short way with the question ('Shall we observe the existing convention or shall we depart from it?') are not exhaustive; for, besides them, there is the alternative of making explicit and examining the principles that have in fact guided the existing usage.

The short way suggested would indeed be appropriate if we were dealing with a proper name. If someone were to ask whether the place called 'London' is *really* London, all we could do would be to remind him of the convention and leave him to abide by it or choose another name to suit his taste. It would be absurd, in such a case, to ask on what principle London was so called and whether this principle was acceptable. This would be absurd because, whereas the allotment of proper names rests *only* on an *ad hoc* convention, the extension of the general terms of any serious discipline is never without its principle or rationale, though it may not be obvious what that is. When as, in the present case, the extension is queried by those who in effect say, 'We know that it is called law, but is it really law?', what is demanded—no doubt obscurely—is that the principle be made explicit and its credentials inspected.

We shall consider two principal sources of doubt concerning the legal character of international law and, with them, the steps which theorists have taken to meet these doubts. Both forms of doubt arise from an adverse comparison of international law with municipal law, which is taken as the clear, standard example of what law is. The first has its roots deep in the conception of law as fundamentally a matter of orders backed by threats and contrasts the character of the *rules* of international law with those of municipal law. The second form of doubt springs from the obscure belief that states are fundamentally incapable of being the subjects of legal obligation, and contrasts the character of the *subjects* of international law with those of municipal law.

2. OBLIGATIONS AND SANCTIONS

The doubts which we shall consider are often expressed in the opening chapters of books on international law in the form of the question 'How can international law be binding?' Yet there is something very confusing in this favourite form of question; and before we can deal with it we must face a prior question to which the answer is by no means clear. This prior question is: what is meant by saying of a whole system of law that it is 'binding'? The statement that a particular rule of a system is binding on a particular person is one familiar to lawyers and tolerably clear in meaning. We may paraphrase it by the assertion that the rule in question is a valid rule, and under it the person in question has some obligation or duty. Besides this, there are some situations in which more general statements of this form are made. We may be doubtful in certain circumstances whether one legal system or another applies to a particular person. Such doubts may arise in the conflict of laws or in public international law. We may ask, in the former case, whether French or English Law is binding on a particular person as regards a particular transaction, and in the latter case we may ask whether the inhabitants of, for example, enemy-occupied Belgium, were bound by what the exiled government claimed was Belgian law or by the ordinances of the occupying power. But in both these cases, the questions are questions of law which arise *within* some system of law (municipal or international) and are settled by reference to the rules or principles of that system. They do not call in question the general character of the rules, but only their scope or applicability in given circumstances to particular persons or transactions. Plainly the question, 'Is international law binding?' and its congeners 'How can international law be binding?' or 'What makes international law binding?' are questions of a different order. They express a doubt not about the applicability, but about the general legal status of international law: this doubt would be more candidly expressed in the form 'Can such rules as these be meaningfully and truthfully said ever to give rise to obligations?' As the discussions in the books show, one source of doubt on this point is simply the absence from the system of centrally organized sanctions. This is one point of adverse comparison with municipal law, the rules of which are taken to be unquestionably 'binding' and to be paradigms of legal obligation. From this stage the further argument is simple: if for this reason the rules of international law are not 'binding', it is surely indefensible to take seriously their classification as law; for however tolerant the modes of common speech may be, this is too great a difference to be overlooked. All speculation about the nature of law begins from the assumption that its existence at least makes certain conduct obligatory.

In considering this argument we shall give it the benefit of every doubt concerning the facts of the international system. We shall take it that neither Article 16 of the Covenant of the League of Nations nor Chapter VII of the United Nations Charter introduced into international law anything which can be equated with the sanctions of municipal law. In spite of the Korean war and of whatever moral may be drawn from the Suez incident, we shall suppose that, whenever their use is of importance, the law enforcement provisions of the Charter are likely to be paralysed by the veto and must be said to exist only on paper.

To argue that international law is not binding because of its lack of organized sanctions is tacitly to accept the analysis of obligation contained in the theory that law is essentially a matter of orders backed by threats. This theory, as we have seen, identifies 'having an obligation' or 'being bound' with 'likely to suffer the sanction or punishment threatened for disobedience'. Yet, as we have argued, this identification distorts the role played in all legal thought and discourse of the ideas of obligation and duty. Even in municipal law, where there are effective organized sanctions, we must distinguish, for the variety of reasons given in Chapter III, the meaning of the external predictive statement 'I (you) are likely to suffer for disobedience', from the internal normative statement 'I (you) have an obligation to act thus' which assesses a particular person's situation from the point of view of rules accepted as guiding standards of behaviour. It is true that not all rules give rise to obligations or duties; and it is also true that the rules which do so generally call for some sacrifice of private interests, and are generally supported by serious demands for conformity and insistent criticism of deviations. Yet once we free ourselves from the predictive analysis and its parent conception of law as essentially an order backed by threats, there seems no good reason for limiting the normative idea of obligation to rules supported by organized sanctions.

We must, however, consider another form of the argument, more plausible because it is not committed to definition of obligation in terms of the likelihood of threatened sanctions. The sceptic may point out that there are in a municipal system, as we have ourselves stressed, certain provisions which are justifiably called necessary; among these are primary rules of obligation, prohibiting the free use of violence, and rules providing for the official use of force as a sanction for these and other rules. If such rules and organized sanctions supporting them are in this sense necessary for municipal law, are they not equally so for international law? That they are may be maintained without insisting that this follows from the very meaning of words like 'binding' or 'obligation'.

The answer to the argument in this form is to be found in those elementary truths about human beings and their environment which constitute the enduring psychological and physical setting of municipal law. In societies of individuals, approximately equal in physical strength and vulnerability, physical sanctions are both necessary and possible. They are required in order that those who would voluntarily submit to the restraints of law shall not be mere victims of malefactors who would, in the absence of such sanctions, reap the advantages of respect for law on the part of others, without respecting it themselves. Among individuals living in close proximity to each other, opportunities for injuring others, by guile, if not by open attack, are so great, and the chances of escape so considerable, that no mere natural deterrents could in any but the simplest forms of society be adequate to restrain those too wicked, too stupid or too weak to obey the law. Yet, because of the same fact of approximate equality and the patent advantages of

submission to a system of restraints, no combination of malefactors is likely to exceed in strength those who would voluntarily co-operate in its maintenance. In these circumstances,
which constitute the background of municipal law, sanctions
may successfully be used against malefactors with relatively
small risks, and the threat of them will add much to whatever
natural deterrents there may be. But, just because the simple
truisms which hold good for individuals do not hold good for
states, and the factual background to international law is so
different from that of municipal law, there is neither a similar
necessity for sanctions (desirable though it may be that international law should be supported by them) nor a similar
prospect of their safe and efficacious use.

This is so because aggression between states is very unlike
that between individuals. The use of violence between states
must be public, and though there is no international police force,
there can be very little certainty that it will remain a matter
between aggressor and victim, as a murder or theft, in the
absence of a police force, might. To initiate a war is, even for
the strongest power, to risk much for an outcome which is
rarely predictable with reasonable confidence. On the other
hand, because of the inequality of states, there can be no
standing assurance that the combined strength of those on the
side of international order is likely to preponderate over the
powers tempted to aggression. Hence the organization and use
of sanctions may involve fearful risks and the threat of them
add little to the natural deterrents. Against this very different
background of fact, international law has developed in a form
different from that of municipal law. In a population of a
modern state, if there were no organized repression and
punishment of crime, violence and theft would be hourly
expected; but for states, long years of peace have intervened
between disastrous wars. These years of peace are only rationally to be expected, given the risks and stakes of war and the
mutual needs of states; but they are worth regulating by rules
which differ from those of municipal law in (among other things)
not providing for their enforcement by any central organ. Yet
what these rules require is thought and spoken of as obligatory;
there is general pressure for conformity to the rules; claims and
admissions are based on them and their breach is held to

justify not only insistent demands for compensation, but re-
prisals and countermeasures. When the rules are disregarded,
it is not on the footing that they are not binding; instead efforts
are made to conceal the facts. It may of course be said that such
rules are efficacious only so far as they concern issues over
which states are unwilling to fight. This may be so, and may
reflect adversely on the importance of the system and its value
to humanity. Yet that even so much may be secured shows that
no simple deduction can be made from the necessity of organized sanctions to municipal law, in its setting of physical
and psychological facts, to the conclusion that without them
international law, in its very different setting, imposes no
obligations, is not 'binding', and so not worth the title of 'law'.

3. OBLIGATION AND THE SOVEREIGNTY OF STATES

Great Britain, Belgium, Greece, Soviet Russia have rights
and obligations under international law and so are among its
subjects. They are random examples of states which the layman
would think of as independent and the lawyer would recognize
as 'sovereign'. One of the most persistent sources of perplexity
about the obligatory character of international law has been
the difficulty felt in accepting or explaining the fact that a state
which is sovereign may also be 'bound' by, or have an obligation under, international law. This form of scepticism is, in a
sense, more extreme than the objection that international law
is not binding because it lacks sanctions. For whereas that would
be met if one day international law were reinforced by a system
of sanctions, the present objection is based on a radical inconsistency, said or felt to exist, in the conception of a state which
is at once sovereign and subject to law.

Examination of this objection involves a scrutiny of the
notion of sovereignty, applied not to a legislature or to some
other element or person *within* a state, but to a state itself.
Whenever the word 'sovereign' appears in jurisprudence, there
is a tendency to associate with it the idea of a person above the
law whose word is law for his inferiors or subjects. We have
seen in the early chapters of this book how bad a guide this
seductive notion is to the structure of a municipal legal system;
but it has been an even more potent source of confusion in the

theory of international law. It is, of course, *possible* to think of
a state along such lines, as if it were a species of Superman—
a Being inherently lawless but the source of law for its subjects.
From the sixteenth century onwards, the symbolical identification of state and monarch ('L'état c'est moi') may have en-
couraged this idea which has been the dubious inspiration of
much political as well as legal theory. But it is important for the
understanding of international law to shake off these associations. The expression 'a state' is not the name of some person
or thing inherently or 'by nature' outside the law; it is a way
of referring to two facts: first, that a population inhabiting a
territory lives under that form of ordered government provided
by a legal system with its characteristic structure of legislature,
courts, and primary rules; and, secondly, that the government
enjoys a vaguely defined degree of independence.

The word 'state' has certainly its own large area of vagueness
but what has been said will suffice to display its central meaning.
States such as Great Britain or Brazil, the United States or
Italy, again to take random examples, possess a very large
measure of independence from both legal and factual control
by any authorities or persons outside their borders, and would
rank as 'sovereign states' in international law. On the other
hand, individual states which are members of a federal union,
such as the United States, are subject in many different ways
to the authority and control of the federal government and
constitution. Yet the independence which even these federated
states retain is large if we compare it with the position, say, of
an English county, of which the word 'state' would not be used
at all. A county may have a local council discharging, for its
area, some of the functions of a legislature, but its meagre
powers are subordinate to those of Parliament and, except in
certain minor respects, the area of the county is subject to the
same laws and government as the rest of the country.

Between these extremes there are many different types and
degrees of dependence (and so of independence) between
territorial units which possess an ordered government. Colonies,
protectorates, suzerainties, trust territories, confederations,
present fascinating problems of classification from this point of
view. In most cases the dependence of one unit on another is
expressed in legal forms, so that what is law in the territory of

the dependent unit will, at least on certain issues, ultimately depend on law-making operations in the other.

In some cases, however, the legal system of the dependent territory may not reflect its dependence. This may be so either because it is merely formally independent and the territory is in fact governed, through puppets, from outside; or it may be so because the dependent territory has a real autonomy over its internal but not its external affairs, and its dependence on another country in external affairs does not require expression as part of its domestic law. Dependence of one territorial unit on another in these various ways is not, however, the only form in which its independence may be limited. The limiting factor may be not the power or authority of another such unit, but an international authority affecting units which are alike independent of each other. It is possible to imagine many different forms of international authority and correspondingly many different limitations on the independence of states. The possibilities include, among many others, a world legislature on the model of the British Parliament, possessing legally unlimited powers to regulate the internal and external affairs of all; a federal legislature on the model of Congress, with legal competence only over specified matters or one limited by guarantees of specific rights of the constituent units; a régime in which the only form of legal control consists of rules generally accepted as applicable to all; and finally a régime in which the only form of obligation recognized is contractual or self-imposed, so that a state's independence is legally limited only by its own act.

It is salutary to consider this range of possibilities because merely to realize that there are many possible forms and degrees of dependence and independence, is a step towards answering the claim that because states are sovereign they 'cannot' be subject to or bound by international law or 'can' only be bound by some specific form of international law. For the word 'sovereign' means here no more than 'independent'; and, like the latter, is negative in force: a sovereign state is one *not* subject to certain types of control, and its sovereignty is that area of conduct in which it is autonomous. Some measure of autonomy is imported, as we have seen, by the very meaning of the word state but the contention that this '*must*' be unlimited or '*can*' only be limited by certain types of obligation is at best the assertion of a claim that states ought to be free of all other restraints, and at worst is an unreasoned dogma. For if in fact we find that there exists among states a given form of international authority, the sovereignty of states is to that extent limited, and it has just that extent which the rules allow. Hence we can only know which states are sovereign, and what the extent of their sovereignty is, when we know what the rules are; just as we can only know whether an Englishman or an American is free and the extent of his freedom when we know what English or American law is. The rules of international law are indeed vague and conflicting on many points, so that doubt about the area of independence left to states is far greater than that concerning the extent of a citizen's freedom under municipal law. Nonetheless, these difficulties do not validate the *a priori* argument which attempts to deduce the general character of international law from an absolute sovereignty, which is assumed, without reference to international law, to belong to states.

It is worth observing that an uncritical use of the idea of sovereignty has spread similar confusion in the theory both of municipal and international law, and demands in both a similar corrective. Under its influence, we are led to believe that there *must* in every municipal legal system be a sovereign legislator subject to no legal limitations; just as we are led to believe that international law *must* be of a certain character because states are sovereign and incapable of legal limitation save by themselves. In both cases, belief in the necessary existence of the legally unlimited sovereign prejudges a question which we can only answer when we examine the actual rules. The question for municipal law is: what is the extent of the supreme legislative authority recognized in this system? For international law it is: what is the maximum area of autonomy which the rules allow to states?

Thus the simplest answer to the present objection is that it inverts the order in which questions must be considered. There is no way of knowing what sovereignty states have, till we know what the forms of international law are and whether or not they are mere empty forms. Much juristic debate has been confused because this principle has been ignored, and it is profitable to consider in its light those theories of international law which are known as 'voluntarist' or theories of 'auto-limitation'. These attempted to reconcile the (absolute) sovereignty of states with the existence of binding rules of international law, by treating all international obligations as self-imposed like the obligation which arises from a promise. Such theories are in fact the counterpart in international law of the social contract theories of political science. The latter sought to explain the facts that individuals, 'naturally' free and independent, were yet bound by municipal law, by treating the obligation to obey the law as one arising from a contract which those bound had made with each other, and in some cases with their rulers. We shall not consider here the well-known objections to this theory when taken literally, nor its value when taken merely as an illuminating analogy. Instead we shall draw from its history a threefold argument against the voluntarist theories of international law.

First, these theories fail completely to explain how it is known that states '*can*' only be bound by self-imposed obligations, or why this view of their sovereignty should be accepted, in advance of any examination of the actual character of international law. Is there anything more to support it besides the fact that it has often been repeated? Secondly, there is something incoherent in the argument designed to show that states, because of their sovereignty, *can* only be subject to or bound by rules which they have imposed upon themselves. In some very extreme forms of 'auto-limitation' theory, a state's agreement or treaty engagements are treated as mere declarations of its proposed future conduct, and failure to perform is not considered to be a breach of any obligation. This, though very much at variance with the facts, has at least the merit of consistency: it is the simple theory that the absolute sovereignty of states is inconsistent with obligation of any kind, so that, like Parliament, a state cannot bind itself. The less extreme view that a state may impose obligations on itself by promise, agreement, or treaty is not, however, consistent with the theory that states are subject only to rules which they have thus imposed on themselves. For, in order that words, spoken or written, should in certain circumstances function as a promise, agreement, or treaty, and so give rise to obligations and confer rights which others may claim, *rules* must already exist providing that a state is bound to do whatever it undertakes by appropriate words to do. Such rules presupposed in the very notion of a self-imposed obligation obviously cannot derive *their* obligatory status from a self-imposed obligation to obey them.

It is true that every specific *action* which a given state was bound to do might in theory derive its obligatory character from a promise; none the less this could only be the case if the *rule* that promises, &c., create obligations is applicable to the state independently of any promise. In any society, whether composed of individuals or states, what is necessary and sufficient, in order that the words of a promise, agreement, or treaty should give rise to obligations, is that rules providing for this and specifying a procedure for these self-binding operations should be generally, though they need not be universally, acknowledged. Where they are acknowledged the individual or state who wittingly uses these procedures is bound thereby, whether he or it chooses to be bound or not. Hence, even this most voluntary form of social obligation involves some rules which are binding independently of the choice of the party bound by them, and this, in the case of states, is inconsistent with the supposition that their sovereignty demands freedom from all such rules.

Thirdly there are the facts. We must distinguish the *a priori* claim just criticized, that states *can* only be bound by self-imposed obligations, from the claim that though they could be bound in other ways under a different system, in fact no other form of obligation for states exists under the present rules of international law. It is, of course, possible that the system might be one of this wholly consensual form, and both assertions and repudiations of this view of its character are to be found in the writings of jurists, in the opinions of judges, even of international courts, and in the declarations of states. Only a dispassionate survey of the actual practice of states can show whether this view is correct or not. It is true that modern international law is very largely treaty law, and elaborate attempts have been made to show that rules which appear to be binding on states without their prior consent do in fact rest on consent, though this may have been given only 'tacitly' or has to be 'inferred'. Though not all are fictions, some at least of these attempts to reduce to one the forms of international obligation excite the same suspicion as the notion of a 'tacit command' which, as we have seen, was designed to perform a similar, though more obviously spurious, simplification of municipal law.

A detailed scrutiny of the claim that all international obligation arises from the consent of the party bound, cannot be undertaken here, but two clear and important exceptions to this doctrine must be noticed. The first is the case of a new state. It has never been doubted that when a new, independent state emerges into existence, as did Iraq in 1932, and Israel in 1948, it is bound by the general obligations of international law including, among others, the rules that give binding force to treaties. Here the attempt to rest the new state's international obligations on a 'tacit' or 'inferred' consent seems wholly threadbare. The second case is that of a state acquiring territory or undergoing some other change, which brings with it, for the first time, the incidence of obligations under rules which previously it had no opportunity either to observe or break, and to which it had no occasion to give or withhold consent. If a state, previously without access to the sea, acquires maritime territory, it is clear that this is enough to make it subject to all the rules of international law relating to the territorial waters and the high seas. Besides these, there are more debatable cases, mainly relating to the effect on non-parties of general or multilateral treaties; but these two important exceptions are enough to justify the suspicion that the general theory that all international obligation is self-imposed has been inspired by too much abstract dogma and too little respect for the facts.

4. INTERNATIONAL LAW AND MORALITY

In Chapter V we considered the simple form of social structure which consists of primary rules of obligation alone, and we saw that, for all but the smallest most tightly knit and isolated societies, it suffered from grave defects. Such a régime must be static, its rules altering only by the slow processes of growth and decay; the identification of the rules must be uncertain; and the ascertainment of the fact of their violation in particular cases, and the application of social pressure to offenders must be haphazard, time-wasting, and weak. We found it illuminating to conceive the secondary rules of recognition, change, and adjudication characteristic of municipal law as different though related remedies for these different defects.

In form, international law resembles such a régime of primary rules, even though the content of its often elaborate rules are very unlike those of a primitive society, and many of its concepts, methods, and techniques are the same as those of modern municipal law. Very often jurists have thought that these formal differences between international and municipal law can best be expressed by classifying the former as 'morality'. Yet it seems clear that to mark the difference in this way is to invite confusion.

Sometimes insistence that the rules governing the relations between states are only moral rules, is inspired by the old dogmatism, that any form of social structure that is not reducible to orders backed by threats can only be a form of 'morality'. It is, of course, possible to use the word 'morality' in this very comprehensive way; so used, it provides a conceptual wastepaper basket into which will go the rules of games, clubs, etiquette, the fundamental provisions of constitutional law and international law, together with rules and principles which we ordinarily think of as moral ones, such as the common prohibitions of cruelty, dishonesty, or lying. The objection to this procedure is that between what is thus classed together as 'morality' there are such important differences of both form and social function, that no conceivable purpose, practical or theoretical, could be served by so crude a classification. Within the category of morality thus artificially widened, we should have to mark out afresh the old distinctions which it blurs.

In the particular case of international law there are a number of different reasons for resisting the classification of its rules as 'morality'. The first is that states often reproach each other for immoral conduct or praise themselves or others for living up to the standard of international morality. No doubt *one* of the virtues which states may show or fail to show is that of abiding by international law, but that does not mean that that law is morality. In fact the appraisal of states' conduct in terms of morality is recognizably different from the formulation of claims, demands, and the acknowledgements of rights and obligations under the rules of international law. In Chapter V we listed certain features which might be taken as defining characteristics of social morality: among them was the distinctive form of moral pressure by which moral rules are primarily supported. This consists not of appeals to fear or threats of retaliation or demands for compensation, but of appeals to conscience, made in the expectation that once the person addressed is reminded of the moral principle at stake, he may be led by guilt or shame to respect it and make amends.

Claims under international law are not couched in such terms though of course, as in municipal law, they may be joined with a moral appeal. What predominate in the arguments, often technical, which states address to each other over disputed matters of international law, are references to precedents, treaties and juristic writings; often no mention is made of moral right or wrong, good or bad. Hence the claim that the Peking Government has or has not a right under international law to expel the Nationalist forces from Formosa is very different from the question whether this is fair, just, or a morally good or bad thing to do, and is backed by characteristically different arguments. No doubt in the relations between states there are halfway houses between what is clearly law and what is clearly morality, analogous to the standards of politeness and courtesy recognized in private life. Such is the sphere of international 'comity' exemplified in the privilege extended to diplomatic envoys of receiving goods intended for personal use free of duty.

A more important ground of distinction is the following. The rules of international law, like those of municipal law, are often morally quite indifferent. A rule may exist because it is convenient or necessary to have some clear fixed rule about the subjects with which it is concerned, but not because any moral importance is attached to the particular rule. It may well be but one of a large number of possible rules, any one of which would have done equally well. Hence legal rules, municipal and international, commonly contain much specific detail, and draw arbitrary distinctions, which would be unintelligible as elements in moral rules or principles. It is true that we must not be dogmatic about the possible content of social morality: as we saw in Chapter V the morality of a social group may contain much by way of injunction which may appear absurd or superstitious when viewed in the light of modern knowledge. So it is possible, though difficult, to imagine that men with general beliefs very different from ours, might come to attach *moral* importance to driving on the left instead of the right of the road or could come to feel moral guilt if they broke a promise witnessed by two witnesses, but no such guilt if it was witnessed by one. Though such strange moralities are possible, it yet remains true that a morality cannot (logically) contain rules which are generally held by those who subscribe to them to be in no way preferable to alternatives and of no intrinsic importance. Law, however, though it also contains much that is of moral importance, can and does contain just such rules, and the arbitrary distinctions, formalities, and highly specific detail which would be most difficult to understand as part of morality, are consequently natural and easily comprehensible features of law. For one of the typical functions of law, unlike morality, is to introduce just these elements in order to maximize certainty and predictability and to facilitate the proof or assessments of claims. Regard for forms and detail carried to excess, has earned for law the reproaches of 'formalism' and 'legalism'; yet it is important to remember that these vices are exaggerations of some of the law's distinctive qualities.

It is for this reason that just as we expect a municipal legal system, but not morality, to tell us how many witnesses a validly executed will must have, so we expect international law, but not morality, to tell us such things as the number of days a belligerent vessel may stay for refuelling or repairs in a neutral port; the width of territorial waters; the methods to be used in their measurement. All these things are necessary and desirable provisions for *legal rules* to make, but so long as the sense is retained that such rules may equally well take any of several forms, or are important only as one among many possible means to specific ends, they remain distinct from rules which have the status in individual or social life characteristic of morality. Of course not all the rules of international law are of this formal, or arbitrary, or morally neutral kind. The point is only that legal rules *can* and moral rules *cannot* be of this kind.

The difference in character between international law and anything which we naturally think of as morality has another aspect. Though the effect of a law requiring or proscribing certain practices might ultimately be to bring about changes in the morality of a group, the notion of a legislature making or repealing moral rules is, as we saw in Chapter VII, an absurd one. A legislature cannot introduce a new rule and give it the status of a moral rule by its *fiat*, just as it cannot, by the same means, give a rule the status of a tradition, though the reasons why this is so may not be the same in the two cases. Accordingly morality does not merely lack or happen not to have a legislature; the very idea of change by human legislative *fiat* is repugnant to the idea of morality. This is so because we conceive of morality as the ultimate standard by which human actions (legislative or otherwise) are evaluated. The contrast with international law is clear. There is nothing in the nature or function of international law which is similarly inconsistent with the idea that the rules might be subject to legislative change; the lack of a legislature is just a lack which many think of as a defect one day to be repaired.

Finally we must notice a parallel in the theory of international law between the argument, criticized in Chapter V, that even if particular rules of municipal law may conflict with morality, none the less the system as a whole must rest on a generally diffused conviction that there is a moral obligation to obey its rules, though this may be overridden in special exceptional cases. It has often been said in the discussion of the 'foundations' of international law, that in the last resort, the rules of international law *must* rest on the conviction of states that there is a moral obligation to obey them; yet, if this means more than that the obligations which they recognize are not enforceable by officially organized sanctions, there seems no reason to accept it. Of course it is possible to think of circumstances which would certainly justify our saying that a state considered some course of conduct required by international law morally obligatory, and acted for that reason. It might, for example, continue to perform the obligations of an onerous treaty because of the manifest harm to humanity that would follow if confidence in treaties was severely shaken, or because of the sense that it was only fair to shoulder the irksome burdens of a code from which it, in its turn, had profited in the past when the burden fell on others. Precisely whose motives, thoughts and feelings on such matters of moral conviction are to be attributed to the state is a question which need not detain us here.

But though there *may* be such a sense of moral obligation it is difficult to see why or in what sense it *must* exist as a condition of the existence of international law. It is clear that in the practice of states certain rules are regularly respected even at the cost of certain sacrifices; claims are formulated by reference to them; breaches of the rules expose the offender to serious criticism and are held to justify claims for compensation or retaliation. These, surely, are all the elements required to support the statement that there exist among states rules imposing obligations upon them. The proof that 'binding' rules in any society exist, is simply that they are thought of, spoken of, and function as such. What more is required by way of 'foundations' and why, if more is required, must it be a foundation of moral obligation? It is, of course, true that rules could not exist or function in the relations between states unless a preponderant majority accepted the rules and voluntarily cooperated in maintaining them. It is true also that the pressure exercised on those who break or threaten to break the rules is often relatively weak, and has usually been decentralized or unorganized. But as in the case of individuals, who voluntarily accept the far more strongly coercive system of municipal law, the motives for voluntarily supporting such a system may be extremely diverse. It may well be that any form of legal order is at its healthiest when there is a generally diffused sense that it is morally obligatory to conform to it. Nonetheless, adherence to law may not be motivated by it, but by calculations of long-term interest, or by the wish to continue a tradition or by disinterested concern for others. There seems no good reason for identifying any of these as a necessary condition of the existence of law either among individuals or states.

5. ANALOGIES OF FORM AND CONTENT

To the innocent eye, the formal structure of international law lacking a legislature, courts with compulsory jurisdiction and officially organized sanctions, appears very different from that of municipal law. It resembles, as we have said, in form though not at all in content, a simple régime of primary or customary law. Yet some theorists, in their anxiety to defend against the sceptic the title of international law to be called 'law', have succumbed to the temptation to minimize these formal differences, and to exaggerate the analogies which can be found in international law to legislation or other desirable formal features of municipal law. Thus, it has been claimed that war, ending with a treaty whereby the defeated power cedes territory, or assumes obligations, or accepts some diminished form of independence, is essentially a legislative act; for, like legislation, it is an imposed legal change. Few would now be impressed by this analogy, or think that it helped to show that international law had an equal title with municipal law to be called 'law'; for one of the salient differences between municipal and international law is that the former usually does not, and the latter does, recognize the validity of agreements extorted by violence.

A variety of other, more respectable analogies have been stressed by those who consider the title of 'law' to depend on them. The fact that in almost all cases the judgment of the International Court and its predecessor, the Permanent Court of International Justice, have been duly carried out by the parties, has often been emphasized as if this somehow offset the fact that, in contrast with municipal courts, no state can be brought before these international tribunals without its prior consent. Analogies have also been found between the use of force, legally regulated and officially administered, as a sanction in municipal law and 'decentralized sanctions', i.e. the resort to war or forceful retaliation by a state which claims that its rights under international law have been violated by another. That there is some analogy is plain; but its significance must be assessed in the light of the equally plain fact that, whereas a municipal court has a compulsory jurisdiction to investigate the rights and wrongs of 'self help', and to punish a wrongful resort to it, no international court has a similar jurisdiction.

Some of these dubious analogies may be considered to have been much strengthened by the obligations which states have assumed under the United Nations Charter. But, again, any assessment of their strength is worth little if it ignores the extent to which the law enforcement provisions of the Charter, admirable on paper, have been paralysed by the veto and the ideological divisions and alliances of the great powers. The reply, sometimes made, that the law-enforcement provisions of municipal law *might* also be paralysed by a general strike is scarcely convincing; for in our comparison between municipal law and international law we are concerned with what exists in fact, and here the facts are undeniably different.

There is, however, one suggested formal analogy between international and municipal law which deserves some scrutiny here. Kelsen and many modern theorists insist that, like municipal law, international law possesses and indeed must possess a 'basic norm', or what we have termed a rule of recognition, by reference to which the validity of the other rules of the system is assessed, and in virtue of which the rules constitute a single system. The opposed view is that this analogy of structure is false: international law simply consists of a *set* of separate primary rules of obligation which are not united in this manner. It is, in the usual terminology of international lawyers, a set of customary rules of which the rule giving binding force to treaties is one. It is notorious that those who have embarked on the task have found very great difficulties in formulating the 'basic norm' of international law. Candidates for this position include the principle *pacta sunt servanda*. This has, however, been abandoned by most theorists, since it seems incompatible with the fact that not all obligations under international law arise from '*pacta*', however widely that term is construed. So it has been replaced by something less familiar: the so-called rule that 'States should behave as they customarily behave'.

We shall not discuss the merits of these and other rival formulations of the basic norm of international law; instead we shall question the assumption that it must contain such an element. Here the first and perhaps the last question to ask is: why should we make this *a priori* assumption (for that is what it is) and so prejudge the actual character of the rules of international law? For it is surely conceivable (and perhaps has often been the case) that a society may live by rules imposing obligations on its members as 'binding', even though they are regarded simply as a set of separate rules, not unified by or deriving their validity from any more basic rule. It is plain that the mere existence of rules does not involve the existence of such a basic rule. In most modern societies there are rules of etiquette, and, though we do not think of them as imposing obligations, we may well talk of such rules as existing; yet we would not look for, nor could we find, a basic rule of etiquette from which the validity of the separate rules was derivable.

Such rules do not form a system but a mere set, and, of course, the inconveniences of this form of social control, where matters more important than those of etiquette are at stake, are considerable. They have already been described in Chapter V. Yet if rules are in fact accepted as standards of conduct, and supported with appropriate forms of social pressure distinctive of obligatory rules, nothing more is required to show that they are binding rules, even though, in this simple form of social structure, we have not something which we do have in municipal law: namely a way of demonstrating the validity of individual rules by reference to some ultimate rule of the system.

There are of course a number of questions which we can ask about rules which constitute not a system but a simple set. We can, for example, ask questions about their historical origin, or questions concerning the causal influences that have fostered the growth of the rules. We can also ask questions about the value of the rules to those who live by them, and whether they regard themselves as morally bound to obey them or obey from some other motive. But we cannot ask in the simpler case one kind of question which we can ask concerning the rules of a system enriched, as municipal law is, by a basic norm or secondary rule of recognition. In the simpler case we cannot ask: 'From what ultimate provision of the system do the separate rules derive their validity or 'binding force'?' For there is no such provision and need be none. It is, therefore, a mistake to suppose that a basic rule or rule of recognition is a generally necessary condition of the existence of rules of obligation or 'binding' rules. This is not a necessity, but a luxury, found in advanced social systems whose members not merely come to accept separate rules piecemeal, but are committed to the acceptance in advance of general classes of rule, marked out by general criteria of validity. In the simpler form of society we must wait and see whether a rule gets accepted as a rule or not; in a system with a basic rule of recognition we can say before a rule is actually made, that it *will* be valid *if* it conforms to the requirements of the rule of recognition.

The same point may be presented in a different form. When such a rule of recognition is added to the simple set of separate rules, it not only brings with it the advantages of system and ease of identification, but it makes possible for the first time a new form

of statement. These are internal statements about the validity of
the rules; for we can now ask in a new sense, 'What provision
of the system makes this rule binding?' or, in Kelsen's language,
'What, within the system, is the reason of its validity?' The
answers to these new questions are provided by the basic rule
of recognition. But though, in the simpler structure, the validity
of the rules cannot thus be demonstrated by reference to any
more basic rule, this does not mean that there is some question
about the rules or their binding force or validity which is left
unexplained. It is not the case that there is some mystery as to
why the rules in such a simple social structure are binding,
which a basic rule, if only we could find it, would resolve.
The rules of the simple structure are, like the basic rule of the
more advanced systems, binding if they are accepted and
function as such. These simple truths about different forms of
social structure can, however, easily be obscured by the obsti-
nate search for unity and system where these desirable elements
are not in fact to be found.

There is indeed something comic in the efforts made to
fashion a basic rule for the most simple forms of social structure
which exist without one. It is as if we were to insist that a
naked savage *must* really be dressed in some invisible variety of
modern dress. Unfortunately, there is also here a standing
possibility of confusion. We may be persuaded to treat as a basic
rule, something which is an empty repetition of the mere fact
that the society concerned (whether of individuals or states)
observes certain standards of conduct as obligatory rules. This
is surely the status of the strange basic norm which has been
suggested for international law: 'States should behave as they
have customarily behaved'. For it says nothing more than that
those who accept certain rules must also observe a rule that the
rules ought to be observed. This is a mere useless reduplication
of the fact that a set of rules are accepted by states as binding
rules.

Again once we emancipate ourselves from the assumption
that international law *must* contain a basic rule, the question to
be faced is one of fact. What is the actual character of the rules
as they function in the relations between states? Different interpretations of the phenomena to be observed are of course
possible; but it is submitted that there is no basic rule providing

general criteria of validity for the rules of international law, and that the rules which are in fact operative constitute not a system but a set of rules, among which are the rules providing for the binding force of treaties. It is true that, on many important matters, the relations between states are regulated by multilateral treaties, and it is sometimes argued that these may bind states that are not parties. If this were generally recognized, such treaties would in fact be legislative enactments and international law would have distinct criteria of validity for its rules. A basic rule of recognition could then be formulated which would represent an actual feature of the system and would be more than an empty restatement of the fact that a set of rules are in fact observed by states. Perhaps international law is at present in a stage of transition towards acceptance of this and other forms which would bring it nearer in structure to a municipal system. If, and when, this transition is completed the formal analogies, which at present seem thin and even delusive, would acquire substance, and the sceptic's last doubts about the legal 'quality' of international law may then be laid to rest. Till this stage is reached the analogies are surely those of function and content, not of form. Those of function emerge most clearly when we reflect on the ways in which international law differs from morality, some of which we examined in the last section. The analogies of content consist in the range of principles, concepts, and methods which are common to both municipal and international law, and make the lawyers' technique freely transferable from the one to the other. Bentham, the inventor of the expression 'international law', defended it simply by saying that it was 'sufficiently analogous'[1] to municipal law. To this, two comments are perhaps worth adding. First that the analogy is one of content not of form: secondly that, in this analogy of content, no other social rules are so close to municipal law as those of international law.

[1] *Principles of Morals and Legislation*, xvii. 25, n. 1.

NOTES

THE text of this book is self-contained, and the reader may find it best to read each chapter through before turning to these notes. The footnotes in the text give only the sources of quotations, and references to cases or statutes cited. The following notes are designed to bring to the reader's attention matters of three different kinds, viz.: (i) further illustrations or examples of general statements made in the text; (ii) writings in which the views adopted or referred to in the text are further expounded or criticized; (iii) suggestions for the further investigation of questions raised in the text. All references to this book are indicated simply by chapter and section numbers. e.g. Chapter I, s. 1. The following abbreviations are used:

Austin, *The Province* Austin, *The Province of Jurisprudence Determined* (ed. Hart, London, 1954).

Austin, *The Lectures* Austin, *Lectures on the Philosophy of Positive Law.*

Kelsen, *General Theory* Kelsen, *General Theory of Law and State.*

B.Y.B.I.L. *British Year Book of International Law.*

H.L.R. *Harvard Law Review.*

L.Q.R. *Law Quarterly Review.*

M.L.R. *Modern Law Review.*

P.A.S. *Proceedings of the Aristotelian Society.*

CHAPTER I

Pages 1–2. Each of the quotations on these pages from Llewellyn, Holmes, Gray, Austin, and Kelsen, are paradoxical or exaggerated ways of emphasizing some aspect of law which, in the author's view, is either obscured by ordinary legal terminology, or has been unduly neglected by previous theorists. In the case of any important jurist, it is frequently profitable to defer consideration of the question whether his statements about law are literally true or false, and to examine first, the detailed reasons given by him in support of his statements and secondly, the conception or theory of law which his statement is designed to displace.

A similar use of paradoxical or exaggerated assertions, as a method of emphasizing neglected truths is familiar in philosophy. See J. Wisdom, 'Metaphysics and Verification' in *Philosophy and Psychoanalysis* (1953); Frank, *Law and the Modern Mind* (London, 1949), Appendix VII ('Notes on Fictions').

The doctrines asserted or implied in each of the five quotations on these pages are examined in Chapter VII, ss. 2 and 3 (Holmes, Gray, and Llewellyn); Chapter IV, ss. 3 and 4 (Austin); and Chapter III, s. 1, pp. 35–41 (Kelsen).

Page 4. Standard cases and borderline cases. The feature of language referred to here is generally discussed under the heading of 'The Open Texture of Law' in Chapter VII, s. 1. It is something to be kept in mind not only when a definition is expressly sought for general terms like 'law', 'state', 'crime', &c., but also when attempts are made to characterize the reasoning involved in the application of rules, framed in general terms, to particular cases. Among legal writers who have stressed the importance of this feature of language are: Austin, *The Province*, Lecture VI, pp. 202–7, and *Lectures in Jurisprudence* (5th ed., 1885), p. 997 ('Note on Interpretation'); Glanville Williams, 'International Law and the Controversy Concerning the Word "Law"', *22 B.Y.B.I.L.* (1945), and 'Language in the Law' (five articles), *61* and *62 L.Q.R.* (1945–6). On the latter, however, see comments by J. Wisdom in 'Gods' and in 'Philosophy, Metaphysics and Psycho-Analysis', both in *Philosophy and Psycho-Analysis* (1953).

Page 6. Austin on obligation. See *The Province*, Lecture I, pp. 14–18; *The Lectures*, Lectures 22 and 23. The idea of obligation and the differences between 'having an obligation' and 'being obliged' by coercion are examined in detail in Chapter V, s. 2. On Austin's analysis see notes to Chapter II, *infra*, p. 236.

Page 7. Legal and moral obligation. The claim that law is best understood through its connexion with morality is examined in Chapters VIII and IX. It has taken very many different forms. Sometimes, as in the classical and scholastic theories of Natural Law, this claim is associated with the assertion that fundamental moral distinctions are 'objective truths' discoverable by human reason; but many other jurists, equally concerned to stress the interdependence of law and morals, are not committed to this view of the nature of morality. See notes to Chapter IX, *infra*, p. 253.

Page 10. Scandinavian legal theory and the idea of a binding rule. The most important works of this school, for English readers, are Hägerström (1868–1939), *Inquiries into the Nature of Law and Morals* (trans. Broad, 1953), and Olivecrona, *Law as Fact* (1939). The clearest statement of their views on the character of legal rules is to be found in Olivecrona, op. cit. His criticism of the predictive analysis of legal rules favoured by many American jurists (see op. cit., pp. 85–88, 213–15) should be compared with the similar criticisms in Kelsen, *General Theory* (pp. 165 ff., 'The Prediction of the Legal Function'). It is worth inquiring why such different conclusions as to the character of legal rules are drawn by these two jurists in spite of their agreement on many points. For criticisms of the Scandinavian School, see Hart, review of Hägerström, op. cit. in *30 Philosophy* (1955); 'Scandinavian Realism', *Cambridge Law Journal* (1959); Marshall, 'Law in a Cold Climate', *Juridical Review* (1956).

Page 12. Rule-scepticism in American legal theory. See Chapter VII, ss. 1 and 2 on 'Formalism and Rule-scepticism', where some of the principal doctrines which have come to be known as 'Legal Realism' are examined.

Page 12. Doubt as to meaning of common words. For cases on the meaning of 'sign' or 'signature' see 34 Halsbury, *Laws of England* (2nd ed.), paras. 165–9 and In the Estate of Cook (1960), 1 A.E.R. 689 and cases there cited.

Page 13. *Definition.* For a general modern view of the forms and functions of definition see Robinson, *Definition* (Oxford, 1952). The inadequacy of the traditional definition *per genus et differentiam* as a method of elucidating legal terms is discussed by Bentham, *Fragment on Government* (notes to Chapter V, s. 6), and Ogden, *Bentham's Theory of Fictions* (pp. 75–104). See also Hart, 'Definition and Theory in Jurisprudence', 70 *L.Q.R.* (1954), and Cohen and Hart, 'Theory and Definition in Jurisprudence,' *P.A.S.* Suppl. vol. xxix (1955).

For the definition of the term 'law' see Glanville Williams, op. cit.; R. Wollheim, 'The Nature of Law' in 2 *Political Studies* (1954); and Kantorowicz, *The Definition of Law* (1958), esp. Chapter I. On the general need for, and clarificatory function of, a definition of terms, though no doubts are felt about their day-to-day use in particular cases, see Ryle, *Philosophical Arguments* (1945); Austin, 'A Plea for Excuses', 57 *P.A.S.* (1956–7), pp. 15 ff.

Page 15. *General terms and common qualities.* The uncritical belief that if a general term (e.g. 'law', 'state', 'nation', 'crime', 'good', 'just') is correctly used, then the range of instances to which it is applied must all share 'common qualities' has been the source of much confusion. Much time and ingenuity has been wasted in jurisprudence in the vain attempt to discover, for the purposes of definition, the common qualities which are, on this view, held to be the *only* respectable reason for using the same word of many different things (see Glanville Williams, op. cit. It is however important to notice that this mistaken view of the character of general words does not always involve the further confusion of 'verbal questions' with questions of fact which this author suggests).

Understanding of the different ways in which the several instances of a general term may be related is of particular importance in the case of legal, moral, and political terms. For analogy: see Aristotle, *Nichomachean Ethics*, i, ch. 6 (where it is suggested that the different instances of 'good' may be so related), Austin, *The Province*, Lecture V, pp. 119–24. For different relationships to a central case, e.g. healthy: see Aristotle, *Categories*, chap. I and examples in *Topics*, I, chap. 15, ii, chap. 9, of 'paronyms'. For the notion of 'family resemblance': see Wittgenstein, *Philosophical Investigations*, i, paras. 66–76. Cf. Chapter VIII, s. 1 on the structure of the term 'just'. Wittgenstein's advice (op. cit., para. 66) is peculiarly relevant to the analysis of legal and political terms. Considering the definition of 'game' he said, 'Don't say there *must* be something common or they would not be called 'games', but *look* and *see* whether there is anything common to all. For if you look at them you will not see anything common to *all* but similarities, relationships, and a whole series at that.'

CHAPTER II

Page 18. *The varieties of imperatives.* The classification of imperatives as 'orders', 'pleas', 'comments', &c., which depends upon many circumstances such as the social situation and relationships of the parties and their intentions as to the use of force, is as yet a virtually untapped subject of inquiry. Most philosophical discussion of imperatives is concerned either with (1) the relationships between imperative and indicative or descriptive language and the possibilities of reducing the former to the latter (see Bohnert, 'The Semiotic Status of Commands', *12 Philosophy of Science* (1945), or (2) the question whether any, and if so what, deductive relationships exist between imperatives (see Hare, 'Imperative Sentences', *Mind*, lviii (1949), also *The Language of Morals* (1952); Hofstadter and McKinsey, 'The Logic of Imperatives', *6 Philosophy of Science* (1939); Hall, *What is Value* (1952), chap. 6; and Ross, 'Imperatives and Logic', *11 Philosophy of Science* (1944)). Study of these logical questions is important; but there is also great need for a discrimination of the varieties of imperatives by reference to contextual social situations. To ask in what standard sorts of situation would the use of sentences in the grammatical imperative mood be normally classed as 'orders', 'pleas', 'requests', 'commands', 'directions', 'instructions', &c., is a method of discovering not merely facts about language, but the similarities and differences, recognized in language, between various social situations and relationships. The appreciation of these is of great importance for the study of law, morals, and sociology.

Page 18. Imperatives as the expressions of the wish that others should act or abstain from action. In characterizing in this way the standard use of the imperative mood in language, care must be taken to distinguish the case where the speaker simply reveals that he wishes another to act in a certain way, as a piece of information about himself, from the case where he speaks with the intention that the other shall be moved thereby to act as the speaker wishes. The indicative not the imperative mood would normally be appropriate in the former case (see on this distinction Hägerström, *Inquiries into the Nature of Law and Morals*, chap. 3, s. 4, pp. 116–26). But though it is necessary, it is not sufficient to characterize the standard use of the imperative mood that the speaker's purpose in speaking is that the other should act in the way he wishes; for it is also necessary that the speaker should intend the person addressed to recognize that this is his purpose in speaking and to be influenced thereby to act as the speaker desires. For this complication (which is neglected in the text) see Grice, 'Meaning', *66 Philosophical Review* (1957) and Hart, 'Signs and Words', *11 Philosophical Quarterly* (1952).

Page 19. The gunman situation, orders and obedience. One of the difficulties to be faced in the analysis of the general notion of an 'imperative' is that no word exists for what is common to orders, commands, requests, and many other varieties, i.e. the expression of intention that another should or should not do some action; similarly no single word exists for the performance of, or abstention from, such action. All the natural expressions (such as 'orders', 'demands', 'obedience', 'compliance') are coloured by the special features of the different situations in which they are normally used. Even the most colourless of these, viz. 'telling to' suggests some ascendancy of one party over the other. For the purpose of describing the gunman situation we have chosen the expressions 'orders' and 'obedience' since it would be perfectly natural to say of the gunman that he *ordered* the clerk to hand over the money, and that the clerk *obeyed*. It is true that the abstract *nouns* 'orders' and 'obedience' would not naturally be used to describe this situation, since some suggestion of authority attaches to the former and the latter is often considered a virtue. But in expounding and criticizing the theory of law as coercive orders we have used the nouns 'orders' and 'obedience' as well as the verbs 'order' and 'obey' without these implications of authority or propriety. This is a matter of convenience and does not prejudge any issue. Both Bentham (in *Fragment of Government*, chap. i, note to para. 12) and Austin (*The Province*, p. 14) use the word 'obedience' in this way. Bentham was aware of all the difficulties mentioned here (see *Of Laws in General*, 298 n.a.).

Page 20. *Law as coercive orders: relation to Austin's doctrine.* The simple model of law as coercive orders constructed in section 2 of this chapter differs from Austin's doctrine in *The Province* in the following respects.

(*a*) *Terminology.* The phrases 'order backed by threats' and 'coercive orders' are used instead of 'command' for the reasons given in the text.

(*b*) *Generality of laws.* Austin (op. cit., p. 19) distinguishes between 'laws' and 'particular commands' and asserts that a command is a law or rule if it 'obliges generally to acts or forbearances of a class'. On this view a command would be a law even if it were 'addressed' by the sovereign to a single individual so long as it required him to do or abstain from a class or kind of action and not merely a single act or a set of different actions specified individually. In the model of a legal system constructed in the text the orders are general, both in the sense that they apply to classes of individuals and refer to classes of acts.

(*c*) *Fear and obligation.* Austin occasionally suggests that a person is bound or obliged only if he *actually* fears the sanction (op. cit., pp. 15 and 24, and *The Lectures*, Lecture 22 (5th ed.), p. 444, 'The party is *bound* or *obliged* to do or forbear because he is obnoxious to the evil and because he fears the evil'). His main doctrine, however, seems to be that it is enough that there is the '*smallest* chance of incurring the slightest evil' whether the person bound fears it or not (*The Province*, p. 16). In the model of law as coercive orders we have stipulated only that there should be a *general belief* that disobedience is likely to be followed by the threatened evil.

(*d*) *Power and legal obligation.* Similarly, in his analysis of command and obligation, Austin at first suggests that the author of the command must actually possess the power (be 'able and willing') to inflict the eventual evil; but he later weakens this requirement to the smallest chance of the smallest evil (op. cit., pp. 14, 16). See on these ambiguities in Austin's definitions of command and obligation Hart, 'Legal and Moral Obligation', in Melden, *Essays in Moral Philosophy* (1958), and Chapter V, s. 2.

(*e*) *Exceptions.* Austin treats declaratory laws, permissive laws (e.g. repealing enactments), and imperfect laws as exceptions to his general definition of law in terms of command (op. cit., pp. 25–29). This has been disregarded in the text of this chapter.

(*f*) *The legislature as sovereign.* Austin held that in a democracy the electorate, and not their representatives in the legislature, constitute or form part of the sovereign body, though in the United Kingdom the only use made by the electorate of its sovereignty is to appoint its representatives, and to delegate to them the rest of their sovereign powers. Though he claimed that 'accurately speaking' this is the true position, he permitted himself to speak (as all constitutional writers do) of Parliament as possessing the sovereignty (op. cit., Lecture VI, pp. 228–35). In the text of this chapter a legislature such as Parliament is identified with the sovereign; but see Chapter IV, s. 4, for a detailed scrutiny of this aspect of Austin's doctrine.

(g) *Refinements and qualifications of Austin's doctrine.* In later chapters of this book certain ideas which have been used in defending Austin's theory against criticisms are considered in detail, though they are not reproduced in the model constructed in this chapter. These ideas were introduced by Austin himself though, in some cases, only in a sketchy or inchoate form, anticipating doctrines of later writers such as Kelsen. They include the notion of a 'tacit' command (see Chapter III, s. 3, *supra*, p. 45, and Chapter IV, s. 2, *supra*, p. 62); nullity as a sanction (Chapter III, s. 1); the doctrine that the 'real' law is a rule addressed to officials requiring them to apply sanctions (Chapter III, s. 1); the electorate as an extraordinary sovereign legislature (Chapter IV, s. 4); the unity and continuity of the sovereign body (Chapter IV, s. 4, p. 74). In any assessment of Austin attention should be paid to W. L. Morison, 'Some Myth about Positivism', *68 Yale Law Journal*, 1958, which corrects serious misunderstandings of earlier writers on Austin. See also A. Agnelli, *John Austin alle origini del positivismo giuridico* (1959), chap. 5.

CHAPTER III

Page 26. The varieties of law. The pursuit of a general definition of law has obscured differences in form and function between different types of legal rules. The argument of this book is that the differences between rules which impose obligations, or duties, and rules which confer powers, is of crucial importance in jurisprudence. Law can be best understood as a union of these two diverse types of rule. This is, accordingly, the main distinction between types of legal rule stressed in this chapter but many other distinctions could and, for some purposes, should be drawn (see Daube, *Forms of Roman Legislation* (1956), for further illuminating classifications of laws, reflecting their diverse social functions which is often evidenced by their linguistic form).

Page 27. Duties in criminal and civil law. In order to focus attention on the distinction between rules imposing duties and rules conferring powers, we have neglected many distinctions between the duties of the criminal law and those in tort and contract. Some theorists, impressed by these differences, have argued that, in contract and tort, the 'primary' or 'antecedent' duties to do or abstain from certain acts (e.g. to perform some act stipulated by contract or to abstain from libel) are illusory and the only 'genuine' duties are remedial or sanctioning duties to pay compensation in certain eventualities, including failure to perform the so-called primary duty (see Holmes, *The Common Law*, chap. 8, criticized by Buckland in *Some Reflections on*

Jurisprudence, p. 96, and in 'The Nature of Contractual Obligation', *8 Cambridge Law Journal* (1944); cf. Jenks, *The New Jurisprudence*, p. 179).

Page 27. Obligation and duty. In Anglo-American Law these terms are now roughly synonymous though, except in abstract discussions of the law's requirements (e.g. the analysis of legal obligation as opposed to moral obligation), it is unusual to refer to the criminal law as imposing obligations. The word 'obligation' is, perhaps, still most commonly used by lawyers to refer to contract or other cases, such as the obligation to pay compensation after the commission of a tort, where a determinate individual has a right against another determinate individual (right *in personam*). In other cases 'duty' is more commonly used. This is all that now survives in modern English legal usage of the original meaning of the Roman *obligatio* as a *vinculum juris* binding together determinate individuals (see Salmond, *Jurisprudence*, 11th ed., chap. 10, p. 260 and chap. 21; cf. also Chapter V, s. 2).

Page 28. Power-conferring rules. In continental jurisprudence rules which confer legal powers are sometimes referred to as 'norms of competence' (see Kelsen, *General Theory*, p. 90 and A. Ross, *On Law and Justice* (1958), pp. 34, 50–59, 203–25). Ross distinguishes between private and social competence (and so between private dispositions such as a contract and public legal acts). He also observes that norms of competence do not prescribe duties. 'The norm of competence is not immediately in itself a directive; it does not prescribe a procedure as a duty. . . . The norm of competence itself does not say that the competent person is obligated to exercise his competence' (op. cit., p. 207). It is, however, to be noted that in spite of making these distinctions, Ross adopts the view criticized in this chapter (*supra*, pp. 35–41) that norms of competence are reducible to 'norms of conduct' since both types of norm must 'be interpreted as directives to the Courts' (op. cit., p.33).

In considering the criticism in the text of the various attempts to eliminate the distinction between these two types of rule or to show that it is merely superficial, forms of social life other than law, where this distinction appears important, should be remembered. In morals, the vague rules which determine whether a person has made a binding promise confer limited powers of moral legislation on individuals and so need to be distinguished from rules which impose duties *in invitum* (see Melden, 'On Promising', 65 *Mind* (1956); Austin, 'Other Minds', *P.A.S.* Suppl. vol. xx (1946), reprinted in *Logic and Language*, 2nd series; Hart, 'Legal and Moral Obligation', in Melden, *Essays on Moral Philosophy*). The rules of any complex game may also be profitably studied from this point of view. Some rules (analogous to the criminal law) prohibit, under penalty, certain types of behaviour, e.g. fouling or disrespect to the referee. Other rules define the jurisdiction of officials of the game (referee, scorer, or umpire); others again define what must be done to score (e.g. goals or runs). Fulfilling the conditions for making a run or a goal marks a crucial phase towards winning; failure to fulfil them is a failure to score and from that point of view a 'nullity'. Here, prima facie, are different types of rule with diverse functions in the game. Yet a theorist might claim that they could and should be reduced to one type either because failure to score ('nullity') might be regarded as a 'sanction' or penalty for prohibited behaviour, or because all rules might be interpreted as directions to the officials to take certain steps (e.g. record a score or send players off the field) under certain circumstances. To reduce the two types of rule in this way to a single type would, however, obscure their character and subordinate what is of central importance in the game to what is merely ancillary. It is worth considering how far the reductionist legal theories, criticized in this chapter, similarly obscure the diverse functions which different types of legal rules have in the system of social activity of which they form part.

Page 29. Rules conferring judicial powers and additional rules imposing duties on the judge. The distinction between these two types of rule remains although the same conduct may be treated *both* as an excess of jurisdiction, rendering a judicial decision liable to be quashed as a nullity, *and* as a breach of duty under a special rule requiring a judge not to exceed his jurisdiction. This would be the case if an injunction could be obtained to prevent a judge trying a case outside his jurisdiction (or behaving in other ways which would invalidate his decision) or if penalties were prescribed for such behaviour. Similarly if a legally disqualified person participates in official proceedings this may expose him to a penalty as well as rendering the proceedings invalid. (See for such a penalty Local Government Act 1933, s. 76; *Rands* v. *Oldroyd* (1958), 3 A.E.R. 344. This Act, however, provides that the proceedings of a local authority shall not be invalidated by a defect in qualifications of its members (ib. Schedule III, Part 5 (5)).

Page 33. Nullity as a sanction. Austin adopts but does not develop this conception in *The Lectures*, Lecture 23, but see the criticisms of Buckland, op. cit., chap. 10.

Page 35. Power-conferring rules as fragments of rules imposing duties. The extreme version of this theory is elaborated by Kelsen in conjunction with the theory that the primary rules of law are the rules requiring courts or officials to apply sanctions under certain conditions (see *General Theory*, pp. 58–63 and (with reference to constitutional law) ib., pp. 143–4. 'The norms of the constitution are thus not independent complete norms; they are intrinsic parts of all the legal norms which the Courts and other organs have to apply'). This doctrine is qualified by its restriction to a 'static' as distinct from a 'dynamic' presentation of the law (ib., p. 144). Kelsen's exposition is also complicated by his claim that in the case of rules conferring private powers, e.g. to make a contract, the 'secondary norm' or duties created by the contract is 'not a mere auxiliary construction of juristic theory' (op. cit., pp. 90 and 137). But in essentials Kelsen's theory is that criticized in this chapter. See, for a simpler version, Ross's doctrine that 'Norms of competence are norms of conduct in indirect formulation' (Ross, op. cit., p. 50). For the more moderate theory reducing all rules to rules creating duties see Bentham, *Of Laws in General*, chap. 16 and Appendices A–B.

Page 39. Legal duties as predictions and sanctions as taxes on conduct. For both these theories see Holmes, 'The Path of the Law (1897), in *Collected Legal Papers*. Holmes thought it was necessary to wash the idea of duty in 'cynical acid', because it had become confused with moral duty. 'We fill the word with all the content which we draw from morals' (op. cit. 173). But the conception of legal rules as standards of conduct does not necessitate their identification with moral standards (see Chapter V, s. 2). For criticisms of Holmes's identification of duty with the 'prophecy that if he [the Bad Man] does certain things he will be subjected to disagreeable consequences' (loc. cit.) see A. H. Campbell, review of Frank's 'Courts on Trial', *13 M.L.R.* (1950); and also Chapter V, s. 2, Chapter VII, ss. 2 and 3.

The American courts have found difficulty in distinguishing a penalty from a tax, for the purposes of Article I, s. 8 of the U.S. constitution which confers power to tax on Congress. See *Charles C. Steward Machine Co.* v. *Davis*, 301 U.S. 548 (1937).

Page 40. The individual as duty-bearer and as private legislator. Cf. Kelsen's account of legal capacity and private autonomy (*General Theory*, pp. 90 and 136).

Page 42. Legislation binding the legislator. For criticisms of imperative theories of law on the ground that orders and commands apply only to others, see Baier, *The Moral Point of View* (1958), pp. 136–9. Some philosophers, however, accept the idea of a self-addressed command, and even use it in their analysis of first person moral judgments (see Hare, *The Language of Morals*, chaps. 11 and 12 on 'Ought'). For the analogy suggested in the text between legislation and the making of a promise see Kelsen, *General Theory*, p. 36.

Page 44. Custom and tacit commands. The doctrine criticized in the text is Austin's (see *The Province*, Lecture I, pp. 30–33 and *The Lectures*, Lecture 30). For the notion of tacit command and its use in explaining, consistently with imperative theory, the recognition of various forms of law, see Bentham's doctrines of 'adoption' and 'susception' in *Of Laws in General*, p. 21; Morison, 'Some Myth about Positivism', *68 Yale Law Journal* (1958); and also Chapter IV, s. 2. For criticism of the notion of a tacit command see Gray, *The Nature and Sources of the Law*, ss. 193–9.

Page 48. Imperative theories and statutory interpretation. The doctrine that laws are essentially orders and so expressions of the will or intention of a legislator is open to many criticisms besides those urged in this chapter. By some critics it has been held responsible for a misleading conception of the task of statutory interpretation as a search for 'the intention' of the legislator, without regard to the fact that where the legislature is a complex artificial body there may not only be difficulties in finding or producing evidence of its intention but no clear meaning is given to the phrase 'the legislature's intention' (see Hägerström, *Inquiries into the Nature of Law and Morals*, chap. iii, pp. 74–97, and for the fiction involved in the idea of legislative intention see Payne, 'The Intention of the Legislature in the Interpretation of Statute', *Current Legal Problems* (1956); cf. Kelsen, *General Theory*, p. 33, on the 'will' of the legislator).

CHAPTER IV

Page 49. *Austin on sovereignty.* The theory of sovereignty examined in this chapter is that expounded by Austin in *The Province*, Lectures V and VI. We have interpreted him as not merely offering certain formal definitions or an abstract scheme for the logical arrangement of a legal system, but as making the factual claim that in all societies, such as England or the United States, where there is law a sovereign with the attributes defined by Austin is somewhere to be found, though this may be obscured by different con-stitutional and legal forms. Some theorists have interpreted Austin dif-ferently as making no such factual claims (see Stone, *The Province and Function of Law*, chaps. 2 and 6, and especially pp. 60, 61, 138, 155 in which Austin's efforts to identify the sovereign in various communities are treated as irrelevant diversions from his main purpose). For criticisms of this view of Austin's doctrine see Morison, 'Some Myth about Positivism', loc. cit., pp. 217–22. Cf. Sidgwick, *The Elements of Politics*, Appendix (A) 'On Austin's Theory of Sovereignty'.

Page 53. *The continuity of legislative authority in Austin.* The brief references in *The Province* to persons who 'take the sovereignty in the way of succession' (Lecture V, pp. 152–4) are suggestive but obscure. Austin seems to admit that to account for the continuity of sovereignty through a succession of changing persons who acquire it, something more is required in addition to his key notions of 'habitual obedience' and 'commands', but he never clearly identifies the further element. He speaks in this connexion of a *'title'*, and of *'claims'* to succeed and also of a *'legitimate'* title, though all these expressions, as normally used, imply the existence of a *rule* regulating the succession and not merely *habits* of obedience to successive sovereigns. Austin's explanation of these terms and of the expressions 'generic title' and 'the generic mode' of acquiring sovereignty which he uses has to be spelt out of his doctrine con-cerning the 'determinate' character of the sovereign (op. cit., Lecture V, pp. 145–55). Here he distinguishes the case where the person or persons who are sovereign are identified individually, e.g. by name, from the case where they are identified 'as answering to some generic description'. Thus (to take the simplest example) in an hereditary monarchy the generic description might be 'the eldest living male descendant' of some given ancestor; in a parliamentary democracy it would be a highly complex description reproducing the qualifications for membership of the legislature.

Austin's view seems to be that when a person satisfies such a 'generic' description he has a 'title' or 'right' to succeed. This explanation in terms of the generic *description* of the sovereign is, as it stands, inadequate, unless Austin means by a 'description' in this context an accepted *rule* regulating the succession. For there is plainly a distinction between the case in which the members of a society each *as a matter of fact* habitually obey whoever for the time being answers to a certain description, and one in which a rule is accepted that whoever answers this description has a *right* or *title* to be obeyed. This is parallel to the difference between the case of persons who move a chess piece habitually in a certain way and those who, as well as doing this, accept the rule that this is the *right* way to move it. If there is to be a 'right' or 'title' to succeed, there must be a rule providing for the succession. Austin's doctrine of generic descriptions cannot take the place of such a rule though it plainly reveals its necessity. For somewhat similar criticism of Austin's failure to admit the notion of a rule qualifying persons as legislators, see Gray, *The Nature and Sources of the Law*, chap. iii, esp. ss. 151–7. Austin's account in Lecture V of the unity and the corporate or 'collegiate' capacity of the sovereign body suffers from the same defect (see s. 4 of this chapter).

Page 54. Rules and habits. The internal aspect of rules which is stressed here is discussed further in Chapters V, s. 2, p. 86 and s. 3, p. 96, VI, s. 1, and VII, s. 3. See also Hart, 'Theory and Definition in Jurisprudence', 29 *P.A.S.* Suppl. vol. (1955), pp. 247–50. For a similar view see Winch on 'Rules and Habits' in *The Idea of a Social Science* (1958), chap. ii, pp. 57–65, chap. iii, pp. 84–94; Piddington, 'Malinowski's Theory of Needs' in *Man and Culture* (ed. Firth).

Page 59. General acceptance of fundamental constitutional rules. The complex of different attitudes to rules of law on the part of officials and private citizens which is involved in the acceptance of a constitution and so in the existence of a legal system is examined further in Chapter V, s. 2, pp. 86–88, and Chapter VI, s. 2, pp. 111–14. See also Jennings, *The Law of the Constitution* (3rd ed.), Appendix 3: 'A Note on the Theory of Law'.

Page 62. Hobbes and the theory of tacit commands. See *ante*, Chapter III, s. 3, and notes thereto; also Sidgwick, *Elements of Politics*, Appendix A. For the partly similar 'realist' theory that even statutes of a contemporary legislature are not law until they are enforced, see Gray, *The Nature and Sources of the Law*, chap. 4; J. Frank, *Law and the Modern Mind*, chap. 13.

Page 64. Legal limitations on legislative power. Unlike Austin, Bentham held that the supreme power might be limited by 'express convention' and that laws made in breach of the convention would be void. See *A Fragment on Government*, chap. 4, paras. 26 and 34–38. Austin's argument against the possibility of a legal limitation on the power of the sovereign rests on the assumption that to be subject to such a limitation is to be subject to a *duty*. See *The Province*, Lecture VI, pp. 254–68. In fact, limitations on legislative authority consist of *disabilities* not duties (see Hohfeld, *Fundamental Legal Conceptions* (1923), chap. i).

Page 66. Provisions as to manner and form of legislation. The difficulty of distinguishing these from substantive limitations on legislative power is considered further in Chapter VII, s. 4, pp. 145–8. See Marshall, *Parliamentary Sovereignty and the Commonwealth* (1957), chaps. 1–6, for an exhaustive discussion of the distinction between 'defining' and 'fettering' the capacities of a sovereign body.

Page 71. Constitutional safeguards and judicial review. For constitutions where no judicial review is permitted see Wheare, *Modern Constitutions*, chap. 7. They include Switzerland (except cantonal legislation), the Third French Republic, Holland, Sweden. For the refusal of the U.S. Supreme Court to adjudicate claims of unconstitutionality which raise 'political questions' see *Luther* v. *Borden*, 7 Howard 1 12 L. Ed. 581 (1849); Frankfurter, 'The Supreme Court', in *14 Encyclopaedia of the Social Sciences*, pp. 474–6.

Page 73. The electorate as an 'extraordinary legislature'. For Austin's use of this notion in the effort to escape the objection that in many systems the ordinary legislature is subject to legal limitations, see *The Province*, Lecture VI, pp. 222–33 and 245–51.

Page 74. Legislators in their private and in their official capacity. Austin frequently distinguishes between members of the sovereign body 'considered severally' and 'considered as members or in their collegiate and sovereign capacity' (*The Province*, Lecture VI, pp. 261–6). But this distinction involves the idea of a rule regulating the legislative activity of the sovereign body. Austin only hints at an analysis of the notion of official or collegiate capacity in the unsatisfactory terms of a 'generic description' (see above note on p. 53).

Page 76. Limited scope of amending powers. See proviso to Article V of the United States Constitution. Articles 1 and 20 of the Basic Law of the German Federal Republic (1949) are placed altogether outside the scope of the amending power conferred by Article 79 (3). See also Article 1 and Article 102 of the Constitution of Turkey (1945).

CHAPTER V

Page 81. Obligation as the likelihood of threatened harm. For 'predictive' analyses of obligation see Austin, *The Province*, Lecture I, pp. 15–24, and *The Lectures*, Lecture 22; Bentham, *A Fragment on Government*, chap. 5, esp. para. 6 and note thereto; Holmes, *The Path of the Law*. Austin's analysis is criticized in Hart, 'Legal and Moral Obligation' in Melden, *Essays in Moral Philosophy*. For the general notion of obligation, cf. Nowell-Smith, *Ethics* (1954), chap. 14.

Page 85. Obligation and the figure of a bond ('*vinculum juris*'). See A. H. Campbell, *The Structure of Stairs Institute* (Glasgow, 1954), p. 31. Duty is derived through the French *devoir* from the Latin *debitum*. Hence the latent idea of a debt.

Page 85. Obligation and feelings of compulsion. Ross analyses the concept of validity in terms of two elements, viz. the effectiveness of the rule and 'the way it is felt to be motivating, that is, socially binding'. This involves an analysis of obligation in terms of a mental experience accompanying experienced patterns of behaviour. See Ross, *On Law and Justice*, chaps. i and ii, and *Kritik der sogennannten praktischen Erkenntniss* (1933), p. 280. For an elaborate discussion of the idea of duty in its relation to feeling see Hägerström, *Inquiries into the Nature of Law and Morals*, pp. 127–200, on which see Broad, 'Hägerström's Account of Sense of Duty and Certain Allied Experiences', *26 Philosophy* (1951); Hart, 'Scandinavian Realism' in *Cambridge Law Journal* (1959), pp. 236–40.

Page 86. The internal aspect of rules. The contrast between the external predictive point of view of the observer and the internal point of view of those who accept and use the rules as guides is made, though not in these terms, by Dickinson, 'Legal Rules. Their Function in the Process of Decision', *79 University of Pennsylvania Law Review*, p. 833 (1931). Cf. L.J. Cohen, *The Principles of World Citizenship* (1954), chap. 3. It is to be noted that from the external point of view, i.e. that of an observer who does not accept the rules of the society which he is observing, many different types of statements may be made, viz. (i) he may merely record the regularities of behaviour on the part of those who comply with the rules as if they were mere habits, without referring to the fact that these patterns are regarded by members of the society as standards of correct behaviour; (ii) he may, in addition, record the regular hostile reaction to deviations from the usual pattern of behaviour as something habitual, again without referring to the fact that such deviations are regarded by members of the society as reasons and justifications for such reactions; (iii) he may record not only such observable regularities of behaviour and reactions but also *the fact that* members of the society accept certain rules as standards of behaviour, and that the observable behaviour and reactions are regarded by *them* as required or justified by the rules. It is important to distinguish the external statement of fact asserting that members of society accept a given rule from the internal statement of the rule made by one who himself accepts it. See Wedberg, 'Some Problems on the Logical Analysis of Legal Science', *17 Theoria* (1951); Hart, 'Theory and Definition in Jurisprudence', *29 P.A.S.* Suppl. vol. (1955), pp. 247–50. See also Chapter VI, s. 1, pp. 99–102 and 106–7.

Page 89. Customary rules in primitive communities. Few societies have existed in which legislative and adjudicative organs and centrally organized sanctions were all entirely lacking. For studies of the nearest approximations to this state see Malinowski, *Crime and Custom in Savage Society*; A. S. Diamond, *Primitive Law* (1935), chap. 18; Llewellyn and Hoebel, *The Cheyenne Way* (1941).

Page 91. Adjudication without organized sanctions. For primitive societies in which provision is made for the settlement of disputes by rudimentary forms of adjudication though no system of centrally organized sanctions for enforcing decisions exists, see Evans-Pritchard on 'ordered anarchy' in *The Nuer* (1940), pp. 117 ff., quoted in Gluckman, *The Judicial Process among the Barotse* (1955), p. 262. In Roman law an elaborate system of litigation long preceded the provision of State machinery for enforcing judgments in civil cases. Until the later empire the successful plaintiff, if the defendant failed to pay, was left to seize him or his property. See Schulz, *Classical Roman Law*, p. 26.

Page 91. The step from the pre-legal into the legal world. See Baier on 'Law and Custom' in *The Moral Point of View*, pp. 127–33.

Page 92. Rule of recognition. For further discussion of this element in a legal system and its relation to Kelsen's Basic Norm (*Grundnorm*) see Chapter VI, s. 1 and Chapter X, s. 5 and notes thereto.

Page 92. *Authoritative texts of rules.* In Rome, according to tradition, the XII Tables were set up on bronze tablets in the market-place in response to the demands of the Plebeians for publication of an authoritative text of the law. From the meagre evidence available it seems unlikely that the XII Tables departed much from the traditional customary rules.

Page 94. *Contracts, wills, &c., as the exercise of legislative powers.* See, for this comparison, Kelsen, *General Theory*, p. 136, on the legal transaction as a 'law creating act'.

CHAPTER VI

Page 97. *Rule of recognition and Kelsen's 'basic norm'.* One of the central theses of this book is that the foundations of a legal system consist not in a general habit of obedience to a legally unlimited sovereign, but in an ultimate rule of recognition providing authoritative criteria for the identification of valid rules of the system. This thesis resembles in some ways Kelsen's conception of a basic norm, and, more closely, Salmond's insufficiently elaborated conception of 'ultimate legal principles' (see Kelsen, *General Theory*, pp. 110–24, 131–4, 369–73, 395–6, and Salmond, *Jurisprudence*, 11th ed., p. 137 and Appendix I). A different terminology from Kelsen's has, however, been adopted in this book because the view taken here differs from Kelsen's in the following major respects.

1. The question whether a rule of recognition exists and what its content is, i.e. what the criteria of validity in any given legal system are, is regarded throughout this book as an empirical, though complex, question of fact. This is true even though it is also true that normally, when a lawyer operating within the system asserts that some particular rule is valid he does not *explicitly state* but *tacitly presupposes* the fact that the rule of recognition (by reference to which he has tested the validity of the particular rule) exists as the accepted rule of recognition of the system. If challenged, what is thus presupposed but left unstated could be established by appeal to the facts, i.e. to the actual practice of the courts and officials of the system when identifying the law which they are to apply. Kelsen's terminology classifying the basic norm as a 'juristic hypothesis' (ib. xv), 'hypothetical' (ib. 396), a 'postulated ultimate rule' (ib. 113), a 'rule existing in the juristic consciousness' (ib. 116), 'an assumption' (ib. 396), obscures, if it is not actually inconsistent with, the point stressed in this book, viz. that the question what the criteria of legal validity in any legal system are is a question of fact. It is a factual question though it is one *about* the existence and content of a rule. Cf. Ago, 'Positive Law and International Law' in *51 American Journal of International Law* (1957), pp. 703–7.

2. Kelsen speaks of 'presupposing the *validity*' of the basic norm. For the reasons given in the text (pp. 105–7) no question concerning the validity or invalidity of the generally accepted rule of recognition as distinct from the factual question of its existence can arise.

3. Kelsen's basic norm has in a sense always the same content; for it is, in all legal systems, simply the rule that the constitution or those 'who laid down the first constitution' ought to be obeyed (*General Theory*, pp. 115–16).

This appearance of uniformity and simplicity may be misleading. If a constitution specifying the various sources of law is a living reality in the sense that the courts and officials of the system actually identify the law in accordance with the criteria it provides, then the constitution is accepted and actually exists. It seems a needless reduplication to suggest that there is a further rule to the effect that the constitution (or those who 'laid it down') are to be obeyed. This is particularly clear where, as in the United Kingdom, there is no written constitution: here there seems no place for the rule 'that the constitution is to be obeyed' in addition to the rule that certain criteria of validity (e.g. enactment by the Queen in Parliament) are to be used in identifying the law. This is the accepted rule and it is mystifying to speak of a rule that this rule be obeyed.

4. Kelsen's view (*General Theory*, pp. 373–5, 408–10) is that it is logically impossible to regard a particular rule of law as valid and at the same time to accept, as morally binding, a moral rule forbidding the behaviour required by the legal rule. No such consequences follow from the account of legal validity given in this book. One reason for using the expression 'rule of recognition' instead of a '*basic* norm' is to avoid any commitment to Kelsen's view of the conflict between law and morals.

Page 98. *Sources of law.* Some writers distinguish 'formal' or 'legal' from 'historical' or 'material' sources of laws (Salmond, *Jurisprudence*, 11th ed., chap. v). This is criticized by Allen, *Law in the Making*, 6th ed., p. 260, but this distinction, interpreted as a differentiation of two senses of the word 'source', is important (see Kelsen, *General Theory*, pp. 131–2, 152–3). In one sense (i.e. 'material', 'historical') a source is simply the causal or historical influences which account for the existence of a given rule of law at a given time and place: in this sense the source of certain contemporary English rules of law may be rules of Roman law or Canon law or even rules of popular morality. But when it is said that 'statute' is a source of law, the word 'source' refers not to mere historical or causal influences but to one of the criteria of legal validity accepted in the legal system in question. Enactment as a statute by a competent legislature is the *reason* why a given statutory rule is valid law and not merely the *cause* of its existence. This distinction between the historical cause and the reason for the validity of a given rule of law can be drawn only where the system contains a rule of recognition, under which certain things (enactment by a legislature, customary practice, or precedent) are accepted as identifying marks of valid law.

But this clear distinction between historical or causal sources and legal or formal ones may be blurred in actual practice and it is this which has led writers such as Allen (op. cit.) to criticize the distinction. In systems where a statute is a formal or legal source of law, a court in deciding a case is bound to attend to a relevant statute though no doubt it is left considerable freedom in interpreting the meaning of the statutory language (see Chapter VII, s. 1). But sometimes much more than freedom of interpretation is left to the judge. Where he considers that no statute or other formal source of law determines the case before him, he may base his decision on e.g. a text of the Digest, or the writings of a French jurist (see, for example, Allen, op. cit.,

260 et seq.). The legal system does not *require* him to use these sources, but it is accepted as perfectly proper that he should do so. They are therefore more than merely historical or causal influences since such writings are recognized as 'good reasons' for decisions. Perhaps we might speak of such sources as 'permissive' legal sources to distinguish them both from 'mandatory' legal or formal sources such as statute and from historical or material sources.

Page 100. *Legal validity and efficacy.* Kelsen distinguishes between the efficacy of a legal order which is, on the whole, efficacious and the efficacy of a particular norm (*General Theory*, pp. 41–42, 118–22). For him a norm is valid if, and only if, it belongs to a system which is *on the whole* efficacious. This view he also expresses, perhaps more obscurely, by saying that the efficacy of the system as a whole is a *conditio sine qua non* (a necessary condition) though not a *conditio per quam* (a sufficient condition: *sed quaere*) of the validity of its rules. The point of this distinction, expressed in the terminology of this book, is as follows. The general efficacy of the system is not a criterion of validity provided by the rule of recognition of a legal system, but is presupposed though not explicitly stated whenever a rule of the system is identified as a valid rule of the system by reference to its criteria of validity, and unless the system is in general efficacious, no meaningful statement of validity can be made. The view adopted in the text differs from Kelsen on this point since it is here argued that though the efficacy of the system is the *normal context* for making statements of validity, nonetheless, in special circumstances, such statements may be meaningful even if the system is no longer efficacious (see *ante*, p. 101).

Kelsen also discusses under the head of *desuetudo* the possibility of a legal system making the validity of a rule depend on its continued efficacy. In such a case efficacy (of a particular rule) would be part of the system's criteria of validity and not a mere 'presupposition' (op. cit., pp. 119–22).

Page 101. *Validity and prediction.* For the view that a statement that a law is valid is a prediction of future judicial behaviour and its special motivating feeling, see Ross, *On Law and Justice*, chaps. 1 and 2, criticized in Hart, 'Scandinavian Realism' in *Cambridge Law Journal* (1959).

Page 103. *Constitutions with limited amending powers.* See the cases of Western Germany and Turkey in notes to chapter V, *ante*, p. 243.

Page 107. *Conventional categories and constitutional structures.* For the allegedly exhaustive division into 'law' and 'convention' see Dicey, *Law of the Constitution*, 10th ed., pp. 23 ff.; Wheare, *Modern Constitutions*, chap. i.

Page 108. *The rule of recognition: law or fact?* See the arguments for and against its classification as political fact in Wade, 'The Basis of Legal Sovereignty', *Cambridge Law Journal* (1955), especially p. 189, and Marshall, *Parliamentary Sovereignty and the Commonwealth*, pp. 43–46.

Page 109. *The existence of a legal system, habitual obedience, and the acceptance of the rule of recognition.* For the dangers of over-simplifying the complex social phenomenon which involves both the ordinary citizen's obedience and acceptance on the part of officials of constitutional rules, see Chapter IV, s. 1, pp. 59–60, and Hughes, 'The Existence of a Legal System', *35 New York University L.R.* (1960), p. 1010, criticizing justly, on this point, the terminology used in Hart, 'Legal and Moral Obligation' in *Essays in Moral Philosophy* (Melden ed., 1958).

Page 114. Partial breakdown of legal order. Only a few of the many possible half-way states between full normal existence and non-existence of a legal system are noticed in the text. Revolution is discussed from the legal point of view in Kelsen, *General Theory*, pp. 117 et seq., 219 et seq., and at length by Cattaneo in *Il Concetto di Revoluzione nella Scienza del Diritto* (1960). The interruption of a legal system by enemy occupation may take many different forms, some of which have been categorized in international law: see McNair, 'Municipal Effects of Belligerent Occupation', *56 L.Q.R.* (1941), and the theoretical discussion by Goodhart in 'An Apology for Jurisprudence' in *Interpretations of Modern Legal Philosophies*, pp. 288 et seq.

Page 116. The embryology of a legal system. The development from colony to dominion traced in Wheare, *The Statute of Westminster and Dominion Status*, 5th ed., is a rewarding field of study for legal theory. See also Latham, *The Law and the Commonwealth* (1949). Latham was the first to interpret the constitutional development of the Commonwealth in terms of the growth of a new basic norm with a 'local root'. See also Marshall, op. cit., esp. chap. vii on Canada, and Wheare, *The Constitutional Structure of the Commonwealth* (1960), chap. 4 on 'Autochthony'.

Page 117. Renunciation of legislative power. See the discussion of the legal effect of s. 4 of the Statute of Westminister in Wheare, *The Statute of Westminster and Dominion Status*, 5th ed., pp. 297–8; *British Coal Corporation v. The King* (1935), A. C. 500; Dixon, 'The Law and the Constitution', *51 L.Q.R.* (1935); Marshall, op. cit., pp. 146 et seq.; also Chapter VII, s. 4.

Page 118. Independence not recognized by the parent system. See the discussion of the Irish Free State in Wheare, op. cit.; *Moore v. A.G. for the Irish Free State* (1935), A. C. 484; *Ryan v. Lennon* (1935), I.R.R. 170.

Page 118. Factual assertions and statements of law concerning the existence of a legal system. Kelsen's account (op. cit., pp. 373–83) of the possible relationships between municipal law and international law ('primacy of national law or primacy of international law') assumes that the statement that a legal system exists *must* be a statement of law, made from the point of view of one legal system about another, accepting the other system as 'valid' and as forming a single system with itself. The common-sense view that municipal law and international law constitute separate legal systems, involves treating the statement that a legal system (national or international) exists, as a statement of fact. This for Kelsen is unacceptable 'pluralism' (Kelsen, loc. cit.; Jones, 'The "Pure" Theory of International Law', *16 B.Y.B.I.L.* 1935), see Hart 'Kelsen's Doctrine of the Unity of Law' in *Ethics and Social Justice*, vol. 4 of *Contemporary Philosophical Thought* (New York, 1970).

Page 118. South Africa. For a full examination of the important juristic lesson to be learnt from the South African constitutional troubles, see Marshall, op. cit., chap. 11.

CHAPTER VII

Page 122. *Communication of rules by examples.* For a characterization of the use of precedent in these terms see Levi, 'An Introduction to Legal Reasoning', s. 1 in *15 University of Chicago Law Review* (1948). Wittgenstein in *Philosophical Investigations* (esp. i, ss. 208–38) makes many important observations concerning the notions of teaching and following rules. See the discussion of Wittgenstein in Winch, *The Idea of a Social Science*, pp. 24–33, 91–93.

Page 123. *Open texture of verbally formulated rules.* For the idea of open texture see Waismann on 'Verifiability' in *Essays on Logic and Language*, i (Flew ed.), pp. 117–30. For its relevance to legal reasoning see Dewey, 'Logical Method and Law', *10 Cornell Law Quarterly* (1924); Stone, *The Province and Function of Law*, chap. vi; Hart, 'Theory and Definition in Jurisprudence,' *29 P.A.S.* Suppl. vol., 1955, pp. 258–64, and 'Positivism and the Separation of Law and Morals', *71 H.L.R.* (1958), pp. 606–12.

Page 126. *Formalism and conceptualism.* Near synonyms for these expressions, used in legal writings, are 'mechanical' or 'automatic' jurisprudence, 'the jurisprudence of conceptions', 'the excessive use of logic'. See Pound, 'Mechanical Jurisprudence', *8 Columbia Law Review* (1908) and *Interpretations of Legal History*, chap. 6. It is not always clear precisely what vice is referred to in these terms. See Jensen, *The Nature of Legal Argument*, chap. i and review by Honoré, *74 L.Q.R.* (1958), p. 296; Hart, op. cit., *71 H.L.R.*, pp. 608–12.

Page 127. *Legal standards and specific rules.* The most illuminating general discussion of the character and relationships between these forms of legal control is in Dickinson, *Administrative Justice and the Supremacy of Law*, pp. 128–40.

Page 128. *Legal standards implemented by administrative rule-making.* In the United States the federal regulatory agencies such as the Interstate Commerce Commission and the Federal Trade Commission make rules implementing broad standards of 'fair competition', 'just and reasonable rates', &c. (See Schwartz, *An Introduction to American Administrative Law*, pp. 6–18, 33–37.) In England a similar rule-making function is carried out by the executive though usually without the formal quasi-judicial hearing of interested parties, familiar in the United States. Cf. the Welfare Regulations made under s. 46 of the Factories Act 1957 and the Building Regulations made under s. 60 of the same Act. The powers of the Transport Tribunal under the Transport Act 1947 to settle a 'charges scheme' after hearing objectors approximates more closely to the American model.

Page 129. *Standards of care.* For an illuminating analysis of the constituents of a duty of care see the opinion of Learned Hand J. in *U.S.* v. *Carroll Towing Co.* (1947), 159 F 2nd 169, 173. For the desirability of replacing general standards by specific rules see Holmes, *The Common Law*, Lecture, 3, pp. 111–19, criticized in Dickinson, op. cit., pp. 146–50.

Page 130. *Control by specific rules.* For the conditions making hard and fast rules rather than flexible standards the appropriate form of control, see Dickinson, op. cit., pp. 128–32, 145–50.

Page 131. *Precedent and the legislative activity of Courts.* For a modern general account of the English use of precedent see R. Cross, *Precedent in English Law* (1961). A well-known illustration of the narrowing process referred to in the text is *L. & S. W. Railway Co.* v. *Gomm* (1880), 20 Ch.D. 562, narrowing the rule in *Tulk* v. *Moxhay* (1848), 2 Ph. 774.

Page 132. *Varieties of rule-scepticism.* American writing on this subject can be illuminatingly read as a debate. Thus the arguments of Frank in *Law and the Modern Mind* (esp. chap. i and Appendix 2, 'Notes on Rule Fetishism and Realism'), and Llewellyn, *The Bramble Bush*, should be considered in the light of Dickinson, 'Legal Rules: Their Function in the Process of Decision', *79 University of Pennsylvania Law Review* (1931); 'The Law behind the Law', *29 Columbia Law Review* (1929); 'The Problem of the Unprovided Case' in *Recueil d'Études sur les sources de droit en l'honneur de F. Geny*, 11 chap. 5; and Kantorowicz, 'Some Rationalism about Realism' in *43 Yale Law Review* (1934).

Page 135. *The sceptic as a disappointed absolutist.* See Miller, 'Rules and Exceptions', *66 International Journal of Ethics* (1956).

Page 136. *Intuitive application of rules.* See Hutcheson, 'The Judgement Intuitive'; 'The Function of the "Hunch" in Judicial Decision', *14 Cornell Law Quarterly* (1928).

Page 138. *'The constitution is what the judges say it is.'* This is attributed to Chief Justice Hughes of the United States in Hendel, *Charles Evan Hughes and the Supreme Court* (1951), pp. 11–12. But see C. E. Hughes, *The Defence Court of the United States* (1966 ed.), pp. 37, 41 on the duty of Judges to interpret the Constitution apart from personal political views.

Page 145. *Alternative analyses of the sovereignty of Parliament.* See H. W. R. Wade, 'The Basis of Legal Sovereignty', *Cambridge Law Journal* (1955), criticized in Marshall, *Parliamentary Sovereignty and the Commonwealth*, chaps. 4 and 5.

Page 146. *Parliamentary sovereignty and divine omnipotence.* See Mackie, 'Evil and Omnipotence', *Mind*, 1955, p. 211.

Page 147. *Binding or redefining Parliament.* On this distinction see Friedmann, 'Trethowan's Case, Parliamentary Sovereignty and the Limits of Legal Change', *24 Australian Law Journal* (1950); Cowen, 'Legislature and Judiciary', *15 M.L.R.* (1952), and *16 M.L.R.* (1953); Dixon, 'The Law and the Constitution', *51 L.Q.R.* (1935); Marshall, op. cit., chap. 4.

Page 147. *Parliament Acts 1911 and 1949.* For the interpretation of these as authorizing a form of delegated legislation see H. W. R. Wade, op. cit., and Marshall, op. cit., pp. 44–46.

Page 148. *Statute of Westminster, s. 4.* The weight of authority supports the view that the enactment of this section could not constitute an irrevocable termination of the power to enact legislation for a dominion without its consent. See *British Coal Corporation* v. *The King* (1935), A.C. 500; Wheare, *The Statute of Westminster and Dominion Status*, 5th ed., pp. 297–8; Marshall, op. cit., pp. 146–7. The contrary view that 'Freedom once conferred cannot be revoked' was expressed by the South African Courts in *Ndlwana* v. *Hofmeyr* (1937), A.D. 229 at 237.

CHAPTER VIII

Page 153. *Justice as a distinct segment of morality*. Aristotle in *Nichomachean Ethics*, Book 5, chaps. 1–3, exhibits justice as specifically concerned with the maintenance or restoration of a balance or proportion (ἀναλογία) between persons. The best modern elucidations of the idea of justice are Sidgwick, *The Method of Ethics*, chap. 6, and Perelman, *De la Justice* (1945), followed in Ross, *On Law and Justice*, chap. 12. There is historical matter of great interest in Del Vecchio's *Justice*, reviewed by Hart in *28 Philosophy* (1953).

Page 156. *Justice in the application of the law*. The temptation to treat this aspect of justice as exhaustive of the idea of justice perhaps accounts for Hobbes's statement that 'no law can be unjust' (*Leviathan*, chap. 30). Austin in *The Province*, Lecture VI, p. 260 n., expresses the view that 'just is a term of relative import' and 'is uttered with relation to a determinate law which a speaker assumes as a standard of comparison'. Thus for him a law may be morally unjust if 'tried by' positive morality or the law of God. Austin thought that Hobbes merely meant that a law cannot be *legally* unjust.

Page 158. *Justice and equality*. For instructive discussions of the status of the principle that prima facie human beings should be treated alike, and its connexions with the idea of justice, see Benn and Peters, *Social Principles and the Democratic State*, chap. 5, 'Justice and Equality'; J. Rawls, 'Justice as Fairness', *Philosophical Review* (1958); Raphael, 'Equality and Equity', *21 Philosophy* (1946), and 'Justice and Liberty', *51 P.A.S.* (1951–2).

Page 158. *Aristotle on slavery*. See *Politics*, i, chap. ii, 3–22. He held that some who were slaves were not so 'by nature' and for them slavery was not just or expedient.

Page 159. *Justice and compensation*. This is clearly distinguished by Aristotle from justice in distribution, op. cit., Book V, chap. 4, though the unifying principle that there is, in all applications of the idea of justice, a 'just' or proper proportion (ἀναλογία) to be maintained or restored is stressed. See H. Jackson, *Book 5 of the Nichomachean Ethics* (Commentary: 1879).

Page 160. *Legal compensation for invasions of privacy*. For the argument that the law should recognize the right to privacy and that the principles of the common law require its recognition, see Warren and Brandeis, 'The Right to Privacy', *4 H.L.R.* (1890) and the dissenting judgment of Gray J., in *Roberson* v. *Rochester Folding Box Co.* (1902), 171 N.Y. 538. The English law of torts does not protect privacy as such, though it is now extensively protected in the United States. See for English law *Tolley* v. *J. S. Fry and Sons Ltd.* (1931), A.C. 333.

Page 161. *Conflict of justice between individuals and wider social interests*. See the discussion of strict liability and of vicarious liability in tort, in Prosser on *Torts*, chaps. 10 and 11, and Friedmann, *Law in a Changing Society*, chap. 5. On the justification of strict liability in crime see Glanville Williams, *The Criminal Law*, chap. 7; Friedmann, op. cit., chap. 6.

Page 162. *Justice and the 'common good'*. See Benn and Peters, *Social Principles and the Democratic State*, chap. 13, where seeking the common good is identified with acting justly or attending to the interests of all members of a society in a spirit of impartiality. This identification of the 'common good' with justice is not universally accepted. See Sidgwick, *The Method of Ethics*, chap. 3.

Page 163. *Moral obligation*. For the need to distinguish the obligation and duties of social morality both from moral ideals and personal morality, see Urmson, 'Saints and Heroes' in *Essays on Moral Philosophy* (Melden ed.); Whiteley, 'On Defining "Morality"', in *20 Analysis* (1960); Strawson, 'Social Morality and Individual Ideal' in *Philosophy* (1961); Bradley, *Ethical Studies*, chaps. 5 and 6.

Page 165. *The morality of a social group*. Austin in *The Province* uses the expression 'positive morality' to distinguish the actual morality observed within a society from the 'law of God', which constitutes for him the ultimate standards by which both positive morality and positive law are to be tested. This marks the very important distinction between a social morality and those moral principles which transcend it and are used in criticism of it. Austin's 'positive morality', however, includes all social rules other than positive law; it embraces rules of etiquette, games, clubs, and international law, as well as what is ordinarily thought and spoken of as morality. This wide use of the term morality obscures too many important distinctions of form and social function. See Chapter X, s. 4.

Page 167. *Essential rules*. See Chapter IX, s. 2, for the development of the idea that rules restricting the use of violence and requiring respect for property and promises constitute a 'minimum content' of Natural Law underlying both positive law and social morality.

Page 168. *Law and external behaviour*. The view criticized in the text that whereas the law requires external behaviour, and morality does not, has been inherited by jurists from Kant's distinction between juridical and ethical laws. See the General Introduction to the Metaphysic of Morals in Hastie, *Kant's Philosophy of Law* (1887), pp. 14 and 20–24. A modern restatement of this doctrine is in Kantorowicz, *The Definition of Law*, pp. 43–51, criticized by Hughes in 'The Existence of a Legal System', *35 New York University L.R.* (1960).

Page 173. *Mens rea and objective standards*. See Holmes, *The Common Law*, Lecture 11; Hall, *Principles of Criminal Law*, chaps. 5 and 6; Hart, 'Legal Responsibility and Excuses', in *Determinism and Freedom* (ed. Hook).

Page 174. *Justification and excuse.* On this distinction in the law of homicide see Kenny, *Outlines of Criminal Law* (24th ed.), pp. 109–16. For its general moral importance see Austin, 'A Plea for Excuses', 57 *P.A.S.* (1956–7); Hart, 'Prolegomenon to the Principles of Punishment', 60 *P.A.S.* (1959–60), p. 12. For a similar distinction see Bentham, *Of Laws in General,* pp. 121–2 on 'exemption' and 'exculpation'.

Page 176. *Morality, human needs, and interests.* For the view that the criterion for calling a rule a moral rule is that it is the product of reasoned and impartial consideration of the interests of those affected, see Benn and Peters, *Social Principles of the Democratic State,* chap. 2. Contrast Devlin, *The Enforcement of Morals* (1959).

CHAPTER IX

Page 181. *Natural Law.* The existence of a vast literature of comment on classical, scholastic, and modern conceptions of Natural Law and the ambiguities of the expression 'positivism' (see *infra*) often make it difficult to see precisely what issue is at stake when Natural Law is opposed to Legal Positivism. An effort is made in the text to identify one such issue. But very little can be gained from a discussion of this subject if only secondary sources are read. Some first-hand acquaintance with the vocabulary and philosophical presuppositions of the primary sources is indispensable. The following represent an easily accessible minimum. Aristotle, *Physics,* ii, chap. 8 (trans. Ross, Oxford); Aquinas, *Summa Theologica,* Quaestiones 90–97 (available with translation in D'Entrèves, *Aquinas: Selected Political Writings,* Oxford, 1948); Grotius, *On the Law of War and Peace; Prolegomena* (trans. in The Classics of International Law, vol. 3, Oxford, 1925); Blackstone, *Commentaries,* Introduction, s. 2.

Page 181. *Legal Positivism.* The expression 'positivism' is used in contemporary Anglo-American literature to designate one or more of the following contentions: (1) that laws are commands of human beings; (2) that there is no necessary connexion between law and morals, or law as it is and law as it ought to be; (3) that the analysis or study of meanings of legal concepts is an important study to be distinguished from (though in no way hostile to) historical inquiries, sociological inquiries, and the critical appraisal of law in terms of morals, social aims, functions, &c; (4) that a legal system is a 'closed logical system' in which correct decisions can be deduced from pre-determined legal rules by logical means alone; (5) that moral judgments cannot be established, as statements of fact can, by rational argument, evidence or proof ('non cognitivism in ethics'). Bentham and Austin held the views expressed in (1), (2), and (3) but not those in (4) and (5); Kelsen holds those expressed in (2), (3), and (5) but not those in (1) or (4). Contention (4) is often ascribed to 'analytical jurists' but apparently without good reason.

In continental literature the expression 'positivism' is often used for the general repudiation of the claim that some principles or rules of human conduct are discoverable by reason alone. See the valuable discussion of the ambiguities of 'positivism' by Ago, op. cit., in *51 American Journal of International Law* (1957).

Page 182. *Mill on Natural Law.* See his Essay on Nature in *Nature, the Utility of Religion and Theism.*

Page 183. *Blackstone and Bentham on Natural Law.* Blackstone, loc. cit., and Bentham, *Comment on the Commentaries*, ss. 1–6.

Page 189. *The minimum content of natural law.* This empirical version of natural law is based on Hobbes, *Leviathan*, chaps. 14 and 15, and Hume, *Treatise of Human Nature*, Book III, part 2; esp. ss. 2 and 4–7.

Page 196. *Huckleberry Finn.* Mark Twain's novel is a profound study of the moral dilemma created by the existence of a social morality which runs counter to the sympathies of an individual and to humanitarianism. It is a valuable corrective of the identification of all morality with the latter.

Page 196. *Slavery.* For Aristotle a slave was 'a living instrument'. (*Politics*, I, chap. 2–4).

Page 199. *The influence of morality on law.* Valuable studies of the ways in which the *development* of law has been influenced by morality are Ames, 'Law and Morals', *22 H.L.R.* (1908); Pound, *Law and Morals* (1926); Goodhart, *English Law and the Moral Law* (1953). Austin fully recognized this factual or causal connexion. See *The Province*, Lecture V, p. 162.

Page 200. *Interpretation.* On the place of moral considerations in the interpretation of law see Lamont, *The Value Judgment*, pp. 296–31; Wechsler, 'Towards Neutral Principles of Constitutional Law', *73 H.L.R.* i, p. 960; Hart, op. cit., in *71 H. L. R.*, pp. 606–15, and Fuller's criticism, ib. 661 *ad fin.* For Austin's recognition of the area left open for judicial choice between 'competing analogies' and his criticism of the judges' failure to adapt their decisions to the standard of utility, see *The Lectures*, Lectures 37 and 38.

Page 201. *Criticism of law and the right of all men to equal consideration.* See Benn and Peters, *Social Principles and the Democratic State*, chaps. 2 and 5, and Baier, *The Moral Point of View*, chap. 8, for the view that the recognition of such a right is not merely one among many possible moralities but a defining feature of true morality.

Page 202. *Principles of legality and justice.* See Hall, *Principles of Criminal Law*, chap. i and, for the 'internal morality of law', see Fuller, op. cit., *71 H.L.R.* (1958), pp. 644–8.

Page 204. *Revival of Natural Law doctrines in post-war Germany.* See for a discussion of the later views of G. Radbruch, Hart, and reply by Fuller in op. cit. in *71 H.L.R.* (1958). The discussion there of the decision of the Oberlandsgericht Bamberg of July 1949, in which a wife who had denounced her husband for an offence against a Nazi statute of 1934 was convicted of unlawfully depriving him of his freedom, proceeded on the footing that the account of the case in *64 H.L.R.* (1951), p. 1005, was correct and that the

German court held the statute of 1934 to be invalid. The accuracy of this account has recently been challenged by Pappe, 'On the Validity of Judicial Decisions in the Nazi Era', *23 M.L.R.* (1960). Dr. Pappe's criticism is well founded and the case as discussed by Hart should strictly be regarded as hypothetical. As Dr. Pappe shows (op. cit., p. 263), in the actual case the court (Provincial Court of Appeal), after accepting the theoretical possibility that statutes might be unlawful if they violated Natural Law, held that the Nazi statute in question did not violate it; the accused was held guilty of an unlawful deprivation of liberty since she had no duty to inform, but did so for purely personal reasons and must have realized that to do so was in the circumstances 'contrary to the sound conscience and sense of justice of all decent human beings'. Dr. Pappe's careful analysis of a decision of the German Supreme Court in a similar case should be studied (ib., p. 268 *ad fin.*).

CHAPTER X

Page 209. '*Is international law really law?*' For the view that this is a merely verbal question mistaken for a question of fact see Glanville Williams, op. cit., in *22 B.Y.B.I.L.* (1945).

Page 210. *Sources of doubt.* For a constructive general survey see A. H. Campbell, 'International Law and the Student of Jurisprudence' in *35 Grotius Society Proceedings* (1950); Gihl, 'The Legal Character and Sources of International Law' in *Scandinavian Studies in Law* (1957).

Page 211. '*How can international law be binding?*' This question (sometimes referred to as 'the problem of the binding force' of international law) is raised by Fischer Williams, *Chapters on Current International Law*, pp. 11–27; Brierly, *The Law of Nations*, 5th ed. (1955), chap. 2; *The Basis of Obligation in International Law* (1958), chap. 1. See also Fitzmaurice, 'The Foundations of the Authority of International Law and the Problem of Enforcement' in *19 M.L.R.* (1956). These authors do not explicitly discuss the meaning of the assertion that a system of rules is (or is not) binding.

Page 212. *Sanctions in International Law.* For the position under Art. 16 of the Covenant of the League of Nations see Fischer Williams, 'Sanctions under the Covenant' in *17 B.Y.B.I.L.* (1936). For sanctions under chapter vii of the U.N. Charter see Kelsen, 'Sanctions in International Law under the Charter of U.N.', *31 Iowa L.R.* (1946), and Tucker, 'The Interpretation of War under present International Law', *4 The International Law Quarterly* (1951). On the Korean War, see Stone, *Legal Controls of International Conflict* (1954), chap. ix, Discourse 14. It is of course arguable that the Uniting for Peace Resolution showed that the United Nations was not 'paralyzed'.

Page 214. *International Law thought and spoken of as obligatory.* See Jessup, *A Modern Law of Nations*, chap. 1, and 'The Reality of International Law', *118 Foreign Affairs* (1940).

Page 215. *The Sovereignty of States.* For a clear exposition of the view that 'sovereignty is only a name given to so much of the international field as is left by law to the individual action of states' see Fischer Williams, op. cit., pp. 10–11, 285–99, and *Aspects of Modern International Law*, pp. 24–26, and Van Kleffens, 'Sovereignty and International Law', *Recueil des Cours* (1953), i, pp. 82–83.

Page 216. The State. For the notion of a 'state' and types of dependent states see Brierly, *The Law of Nations*, chap. 4.

Page 219. Voluntarist and 'Auto-limitation' theories. The principal authors are Jellinek, *Die Rechtliche Natur der Staatsverträge*; Triepel, 'Les Rapports entre le droit interne et la droit internationale', *Recueil des Cours* (1923). The extreme view is that of Zorn, *Grundzüge des Völkerrechts*. See the critical discussion of this form of 'positivism' in Gihl, op. cit., in *Scandinavian Studies in Law* (1957); Starke, *An Introduction to International Law*, chap. 1; Fischer Williams, *Chapters on Current International Law*, pp. 11–16.

Page 219. Obligation and consent. The view that no rule of international law is binding on a state without its prior consent, express or tacit, has been expressed by English courts (see *R. v. Keyn* 1876, 2 Ex. Div. 63, 'The Franconia') and also by the Permanent Court of International Justice. See *The Lotus*, P.C.I.J. Series A, No. 10.

Page 221. New States and States acquiring maritime territory. See Kelsen, *Principles of International Law*, pp. 312–13.

Page 221. Effect on non-parties of general international treaties. See Kelsen, op. cit., 345 ff.; Starke, op. cit., chap. 1; Brierly, op. cit., chap. vii, pp. 251–2.

Page 222. Comprehensive use of term 'morality'. See Austin on 'positive morality' in *The Province*, Lecture V, pp. 125–9, 141–2.

Page 225. Moral obligation to obey international law. For the view that this is 'the foundation' of international law see Lauterpacht, Introduction to Brierly's *The Base of Obligation in International Law*, xviii, and Brierly, ib., chap. 1.

Page 227. Treaty imposed by force as legislation. See Scott, 'The Legal Nature of International Law' in *American Journal of International Law* (1907) at pp. 837, 862–4. For criticism of the common description of general treaties as 'international legislation' see Jennings, 'The Progressive Development of International Law and its Codification', *24 B.Y.B.I.L.* (1947) at p. 303.

Page 227. Decentralized sanctions. See Kelsen, op. cit., p. 20, and Tucker in op. cit., *4 International Law Quarterly* (1951).

Page 228. The basic norm of international law. For its formulation as *pacta sunt servanda* see Anzilotti, *Corso di diritto internazionale* (1923), p. 40. For the substitution of 'States ought to behave as they have customarily behaved' see Kelsen, *General Theory*, p. 369, and *Principles of International Law*, p. 418. See the important critical discussion by Gihl, *International Legislation* (1937) and op. cit. in *Scandinavian Studies in Law* (1957), pp. 62 et seq. For the fuller development of the interpretation of international law as containing no basic norm see Ago, 'Positive Law and International Law' in *51 American Journal of International Law* (1957) and *Scienza giuridica e diritto internazionale* (1958). Gihl draws the conclusion that in spite of Article 38 of the Statute of the International Court international law has no formal sources of law. See for an attempt to formulate for international law an 'initial hypothesis' which seems open to similar criticisms to those urged in the text, Lauterpacht, *The Future of Law in the International Community*, pp. 420-3.

Page 231. Analogy of content between international law and municipal law. See Campbell, op. cit. in *35 Grotius Society Proceedings* (1950), p. 121 *ad fin.*, and the discussion of treaties and the rules governing acquisition of territory, prescriptions, leases, mandates, servitudes, &c., in Lauterpacht, *Private Law Sources and Analogies of International Law* (1927).

SELECT BIBLIOGRAPHY OF CRITICAL WRITINGS

I

BOOKS

Carrio, *Legal Principles and Legal Positivism*, Buenos Aires, 1971.

Eckmann, *Rechtspositivismus und Sprachanalytische Philosophie*, Berlin, 1969.

Fuller, *The Morality of Law*, ch. V, revised ed., Yale, 1969.

Gavazzi, *Norme primarie e norme secondarie*, Turin, 1967.

Raz, *The Concept of a Legal System*, chs. VI and VIII, Oxford, 1970.

Scarpelli, *Cos' è il positivismo giuridico*, ch. VII, Milan, 1965.

II

ARTICLES

Bedau, 'Law, Legal Systems and Types of Legal Rules' in *Memoria del XIII Congreso Internacional de Filosofia* (Mexico), vol. VII (1964). 17.

Bobbio, 'Nouvelles Réflexions sur les normes primaires et secondaires' in *La Règle de Droit* ed. Perelman, Brussels (1971). 104.

— 'Ancora delle norme primarie e secondarie' 59 *Rivista di filosofia* (1968). 35.

258   SELECT BIBLIOGRAPHY OF CRITICAL WRITINGS

Catania, 'L'Accettazione nel Pensiero di H. L. A. Hart' in 48 *Rivista Internazionale di Filosofia del Diritto* (1971). 261.

Cattaneo, 'Il Diritto Naturale nel Pensiero di H. L. A. Hart' in 42 *Rivista Internazionale di Filosofia del Diritto* (1965). 673.

Cohen, 'The Concept of Law' 71 *Mind* (1962). 395.

Dworkin, 'The Model of Rules' in 35 *University of Chicago Law Review* (1967). 14, reprinted in *Essays on Legal Philosophy* as 'Is Law a System of Rules?' ed. Summers, Oxford, 1968.

Dworkin and MacCallum, Symposium on 'Judicial Discretion' in 60 *Journal of Philosophy* (1963). 624, 638.

Hughes, 'Rules, Policy and Decision Making' in 77 *Yale Law Review* (1968). 411.

— 'Validity and the Basic Norm' in 59 *California Law Review* (1971). 695.

Macbride, 'The Acceptance of a Legal System' in 49 *The Monist* (1965). 377.

Morris, 'The Concept of Law' in 75 *Harvard Law Review* (1962). 452.

Raz, 'The Identity of Legal Systems' in 59 *California Law Review* (1971). 795.

Sartorius, 'The Concept of Law' in 52/2 *Archiv für Recht- und Sozialphilosophie* (1966). 161.

— 'Social Policy and Judicial Legislation' in 8 *American Philosophical Quarterly* (1971). 151.

Singer, 'Hart's Concept of Law' in 60 *Journal of Philosophy* (1963). 197.

Woozley, 'The Existence of Rules' in 1 *Nous* (1967). 63.

Essays by Finnis, Hacker, MacCormick, Raz and Tapper in *Oxford Essays in Jurisprudence* II (forthcoming) Oxford.

INDEX

(N.B. References to pages after p. 231 are to the Notes)

Adjudication, rules of, 94–96; *and see* Courts, Judges.

Agnelli, A., 237.

Ago, 245, 254, 257.

Allen, C. K., 246.

Ames, J. B., 254.

Analogy, 15, 79, 234, 257.

Anzilotti, D., 256.

Aquinas, 8n., 187, 253.

Aristotle, 158, 187, 234, 251, 253, 254.

Augustine, St., 8n., 13, 152.

Austin, John, 1, 6, 7, 16, 18, 19, 20, 21n., 23, 25, 59, 62, 72, 79, 145, 203, 206, 232, 233, 234, 236, 237, 238, 239, 240, 241, 242, 243, 251, 252, 253, 254, 256.

Austin, J. L., 14, 234, 253.

Authority, 19–20, 95;
legislative, 57–62, 69.
distinguished from power, 62, 196, 198–9.

Baier, K., 240, 244, 254.

Basic Norm, *see* Kelsen, H., and Recognition, Rule of.

Benn, S. I., and Peters, R. S., 251, 252, 253, 254.

Bentham, Jeremy, 16, 62, 183, 206, 231, 234, 236, 239, 240, 242, 243, 253, 254.

Blackstone, 183, 253, 254.

Bohnert, H. G., 235.

Bradley, F. H., 252.

Brierly, J. L., 255, 256.

Broad, C. D., 243.

Buckland, W. W., 237–8, 239.

Campbell, A. H., 240, 243, 255, 257.

Cattaneo, M., 248.

Certainty of Law, *see* Uncertainty.

Change, rule of, 93–96; *and see* Legislation.

Cohen, L. J., 234, 244.

Commands, 16, 19–20; *and see* Imperatives; Orders; Tacit commands.

Commonwealth, emergence of independent legal systems in, 116–18, 248; *and see* Constitutional Law; Westminster, Statute of.

Conceptualism, 120, 126–7, 249; *and see* Formalism.

Constitutional Law:
as 'positive morality', 1.
restricting legislature, 67–68, 70–76, 242.
amendment of, 71–72, 76, 243.
And see Legislature; Limitations, Legal; Parliament; Recognition, Rule of; South Africa; United States.

Contracts, 9, 28, 37, 40, 94; *and see* Promises.

Conventions of British Constitution, 108, 247.

Courts, 2, 5, 29–30, 39, 94, 133.
and rule of recognition, 64, 110–14, 145, 149–50.
creative function of, 128–32, 138–44.
finality and infallibility of, 138–44.
And see Adjudication; Judge; Precedent; Realism.

Cowen, D. V., 250.

Criminal Law, 6–7, 9, 24, 27, 28, 31, 32, 37, 38, 39, 40, 77, 85.

Cross, R., 250.

Custom, legal status of, 44–47, 63, 67, 89, 240, 244; *and see* Rules, Primary; Tacit Command.

Daube, D., 237.

Definition, 13–17: of law, 6, 204–7, 208–10, 234.

Del Vecchio, G., 251.

Democracy:
legislators in a, 59.
sovereign in a, 49, 72–74.

Devlin, L. J., 253.

Dewey, J., 249.

Diamond, A. S., 244.

Dicey, A. V., 107, 148, 247.

Dickinson, J., 244, 249, 250.

Discretion:
of rule-making bodies, 128.
of Courts, 138–44.
of scorer in a game, 139–42.
Dixon, Sir O., 248, 250.
Duties, 7, 27, 32–33, 40–41, 166.
distinguished from disability, 68–69.
character of rules imposing, 85.
and obligation, 238.
and predictions, 239–40.
And see Obligation; Rules.

Efficacy of Law, 100–1, 247.
Electorate as sovereign, 47, 70–76, 243.
Evans-Pritchard, E. E., 244.
Existence:
of a legal system, 59–60, 109–14, 247–8.
of a rule, 106–7.

Fiction involved in rules, 11.
Fitzmaurice, G. G., 255.
Formalism, 121–50, 249; *and see* Conceptualism.
Frank, Jerome, 232, 240, 242, 250.
Frankfurter, F., 243.
Friedmann, W., 250, 252.
Fuller, L. L., 204n., 254.

Games:
variety of rules in, 9, 30.
scoring rule in, 34, 58, 99.
theory that all rules are addressed to officials applied to, 40, 238–9.
internal aspect of rules in, 55–56.
persistence of law illustrated by umpire's decision in, 62.
move in chess and compliance with rules in, 136–7.
scorer's discretion in and theory that law is what Courts do, 138–41.
definition of, 234.
Germany:
Nazi, 196, 204.
revival of natural law arguments in post-war, 204–7, 254–5.
Gihl, T., 255, 256, 257.
Gluckman, M., 244.
Goodhart, A. L., 248, 254.
Gray, J. C., 1, 137, 203, 232, 240, 242.
Grice, P., 235.
Grotius, 253.

Habits and rules, 9–11, 54–59, 242; *and see* Obedience; Rules.
Hägerström, A., 233, 235, 240, 243.
Hall, J., 254.
Hand Learned, 249.
Hare, R. M., 235, 240.
Hart, H. L. A., 204 n.1, 233, 234, 235, 236, 238, 242, 243, 244, 247, 248, 249, 251, 252, 253, 254, 255.
Hoadly, Bishop, 137, 142.
Hobbes, T., 62, 187, 242, 251, 254.
Hofstadter, A., and McKinvey, J. C. C., 235.
Hohfeld, W. N., 242.
Holmes, O. W., J., 1, 8, 232, 239–40, 243, 249, 252.
Huckleberry Finn, 196, 254.
Hughes, C. E., C.J., 250.
Hughes, G., 248, 252.
Honoré, A. M., 249.
Hume, D., 187, 254.
Hutcheson, J. C., 250.

Imperatives, varieties of, 18–20, 234–6; *and see* Commands; Orders; Tacit Command.
Independence:
of a legal system, 24, 25, 116–18, 248.
of a state, 216–21.
International Law, 3, 4, 67, 77, 115, 118, 152, 173, 191, 194, 208–31, 255–7.
Iraq, 221.
Israel, 221.

Jackson, H., 251.
Jellinek, G., 256.
Jenks, E., 238.
Jennings, R., 256.
Jennings, W. Ivor, 242.
Jensen, O. C., 249.
Jessup, P. C., 255.
Jones, J. W., 248.
Judge:
powers of, 29, 41, 94.
duties of, 29.
And see Courts.
Jurisdiction, 29–30, 36, 94; *and see* Courts.
Justice, 7, 151–63, 251–2.
in distribution, 153–9, 162–3.
in compensation, 159–62.
natural, 156, 202.

Kant, I., 252.
Kantorowicz, H., 234, 250, 252.
Kelsen, H., 2, 18, 35–36, 203, 228, 232, 233, 237, 238, 239, 240, 244, 245–6, 247, 248, 253, 255, 256; *and see* Recognition, Rule of.

Lamont, W. D., 254.
Latham, R. T., 248.
Lauterpacht, H., 256, 257.
League of Nations, 212.
Legal System:
  existence of, 59–60, 109–14, 247.
  distinguished from a set of separate rules, 90–91, 228–31.
  interruption of, 115–16.
  emergence of new, 116–18.
  partial breakdown of, 118–19.
  And see Revolution.
Legislation, 22, 30–31, 96, 236–7, 240–1.
  self-binding, 42–43, 240.
  authority of, 53–54, 57–62, 241–2.
  legal limits on, 64–69.
  manner and form of, 66, 67, 70, 146–8, 242.
  dependence on language of, 121–5.
  and morality, 171–3, 224–5.
  and international law, 224–5, 227, 256.
Legislature, 5, 47, 236–7; *and see* Legislation; Sovereign.
Limitations, legal on legislature, 64–69, 73, 75, 103.

Marshall, G., 233, 242, 247, 248, 250, 251.
Melden, A., 236, 238, 243, 252.
Mill, J. S., 182, 183, 254.
Miller, 250.
Montesquieu, 182, 183.
Morality:
  and law, 7–8, 17, 84, 181–207.
  characterization of, 151–80, 222–5, 252.
  obligations of, 165–77.
  'internality' of, 168–9, 175–6.
  importance of, 169–70.
  immunity of from deliberate change, 171–3.
  and voluntary action, 173–5.
  social pressure supporting, 175–6.
  ideals of, 177–8.

  personal forms of, 179–80.
  and human interests, 176–7.
  and criticism of law, 151–63, 178–9, 201–2.
  and legal validity, 195–207.
  and development of law, 199–200, 254.
  and international Law, 221–6.
  And see Natural Law.
Morison, W. L., 237, 240, 241.

Natural Justice, 156, 202.
Natural Law, 7, 152, 176, 181–95, 253–4.
  concept of nature in, 184–7.
  empirical version of, 187–9.
  minimum content of, 189–95.
  revival of in post-war Germany, 204–7, 254–5.
Negligence, 129–30.
Normative language, 56, 84, 114; *and see* Obligation; Rules.
Nowell-Smith, P., 243.
Nuer, The, 244.
Nullity, 28, 29–31, 33–35, 48, 239.

Obedience, 19, 30, 31.
  Habit of, 23–24, 49–64, 73, 75.
  and continuity of legislative authority, 50–60.
  and persistence of laws, 60–64.
  and existence of a legal system, 109–14. *And see* Habit.
Obligation, 6–7, 27, 43, 79–88, 238.
  analysis of in terms of rules, 79–88, 243.
  and feelings of compulsion, 85–86, 135, 243.
  and prediction of sanction, 10–11, 81–83, 86–88, 134–5.
  having an, distinguished from being obliged, 80–81, 88, 236.
  moral and legal, 163–76.
  in international law, 211–21.
  and duty, 238.
Officials, 20–21, 38, 59–60, 88–95, 109–14.
Olivecrona, K., 233.
Open texture of law, 120, 124–32, 233, 249.
Orders:
  backed by threats or coercive, 6, 16, 19, 20–25.

Orders (*cont.*):
and rules conferring powers, 28–32.
and legislation, 42.
inadequacy of for analysis of law, 47–48, 77–78.
And see Imperatives; Commands; Tacit Command; Rules.

Pappe, H., 255.
Parliament, 24–25, 103–4.
Sovereignty of, 66, 72–77, 103, 108, 145–8, 237, 246, 250–1.
and Commonwealth, 116–18, 248.
Parliament Acts 1911 and 1949, 147–8.
Payne, D. J., 240.
Perelman, Ch., 251.
Piddington, R., 242.
Plato, 158, 182.
Positivism, legal, 7, 181–2, 203, 207, 253–4.
Pound, R., 249, 254.
Powers, *see* Rules, conferring powers.
Precedent, 121–3, 124, 131–2, 150, 249, 250.
Primitive law, 3, 4, 82, 89–90, 152, 244.
Promises, 34, 42–43, 192–3, 219–21.
Prosser, W. L., 252.
Punishment, 7, 10, 27, 34, 36, 39, 87, 168–9, 175–6; *and see* Sanction; Criminal Law.

Radbruch, G., 254.
Raphael, D., 251.
Rawls, J., 251.
Realism, legal, 64, 132–44, 242, 250; *and see* Courts, Rules.
Recognition, Rule of, 92–93, 94–96, 97–107, 245–6, 247.
uncertainty of, 118, 120, 144–50.
and Courts, 112–14.
in international law, 228–30, 256, 257.
And see Kelsen, Validity.
Revolution, 114–16, 248.
Rights, 7, 53–54, 57–58, 85.
Robinson, R., 234.
Ross, A., 235, 238, 239, 243, 247, 251.
Rules:
varieties of, 8–9, 27–32, 166–7.
conferring powers distinguished from

rules imposing obligations or duties, 26–48, 78–79, 238–40.
contrasted with habits, 9–11, 54–59, 242.
internal aspect of, 55–56, 86–88, 96, 99–100, 101, 105, 112, 114, 197, 242, 244.
scepticism as to existence of, 11–13, 121–50.
and obligations, 83–88.
and predictions, 134–44.
different social functions of, 38–41, 238–9.
acceptance of, 54–60, 110–14.
primary, régime of, 89–91.
law as combination of primary and secondary, 77–96, 114.
distinguished from variable standards, 128–31, 249–50.
connexion with justice, 156–7, 202.
And see Recognition, Rule of; Normative language.

Ryle, G., 234.

Salmond, J., 238, 245, 246.
Sanction, 27, 33–35, 36–38, 39, 48, 95, 193–5, 211–15, 244, 255–6; *and see* Nullity; Orders.
Sankey, Lord, 148.
Scandinavian legal theory, 10, 233; *and see* Hägerström, Olivecrona; Ross.
Schulz, F., 244.
Scott, J. B., 256.
Sidgwick, H., 241, 242, 251.
Sources of Law, 93, 95, 98, 103, 246–7; *and see* Recognition, Rule of; Validity.
South Africa, constitutional problems in, 70–72, 118–19, 149–50, 196, 248, 251.
Sovereign, 24–27, 49–76, 145–9, 218–21, 241–2.
Sovereignty of States, 215–21, 255–6.
State, 49, 52, 95, 191, 215–21, 256.
Statutes as merely sources of law, 2, 63–64, 133–4.
Statute of Westminster, 148, 250–1.
Starke, J. G., 256.
Stone, J., 241, 249, 255.
Strawson, P. F., 252.
Strict liability, 162, 168–9, 173–5.
Switzerland, constitution of, 71, 242.

Tacit command or order, 43–46, 62–64, 76, 78, 220, 240, 242.
Taxes contrasted with punishment, 39.
Tort, laws of, 27, 251, 252.
Triepel, H., 256.
Tucker, R. W., 255, 256.
Twain, Mark, 254.

Uncertainty:
of legal rules, 12, 119–30, 144–51.
of precedent, 122, 131–2.
And see Open texture.
United Nations Charter, 212, 227, 255.
United States of America, constitution of, 12, 36, 70, 71, 72, 73, 76, 103, 141, 242–3.
Urmson, J. O., 252.

Validity:
of laws, 68, 96, 97–107, 195, 247.

of morally iniquitous rules, 203–7.
And see Recognition, Rule of.
Van Kleffens, E. N., 256.

Wade, H. W. R., 247, 250.
Waismann, F., 249.
Warren, S. D., and Brandeis, L. D., 251.
Wechsler, H., 254.
Wedberg, A., 244.
Wheare, K. C., 242, 247, 248, 251.
Wills, 9, 12, 28, 30, 33, 34–37, 40, 94.
Williams, Glanville L., 233, 234, 252, 255.
Williams, John Fischer, 255, 256.
Winch, P., 242, 249.
Wisdom, J., 233.
Wittgenstein, L., 234, 242, 249.
Wollheim, R., 234.

Zorn, P., 256.